COASTAL DEMES OF ATTIKA

The way in which the demes and trittyes of Attika were grouped for the formation of the Kleisthenic tribes is an important historical problem. The ten coastal demes lying between Athens and Sounion constituted the three coastal trittyes for three of the Athenian tribes, and in concentrating his study on these coastal demes Professor Eliot has not only made a substantial contribution to our knowledge of ancient Athens but has come to important conclusions about Kleisthenes' constitution of the tribes.

The research for this book was done in Athens. Professor Eliot was therefore able to make repeated visits to each area in order to study the terrain and the ancient remains. He could examine the finds for each deme, and he had access to all the excavation reports, including the accounts of the early travellers, collectors, and excavators.

Professor Eliot handles this variety of evidence with a sure hand. He examines each item of evidence in its own context and refrains from a general assessment until all of the items can be viewed in relation to each other. To join Professor Eliot in the search for clues in the ancient literature, read the travellers' notes, watch the piecing together of the epigraphical remains, and walk the actual ground in his company is to share in intellectual pursuits of a very high order.

C. W. J. ELIOT received his undergraduate education at the University of Toronto, and was awarded the Ph.D. degree there in 1961. He has held various posts at the American School of Classical Studies at Athens and is now Assistant Professor of Classics, University of British Columbia.

PHOENIX
SUPPLEMENTARY VOLUMES

COASTAL DEMES
OF ATTIKA

A STUDY OF
THE POLICY OF
KLEISTHENES

C. W. J. ELIOT

PHOENIX

JOURNAL OF THE CLASSICAL

ASSOCIATION OF CANADA

SUPPLEMENTARY VOLUME V

UNIVERSITY OF TORONTO PRESS

© UNIVERSITY OF TORONTO PRESS 1962
Reprinted 2017
ISBN 978-1-4875-9833-4 (paper)

PREFACE

IN the spring of 1961 this study, in a different form, was submitted as a thesis in conformity with the requirements for the Degree of Doctor of Philosophy in the University of Toronto. The most important changes, apart from minor additions and rewriting, are the incorporation of a second appendix to chapter v ("Lamptrai") and an appendix to chapter xii ("Conclusion"), and the reworking of a long section in each of chapters iv ("Anagyrous") and viii ("Anaphlystos"). The Bibliography has been adjusted to include the most recent literature and to exclude a few items not strictly relevant.

My introduction to the two subjects that directly and indirectly form the basis of this work occurred when I was a student at Toronto. To Mary E. White I owe my curiosity about the reforms of Kleisthenes, to J. Walter Graham my interest in Attika. A stay of five years (1952–1957) at the American School of Classical Studies at Athens gave me the opportunity to combine these two subjects in a study of certain Attic demes. During these years John L. Caskey was Director of the School: he and other officials were always generous in allowing me time from my duties, first as Fellow, then as Secretary, to carry on this project.

A further stay in Athens of two months in the summer of 1960 enabled me to study the physical remains of these demes once again, to take into account finds made between 1957 and 1960, and to do the research needed for the appendix to chapter xi ("Atene"). For this fruitful experience, I thank the Canada Council for a generous grant and the University of British Columbia for leave of absence.

Mere proximity to the monuments and sites, however, is not enough. There must also be intelligent guidance and thoughtful encouragement while one is mastering the subject. This help I received from Eugene Vanderpool, Professor of Archaeology at the American School. No American, perhaps no European, knows more about Attika than he, and this knowledge he shares with anyone who wants to learn. I have visited all the demes studied here in his company and discussed with him all the problems of identification. It is therefore an embarrassment to me that his name appears only infrequently in the following pages; yet such is his nature that were it otherwise he would be embarrassed.

My indebtedness, moreover, is not limited to one man alone. I am happy to acknowledge the help I have received from many fellow students and colleagues through discussion and criticism. From among them I name five, all of whom have read the complete manuscript at least once. Mary E. White and William P. Wallace directed this study in its original form and there are very few pages that have not gained in force of argument and presentation from their rigorous examination of fact, interpretation, and style. Benjamin D. Meritt allowed me access to Agora inscriptions and made available significant information before publication; I am grateful for these courtesies, but I am even more appreciative of his continual encouragement. Malcolm F. McGregor has proved a critical listener as well as reader, and chapter XII ("Conclusion") has been much improved through his acute observations, accepted by me, I hope not too grudgingly, only after rugged debate. His interest and that of his friend John L. Caskey have made it possible for me, whether in Athens or Vancouver, to compose this study in an atmosphere always conducive to research. Finally, I single out Miss Jean C. Jamieson of the University of Toronto Press; she has prepared this manuscript for publication with great care and has saved me from many a fault.

I also thank those who have given me permission to use special material: Basil Blackwell Ltd.; La Bibliothèque nationale in Paris; Dr. H. Brunsting of the Rijksmuseum at Leiden; Dr. Harry J. Carroll of Pomona College, California; Dr. Markellos T. Mitsos of the Epigraphical Museum at Athens; and Mr. Eugene Vanderpool.

Finally, I express my special gratitude to the Classical Association of Canada and the Publications Fund of the University of Toronto Press for making possible the publishing of this work.

C.W.J.E.

Vancouver
April 16, 1962

CONTENTS

LIST OF FIGURES

(The outlines and prominent geographic features of
Figures 1 to 4 and 6 to 8 are adapted from the
Karten; of Figure 9 from Gomme, *Population*
endpiece, through the kindness of Basil Blackwell
Ltd.)

COASTAL DEMES OF ATTIKA

LIST OF ABBREVIATIONS

AA   *Archäologischer Anzeiger, Beiblatt zum Jahrbuch des deutschen archäologischen Instituts*

AJA   *American Journal of Archaeology and of the History of the Fine Arts* (1885–1896), and *American Journal of Archaeology* (1897–)

AJP   *American Journal of Philology*

AM   *Mitteilungen des deutschen archäologischen Instituts. Athenische Abteilung*

ArchEph   Ἀρχαιολογικὴ Ἐφημερίς or Ἐφημερίς Ἀρχαιολογική

Ath. Pol.   Ἀθηναίων πολιτεία

BCH   *Bulletin de Correspondance hellénique*

BSA   *Annual of the British School at Athens*

CAH   *Cambridge Ancient History*

CIG   *Corpus Inscriptionum Graecarum*

CQ   *Classical Quarterly*

Deltion   Δελτίον Ἀρχαιολογικόν

EM   Epigraphical Museum (Athens)

FGrH   *Die Fragmente der griechischen Historiker*

Hermes   *Hermes, Zeitschrift für classische Philologie*

Hesperia   *Hesperia, Journal of the American School of Classical Studies at Athens*

IG   *Inscriptiones Graecae*

JHS   *Journal of Hellenic Studies*

Karten   Curtius and Kaupert, *Karten von Attika*. Berlin, 1881–1900.

LSJ[9]   Liddell-Scott-Jones-McKenzie, *A Greek-English Lexicon*. Ninth edition, 1940.

MSAF   *Mémoires de la Société nationale des Antiquaires de France*

Polemon   Πολέμων, ἐπιστημονικὸν ἀρχαιολογικὸν περιοδικόν

Praktika   Πρακτικὰ τῆς ἐν Ἀθήναις Ἀρχαιολογικῆς Ἑταιρείας

RA   *Revue archéologique*

RE   *Paulys Real-Encyclopädie der classischen Altertumswissenschaft*

SEG   *Supplementum Epigraphicum Graecum*

TAPA   *Transactions and Proceedings of the American Philological Association*

I

INTRODUCTION

THIS is a detailed examination of ten demes that form three coastal trittyes in southern Attika between Halimous and Sounion. Since the word "deme" has several meanings, and since it is important to clarify its use here, it is essential to begin with a general statement that sets out the limits of meaning applicable in this study.

It was at the end of the sixth century B.C. that the whole of Attika, including Athens, was divided for political and administrative purposes into demes, the number of which according to Strabo (9.1.16) was either 170 or 174, an accurate count to judge from the number of deme names known today. This division was brought about by the reforms of Kleisthenes (508/7 B.C.), in which the demes thus formed were combined into thirty trittyes and the trittyes into ten phylai.

The post-Kleisthenic demes had certain features in common, of which the following should be noted. First, each rural deme possessed one or more inhabited centres or villages and an area of land around the settlement or settlements determined at the time of the Kleisthenic organization. The population of the villages showed the normal range of small to large, as did the extent of land assigned to each deme. The city demes differed from the rural demes in that they were not independent villages but were parts of a large inhabited centre, and those within the city walls of Athens probably had no farming lands assigned to them. Secondly, each deme administered its own religious and secular affairs, and, where necessary, had appropriate buildings and shrines. Thirdly, each deme kept a list of its demesmen and in accordance with its population was given representation on the Council of 500 at Athens.

Two aspects of a deme were therefore of considerable importance, its physical size and the number of its members. Kleisthenes dealt with the first by establishing the geographical extent of each deme, and, as far as is known, these limits were kept for centuries, except where it was necessary to create additional demes. He could not so easily control membership, since population is affected by factors independent of a lawgiver. Here, Kleisthenes laid down the principle that membership in a deme was to be hereditary and passed from father to son irrespective of changes of residence within Attika. Thus in the course of time the membership of each deme consisted of two classes— those who lived in their own deme and those who lived elsewhere, while the population resident in each deme consisted of those who were members of that deme and those who were members of other demes.

A Kleisthenic deme was a fixed area of land with an inhabited centre from which the deme was administered. If the word "deme" had always been used in this technical sense, its occurrence would raise no doubts about the precise meaning attached to it. But "deme," both before and after the reforms of Kleisthenes, also meant a village. Since the name of the chief settlement in a rural deme and the name of the deme itself were generally the same, the use of "deme" can prove ambiguous. "The deme of Dekeleia," for example, lacks precision unless the context makes it clear whether the point of reference is the village of Dekeleia or the administrative unit established by Kleisthenes. In order to avoid ambiguity, in this study "deme" refers solely to the Kleisthenic institution, "village" to the settlement. Where a particular context makes such distinctions impossible to maintain, this will be noted.

The demes studied are Aixone, Halai Aixonides, Anagyrous, Lamp-trai (Upper and Lower), Thorai, Aigilia, Anaphlystos, Amphitrope, Besa, and Atene. In each case all the evidence concerning the position and the extent of both deme and village is assembled, and, if the evidence warrants such conclusions, the village is then located and the boundaries of the deme are described. The evidence is presented under four headings: ancient references, name, inscriptions, and remains.

Each of the ten demes is referred to by some ancient authority. The most prominent are Aischines (1.101), Athenaios (652 e), Harpo-kration (s.v. Ἀναφλύστιοι), Herodotos (4.99), Isaios (3.22), Pausanias (1.31.1, and 2.30.9), Ptolemy (*Geographia* 3.15.22), Skylax (*Periplus* 57), Stephanos (s.v. Ἁλαὶ Ἀραφηνίδες καὶ Ἁλαὶ Αἰξωνίδες, and Ἀτήνη), Strabo (9.1.21), and Xenophon (περὶ πόρων 4.43–44). There can be no general assessment of the value of these notices. Rather, each entry must be considered independently and in the context of the rest of the evidence for the deme under discussion.

The names of four of the demes have survived from ancient times in some form or other. This evidence is very useful for the general location of both the ancient deme and the village, although it must be remembered that a name may have moved from one locality to another in the course of more than twenty-five hundred years, and that the present occurrence of an ancient name is occasionally due to modern revival.

Evidence from inscriptions, apart from the bouleutic and prytany lists, is available for eight of the demes. Various categories of inscriptions are represented: deme decrees, mining leases, dedications to the gods, dedications on account of choregic victories, and tombstones. Again, no general value can be placed on this type of evidence. Much will obviously depend on the circumstances in which it was found, the degree of preservation, and the information presented. Each inscription therefore is best studied separately, so that its evidence may be rated on the basis not of its class but of its individual character.

The number of representatives sent to the Boule by each of these ten demes during the fourth century B.C. is preserved in various bouleutic and prytany lists. From these figures the relative sizes of the demes can be established in general terms, but such deductions are significant only when there are considerable differences in the number of representatives from the demes under discussion. Small differences should be discounted, especially since the representation of many of the demes might occasionally have fluctuated by one member even though there is no reason to suspect a change in population, and since local conditions, quite apart from population, might sometimes have affected the number of representatives sent by a deme in any given year.

Finally, there are the remains, which may be of a village or a cemetery, of pottery or sculpture. In each of the ten demes there are some remains, usually representing several periods of time from the prehistoric to the Turkish. In only one deme are the finds from the classical period sufficiently slight to cause special comment. In the other nine the locations of the classical villages are easy to determine from the evidence of the various sites, although two of the demes seem to have contained more than one settlement during the classical period. Such problems, however, will be discussed in the context of the particular deme; but in general the evidence of dated remains is unequivocal, and is a reliable indication of an inhabited settlement.

In none of the ten demes is the evidence from any one of these four categories sufficient to establish the position and limits of the village and deme. But in no case are we dependent on evidence from a single category, and the identifications here proposed fall short of certainty only in the case of Amphitrope.

II

AIXONE

ATHENAIOS and the lexicographers make it clear that the town of Aixone was on the coast, for they say it was famous for its red mullet or "barbouni,"[1] but this information is too general to be useful in establishing the position of the deme of Aixone. For this purpose only one reference is helpful. In his catalogue of the coastal demes from Phaleron to Sounion, Strabo (9.1.21) places Aixone between Halimous and Halai Aixonides: Μετὰ δὲ τὸν Πειραιᾶ, Φαληρεῖς δῆμος ἐν τῇ ἐφεξῆς παραλίᾳ· εἶθ' Ἁλιμούσιοι, Αἰξωνεῖς, Ἁλαιεῖς οἱ Αἰξωνικοί. . . . He adds that the island of Hydroussa, the present Prasonisi, was off Aixone.[2]

The position of Halimous, the last of the city demes as one goes down the coast towards Sounion, has been fixed with certainty; its territory included Chasani and the promontory of Hagios Kosmas.[3] Halai Aixonides, on the other hand, has never been securely placed;[4] there

[1]See Athenaios, 325 d–f, and Hesychios, s.v. Αἰξωνίδα τρίγλην.

[2]Strabo tells us that the island off Cape Zoster was Phabra; this island is the modern Phleva. Between Lipsokoutali and Phleva there is only one island of sufficient size to be worthy of mention along with Phabra and Eleoussa and that is the island of Prasonisi. Even without determining the exact boundaries of Aixone we can say that Prasonisi lies near that deme. Its identification as Hydroussa seems both economical and natural. As for Strabo's text, it reads καὶ κατὰ τοὺς Αἰξωνέας δ'ἐστὶν Ὑδροῦσσα. The manuscript tradition is strong at this point with no major variants. But Kourouniotes ("Τὸ ἱερόν," 9) gives a text reading καὶ μετὰ τοὺς Αἰξωνέας. . . . He cites no authority for the change of preposition, nor is there any justification for this emendation unless one assumes that because Strabo has already used μετά twice in this sentence he really meant to use it a third time. Even if we could prove the topographical reference to be wrong, that would still not constitute a sufficient reason for changing a text that makes good sense. The possibility should also be considered that Kourouniotes' change was inadvertent, perhaps an unfortunate repetition of the phrase μετὰ τοὺς Αἰξωνέας from two lines above.

[3]Hondius, "A New Inscription of the Deme Halimous," 151–160, esp. 156–157; Day, "Cape Colias Phalerum and the Phaleric Wall," 1–2.

[4]In chapter III I hope to show that it is possible to locate this deme accurately. For the present argument, however, this is not necessary.

can be no doubt, however, that it controlled Vouliagmene.[5] The limits supplied by Strabo are, therefore, the two capes, Kolias[6] and Zoster.

NAME

The name has no topographical significance nor can it be connected with any place name in use today. Nevertheless, a few suggestions about possible modern derivatives have been made. J. Stuart proposed AΞAONA as well as Chasani, whereas W. M. Leake tentatively supported Chasani.[7] Neither theory is convincing: Axaona[8] is far too close to the city to merit consideration; Chasani is basically a Turkish word.[9]

INSCRIPTIONS

Nine deme decrees of Aixone are preserved. Some are reported to have come from Trachones, some from Vari, others from elsewhere. Since Trachones is in the deme of Euonymon and Vari in Anagyrous, it appears that we have the extraordinary situation of the decrees of one deme having been discovered in the territories of at least two other demes. It is worth while, therefore, to examine what is known of the finding places of these nine inscriptions.

1. *IG* II[2] 1196

This inscription, along with *IG* II[2] 1197 and 1200, was first published by H. Lolling in 1879. On the finding place he reported: "Inschriften stammen aus den Ruinen des alten Demos Aixone im jetzigen Prinari, halbwegs zwischen Trachones und Vari."[10] This corresponds both in name and distance to the area around the Byzantine church of Ἅγιος

[5]The deme inscriptions discovered by Kourouniotes ("Τὸ ἱερόν," 40–43) prove this point.

[6]This identification of the promontory of Hagios Kosmas with Cape Kolias has been rightly accepted by most scholars. See Mylonas, *Aghios Kosmas* 5–9. Hammond ("The Battle of Salamis," 48 n. 65) holds a contrary view and feels that Cape Kolias should be identified with Cape Anavyso. His suggestion would carry more weight if he quoted Day's article (see n. 3) and tried to disprove his thesis.

[7]Stuart and Revett, *Antiquities* 3.viii; Leake, *Demi* 55.

[8]Stuart and Revett, *Antiquities* Vol. 3, spell this name "Axona" on the map of Attika facing p. 1. Thus they make it appear even more like Aixone. Their suggestion might receive more support if one were certain that "Axaona" actually existed. No one, other than Stuart and Revett, seems to have recorded it.

[9]Lampros, Ἡ ὀνοματολογία τῆς Ἀττικῆς 11.

[10]Lolling, "Inschriften," 193.

Νικόλαος στὸ κάτω Πιρναρί.[11] Lolling also noted that this inscription and the other two mentioned above were in a collection of antiquities gathered together in the courtyard of the estate of Komninos. This property had been previously owned by a certain Luriotis who lived at Trachones in the same place where Mr. J. Geroulanos resides today. The estate of Luriotis stretched from near Kara to Voula and had its headquarters at Trachones. Until the estate was divided into three sections in the late nineteenth century, the only buildings on it were those at Trachones and the church at Pirnari.[12] It must have been this fact that caused the inscriptions to have been housed so far from their original finding place. Possibly this also explains the misleading information in *IG* II², which for the finding places of most of the Aixone decrees records "In vico Trachones (= ΑΙΞΩΝΗ)," the location given being only a half truth, the equation wrong.[13]

2. *IG* II² 1197

See under No. 1, *IG* II² 1196.

3. *IG* II² 1198

This was first published along with *IG* II² 1202 by A. S. Rusopoulos in 1864. He reported that both inscriptions were found "in un piccolo scavo impreso in un podere situato a *Trachones* fra l'Imetto ed il mare."[14] To the above information we can add that the leader of the excavation was Count Blourdorff, the Russian Minister to Greece. Another description of the finding place is given by E. Miller who published *IG* II² 1202 in 1865.[15] Miller received the following information from Blourdorff himself, who seems to have been deliberately uninformative: "Ce marbre provient d'un commencement de fouilles que M. le comte Blourdorff a exécutées dans une propriété rurale située non loin d'Athènes, sur la route qui conduit au cap Colonne."[16] After an interval of nearly a century, neither description will permit

---

[11]There is no difference in meaning between "prinari" and "pirnari." They are merely two words for the same thing and both derive from "prinos." See Gennadios, Λεξικὸν φυτολογικόν 258 and Heldreich, Τὰ δημώδη ὀνόματα τῶν φυτῶν 110, s.v. Q. Smilax.

[12]I owe this and other information about Trachones and its surroundings to Mr. J. Geroulanos, to whom I am grateful.

[13]*IG* II² 1196, 1197, 1198 (where Milchhöfer seems to be given credit for the equation), 1200, and 1202.

[14]Rusopoulos, "Scavi attici di Aixone," 129.

[15]Miller, "Inscription grecque nouvellement découverte," 154–159.

[16]*Ibid*. 154.

accurate location, since we know that the estate of Trachones in the time of Rusopoulos and Miller covered a large area both north and southeast of the present Trachones. Rusopoulos' comment "between Hymettos and the sea" is more applicable, however, to a place southeast of Trachones than to Trachones or to a place north of that. It should be observed that nothing in either description demands that Trachones be the location of the excavation.

Lolling, some fifteen years later, considered that the inscriptions published by Rusopoulos and Miller came from the same place as the three which he reported (see under No. 1) from Pirnari.[17] One cannot tell, however, whether this observation was based on a natural inference from the contents of the inscriptions themselves or from independent evidence. Nevertheless, we should note that a location near Hagios Nikolaos of Pirnari would accord with the descriptions of Rusopoulos and Miller, since the church lies between Hymettos and the sea and is directly on the old road from Athens to Sounion.

4. *IG* II² 1199

This inscription was first published in 1828 by A. Böckh from copies supplied to him by K. S. Pittakys and B. G. Niebuhr.[18] Böckh's description of the finding place—"in loco pagi Aixonae effosus"—is not helpful, and is probably based on inference rather than actual knowledge. In fact, one is tempted to believe that actual knowledge was deliberately withheld from him by Pittakys, who in 1859 was able to write: Εὑρέθη τὸ 1819 ἐν τὰς ἀνασκαφὰς ἃς ὁ μακαρίτης Γεώργιος Γρόπιος ἐνήργησεν εἰς τὸ χωρίον τῆς Ἀττικῆς, καλούμενον νῦν Βάρη. . . ."[19] Pittakys goes on to relate that the antiquities unearthed in this excavation, which also included No. 8, *IG* II² 2492, were sold to Rottiers, the Dutch General, with the exception of the inscription under discussion, which Pittakys was able to save and which he took to his home in Athens. This information is clear, authoritative, and obviously based on first-hand knowledge. Nevertheless, it must not be accepted as beyond criticism, and there are several features that must be examined. First, it would be unusual to find a deme decree of Aixone in the deme of Anagyrous; even more unusual to find two such decrees, as the information of Pittakys would lead us to believe. Secondly, we have no reference other than this to an excavation at Vari by Gropius in 1819, whereas there exists ample documentation for the fact that

[17]Lolling, "Inschriften," 194.
[18]*CIG* 214: 1.345.
[19]Pittakys published this inscription in *ArchEph* (1859) 1846–1848: No. 3545.

Gropius did excavate "in Trachones" during the same year.[20] Thirdly, Pittakys wrote his description forty years after the events that he recorded and we know that at least on one occasion his memory did not serve him well after a much shorter period of time had elapsed between field work and writing.[21] For further remarks on the finding place of this inscription, see the discussion of No. 8, below.

5. *IG* II² 1200

See under No. 1, *IG* II² 1196.

6. *IG* II² 1201

This inscription was first published by Pittakys in 1842. He reported: "Εὑρέθη εἰς τὰς κατὰ τὸν Δῆμον Αἰξωνέα ἀρχαιολογικὰς ἐρεύνας."[22] This description is of no help in this study, since today it is at best only a vague location.

7. *IG* II² 1202[23]

See under No. 3, *IG* II² 1198.

8. *IG* II² 2492

This was first published by Böckh in 1828 from a copy supplied by Niebuhr. Böckh wrote: "ex Attica, et haud dubie ex pago Aexonien-sium, attulit Rotiers."[24] It is clear that he did not know the exact provenance of this inscription and consequently made a logical deduc-tion from its content. Pittakys,[25] on the other hand, stated authori-tatively in 1859 that this inscription, along with No. 4, *IG* II² 1199, came from Vari as a result of excavations conducted by Gropius. We have already suggested that Pittakys' remarks, despite their clarity, are not free from difficulties. We can accept as correct Pittakys' statement that both inscriptions came from the same place—two decrees from the same deme should be found reasonably close together under normal conditions—and that they were both found by Gropius

---

[20]Gropius' archaeological activities are fully described by Protopsaltes, *Gropius* 64–84. On p. 82 the excavations at Trachones are mentioned.

[21]Parsons, "Klepsydra," 195 n. 5.

[22]*ArchEph* (1842) 519: No. 858.

[23]Although this inscription was first published by Rusopoulos in 1864, Miller thought that he was giving the inscription its first edition in 1865, having previously obtained permission from Count Blourdorff, the excavator, as well as assurances that it had not been made public.

[24]*CIG* 93: 1.132–134.

[25]*ArchEph* (1859) 1847.

in 1819; from other sources we know that Gropius was excavating in
that year near, but not at, Vari, unless this name had a much wider
application for Pittakys than it has for us today. Nevertheless, if we
can determine the finding place of one inscription, we shall have
established it for both. No additional information about No. 4 exists
other than that given above. Fortunately this is not the case with
No. 8.

On April 11, 1819, L. F. S. Fauvel wrote from Athens a letter containing a report on his most recent excavation. The pertinent passage
reads:[26]

> Je viens de faire des fouilles entre alace et
> exone dans les champs felleens a 2 lieues
> d'athenes, imaginez vous une plaine de
> roches couverte de quelques pouces de
> 5 terre, de plus de 2 lieues d'etendue de 3/4
> lieue[27] de large de pied de l'himette
> à la mer, couverte d'une multitude de
> tumulus qui la plus part sont des amas
> de pierailles qui couvrent des sarcophages
> 10 des urnes de cuivre, ou bronze des cipes
> brizes des bas reliefs renversés beaucoup
> de vases des disques dont se servoient
> les atheletes. un cipe de 12 pieds avec
> un beau fleuron peint porte le nom de
> ϚΟΝΟΑϞΘ,
> 15 nom qui j'ai lu aussi sur un casque qui
> avoit ete trouvé a Olympie. on y a trouvé
> des medailles des atheniens, des empereurs
> romains de gordien de maxime des constantin
> et plus bas — un lion, une lione que je
> 20 crois representer leana maitresse d'armodius —
> un beuf grand comme nature. j'ai eu pour ma
> part un bas relief conservé de 4 figures du
> bon tems d'environ deux pieds representant
> l'affranchissement d'un esclave une urne d'un
> 25 pied de haut et d'un pied et demi de large en
> cuivre encore dorée et poli en certains

---

[26]This letter is among the papers of Fauvel in La Bibliothèque nationale in Paris.
It is numbered Vol. II (=mss. franç. 22871), folio 28. It has not been published, but
Legrand knew of it and mentions its existence in "Biographie de Louis-François-
Sébastien Fauvel" (1897) 393–394. In the transcription here presented, the only
departures from the original text, which I know through photostat copies, are the
addition of a few apostrophes.

[27]Fauvel originally wrote "d'une demi lieue" but he crossed this out and sub-
stituted "3/4."

           endroits elle contenoit des os a demi brulés
           des vases des coupes, dans une des pommes
           tres reconnaissables, des tablettes encore
30   enduites de cire ou j'ai lu les caracteres
           qui donnent l'epoque qui est celle des monuments
           d'athenes de pericles.[28] dans cette urne, par-
           dessus les os brulés et les vases, il y avoit
           une piece de toile fine de lin de 4 pieds de
35   large et de huit de long roulée fort serrée
           de maniere a occuper le vide que laissoient
           les os et les vases, cette toile a pu etre
           deroulée, et c'est devenue verte par le
           voisinage du cuivre, les anses de l'urne
40   sont garnis d'etoffe. on a trouvé des
           inscriptions dont des donations de
           terreins par les habitans d'exone . . .[29]
           la plus part de ces urnes sont renfermées
           dans des marbres, ou de gros vases de
45   terre. il est difficile de les avoir
           entieres. quand il se fera quelques
           decouvertes, mon ami, je vous en ferai
           part et vous au public, si vous le jugez
           à propos.

Our interest is caught by the phrase "les champs felleens" in the first sentence. The same expression is used by Fauvel in a letter written on October 2, 1820: "Elles [sc. les échantillons des toiles] ont été trouvées aux environs du cap Zoster, dans les champs Phelléens, dans une urne grande d'airain et non de bronze. . . ." Fauvel is clearly describing his excavation of the previous year. Le comte de la Rochefoucauld also employed the phrase in a letter dated October 8, 1824: "Ce morceau, qu'il juge être un véritable antique, a été trouvé en terre dans les champs Phelléens, entre Athènes et le cap Sunium." Rochefoucauld is referring to a lion, the "un lion" mentioned in Fauvel's letter of 1819.[30]

[28]This sentence from line 30 to the end is broken up by sketches of the letters visible on two of the tablets.

[29]The sentence is left unfinished and the three dots represent a similar number of dots in the original. Between "exone" and the first dot there is an unreadable letter or ligature.

[30]The three references to "les champs felléens" are collected together by Michon, "Notes," 36–43. I quote here another reference for completeness: "ce lion-ci, trouvé dans les champs Phelléens, près de Platée, en Grèce . . ." (excerpt from the *Second Supplément à la description des antiques du Musée royal*, which appeared in 1825). The lion in question is now catalogued No. 827, *Catalogue sommaire* 9. Michon made out a good case for this lion's coming from Fauvel's excavation, but, as he had not read the letter of 1819, he was unable to make the identification noted above.

The adjective "felléen" is derived from an infrequently used Greek word φελλεύς meaning "rocky" or "stony ground." In addition to this general meaning, it had a particular application in Attika because, according to Suidas, there was a place so named: Φελλεὺς τόπος τῆς ’Αττικῆς οὕτω καλούμενος τραχύς.[31] It might be maintained that Fauvel took the name from this source, especially since the area in which he excavated was both covered with stones and not far distant from the farmstead of Trachones, a name obviously derived from τραχύς and in meaning similar to φελλεύς.[32] But a much more likely explanation lies to hand, the simplicity of which is entirely in keeping with what we know of Fauvel. Despite the unfinished sentence in the passage from his letter of April 11, 1819 (lines 40–42) we recognize at once that among the inscriptions discovered in this excavation was *IG* II² 2492; we also note that it was not found by Fauvel but by someone else—the contrast between "on a trouvé" and "j'ai eu pour ma part" is strong and deliberate—whom we can identify as Gropius on Pittakys' authority.

The first line of *IG* II² 2492 reads κατάδε ἐμίσθωσαν Αἰξωνεῖς τὴν Φελλεῖδα, and the complete text is a detailed rental agreement between the deme of Aixone and two private individuals for a property known to the people of Aixone as ἡ φελληίς, "the stony land." There can be little doubt that Fauvel read the first line of the inscription, realized that the property referred to must be near by, saw the appropriateness of the designation to the area in which he and his colleagues were excavating, and promptly dubbed the region "les champs felléens."

Having established links between Fauvel, Gropius, this inscription, and the excavations of 1819 in "les champs felléens," we must now see if we can establish with any accuracy the place of excavation in modern terms. Fauvel speaks of his own excavation as "two leagues" from Athens, which would place it in the neighbourhood of Helleniko, probably near the ancient road, since he was clearly excavating a cemetery and cemeteries were usually placed alongside the roads outside the limits of towns and villages. The third member of the group, the Dutch General, B. E. A. Rottiers, was also an excavator,[33] not just a

[31]S.v. φελλέα.

[32]Ross (*Archäologische Aufsätze* 1.16) discusses the words φελλεύς and Trachones. His views about the former are distorted by his notion that the stone fields belong to a vast cemetery. His suggestion that Trachones is an ancient name (as it may well be) is not, however, supported by his citation from Suidas: Τραχωνῖτις χώρα does not refer to a place in Attika but to the region mentioned in St. Luke 3.1, which was governed by Herod's brother Philip.

[33]The only published record of Rottiers' having taken part in an excavation in

buyer. His great find was the Archestrate relief,[34] and about it he wrote that it "fut découvert en 1819 dans une fouille près de l'endroit où était anciennement le bourg d'Exones, . . . il fut trouvé, renversé avec le fronton, à neuf pieds sous terre et au milieu d'une grande masse de débris de marbres, ce que peut faire supposer, qu'il avait été érigé en forme d'autel. . . . l'ancienne route d'Athènes à Sounion passait à côté de l'endroit où le bas-relief fut déterré." Again, in some lists which the General prepared when he sold his finds to the Netherlands government in 1821, he wrote: "il fut trouvé dans le courant de mars 1819 aux fouilles des tombeaux près de l'endroit où était anciennement le Bourg d'Exones à trois lieues ou 9 milles d'Athènes, sur l'ancienne route à Sunium." Another list, originally in Dutch, has the following: "found March 1819 by some working together in Athens. . . ." Finally, in 1823, he wrote of P. Giuracich that he "n'a joué aucun rôle comme antiquaire à Athènes. Il était chancelier d'Autriche ainsi que de notre consulat dans cette ville. Souvent il avait des articles en vente et surveillait les fouilles dont il payait les ouvriers comme cela fut le cas pour moi durant mon séjour en Grèce."[35] Rottiers, then, was also digging tombs alongside the ancient road but three leagues from Athens, which would place his field of excavation between Glyphada and Voula.

1819 is by Rottiers himself. He writes (*Monumens de Rhodes* 273 n. 1): "J'ai eu le plaisir de rencontrer M. Barrois à Athènes, qu'il vint visiter en 1819, pendant que je m'occupais, dans les environs de cette ville, de fouilles qui furent assez heureuses, et dont on peut voir les résultats au Musée Royal de Leyde." There can be no doubt both from this and the references cited below that he did excavate with Gropius and Fauvel. Perhaps he was not always at the excavation in person but sent his agent, to whom he refers in the note of 1823, to look after the everyday details. This may explain why later writers mention only Gropius and Fauvel.

[34]*IG* II² 7423: Conze, *Die attischen Grabreliefs* 1.66–67, No. 297. The statement made (or quoted) by Conze that Rottiers acquired this stele from Gropius is not, so far as I know, based on sound evidence but on inference: because Rottiers obtained some of his antiquities from Gropius, it could be inferred that he obtained all of them from the same source. This, however, does not take into account the fact that he assisted in the excavation. There are, moreover, some items in Leiden that Rottiers admitted were bought from Gropius and Fauvel. The Archestrate stele is not one of them and Rottiers' descriptions of the finding place read like those of an excavator, not a purchaser. One might entertain a compromise solution: Rottiers made some arrangement with Gropius and Fauvel whereby he became a member of their group, but, in return for this honour, he had to pay them for any antiquities he decided to retain, even though he had found them.

[35]I owe these references to the kindness of Dr. H. Brunsting, Keeper in the Rijksmuseum at Leiden. The first citation was published, he tells me, in *Messager des sciences et des arts* (Gand, May 1823) 1, to which Conze refers. The others do not seem to have been published.

We have no precise information about the position of Gropius' sector. He was obviously not with Fauvel and it is unlikely that he was with Rottiers because Rottiers purchased antiquities that were unearthed in this exploration from both Fauvel and Gropius. In addition, the nature of the finds made by Gropius, two deme decrees as opposed to graves and grave offerings, supports the contention that the three men were digging in different sections. Excavations both at Helleniko and Voula would leave a large gap near Hagios Nikolaos, an area already noticed by Dodwell as abounding in traces of antiquity that suggested habitation by the living rather than by the dead. It is most unlikely that this area was neglected. A plan whereby one excavator explored the region around Hagios Nikolaos while two others concentrated on sectors straddling the ancient road leading to and from Hagios Nikolaos would not only be considered a good one today but also is entirely plausible on the basis of the surface evidence visible in the first years of the nineteenth century.

There remains one other piece of evidence that connects the activities of Fauvel and Gropius with the area near Hagios Nikolaos. On November 22, 1805, Dodwell visited the area between Hagios Nikolaos and Cape Punta. He noted: "Among the bushes I discovered a marble lion, admirably sculptured in the style of those at Mycenae: it is in a recumbent posture; its length is four feet nine inches; but its head is mutilated."[36] This same lion is described in 1825 by Ritter Prokesch von Osten as lying at the entrance to the Acropolis at Athens. He further states that it was found by Gropius and Fauvel a few hours from Athens towards Sounion and that it very probably marked the tomb of Harmodios' mistress.[37] This lion, or rather lioness as Prokesch says, can be none other than "une lione que je crois representer leana maitresse d'armodius" which Fauvel mentions in his letter of 1819 (lines 19–20). Since this lion was in the neighbourhood of Hagios Nikolaos before being rediscovered by Fauvel and Gropius, we

[36]Dodwell, *Classical Tour* 1.525.

[37]Prokesch von Osten, *Denkwürdigkeiten* 2.394. Michon ("Notes," 49–51) first made the observation that Dodwell's lion was the same as that described by Prokesch. There are slight differences in the two accounts. Dodwell measured the lion as 4′ 9″ long: Prokesch wrote "nicht über 4 Fuss lang." They either measured from different places, quite easily done when an object is broken, or else Prokesch was guessing. A second difference is Prokesch's statement that the lion was found "auf einem Tumulus." Since it was "among the bushes" (and Dodwell had no reason to conceal the truth), I am inclined to suspect Fauvel of enlarging on the truth so as to make his theory about Harmodios' mistress appear the more likely. Perhaps Fauvel concealed the facts by saying that "it was once on a tumulus," but then omitted to state that it was no longer so placed when he and Gropius found it.

have proof that they did conduct some exploration in that area, and, since Fauvel says that "on a trouvé . . ." various finds including the lion, we can suppose that it was actually Gropius who was responsible for the rediscovery.

It cannot be proved conclusively that Gropius found the two decrees of the deme of Aixone in the neighbourhood of Hagios Nikolaos. It seems, however, a reasonable deduction from the evidence presented above. The fact that three other deme inscriptions (nos. 1, 2, and 5) are said to have come from "the present Prinari" (i.e., from near Hagios Nikolaos) strengthens our conclusions.

9. *AM* 66 (1941) 218-219

This inscription was found in 1941 in Glyphada and subsequently published by N. Kyparissis and W. Peek.[38] Attempts to find out exactly where it was found have met with no success.

Such is the catalogue of the deme decrees. Our examination has shown that none of the inscriptions was found at Vari, and that none was conclusively from Trachones. On the other hand, nos. 1, 2, and 5 were said to have come from Pirnari, and nos. 3 and 7 may have been found in the same location. We have demonstrated above that in all probability nos. 4 and 8 were discovered near Hagios Nikolaos, a church at Pirnari. Modern Glyphada now stretches towards Hymettos as far as this church and so the vague location "in Glyphada" might indicate the same general area for No. 9. As for No. 6, we shall never know where it was found, only that it was discovered at the place where Pittakys thought the deme of Aixone was.

Despite uncertainties about any single decree, the combined evidence of them all and the lack of any definite conflict between them about finding place make it clear that the religious and secular centre of the deme of Aixone was near the church of Hagios Nikolaos at Pirnari.[39]

---

[38]Kyparissis and Peek, "Attische Urkunden," 218-219.

[39]A number of grave inscriptions with an Aixonian demotic have been found in the area of Pirnari and Glyphada. However, since we have this wealth of evidence from deme inscriptions, it is better not to introduce the grave inscriptions as evidence, for their value can only be corroborative: *IG* II² 5417, 5430 (?), 5448, 5453 (?), and 5454 (where the restoration of the demotic Αἰξων]εύς is not demanded by the existing three letters). Pleket (*Greek Inscriptions* 95) recorded *IG* II² 5416 as if from Aixone, even though he quotes a catalogue entry "near the sacred way to Eleusis." He may be right, but there is no particular reason to suppose that Rottiers acquired all his antiquities from one excavation or that all grave steles with the demotic of Aixone came from Aixone.

REMAINS

The area between the church of Hagios Nikolaos and Cape Punta has been recognized for many years as a place rich in antiquities. Dodwell visited the region on November 22, 1805, and subsequently wrote:

The whole plain from which the peninsula projects is strewed with ancient remains, that are overgrown with the impenetrable lentiscus. The small church of St. Nicolo seems to occupy the site of an ancient temple. Among the bushes I discovered a marble lion. . . . Not many paces from the lion is a marble statue of a female figure. . . . These ruins seem the remains of a considerable demos.[40]

It was doubtless this picture of antiquities lying around so easily accessible that prompted the first excavation of which we have any knowledge, that done by Fauvel in the company of Gropius and Rottiers in 1819. It has already been pointed out that the area in which they dug seems to have extended from Helleniko to Voula. Some of the objects they found have been noted above, others are discussed in the appendix to this chapter.

Further exploration of the area took place during the middle of the nineteenth century: Count Blourdorff excavated in 1864[41] and he may have been preceded by Pittakys some time before 1842.[42]

Mycenaean tombs were discovered ca. 1880 near Cape Punta by grave robbers who may also have found a few Geometric graves at the same time.[43] The Archaeological Society sent D. Philios to make enquiries on the spot but he spent only a day in the area. During his short visit he was shown traces of other graves which had not been opened.[44]

The first scientific excavation was undertaken in 1919 by A. D. Keramopoullos who investigated a number of remains between Cape

[40]*Classical Tour* 1.525.
[41]See inscription No. 3.
[42]See inscription No. 6.
[43]Some of these finds made their way to Berlin where they are recorded as coming from "Aliki," "Aliki nahe dem Phaleron 1881," or "Aliki beim Phaleron 1881." Keramopoullos ("Ἀνασκαφὴ ἐν Αἰξωνῇ," 34) makes it clear that Aliki in this instance is equivalent to the waist of land joining Cape Punta to the mainland. See Furtwängler, *Beschreibung* 4-8 and 11: nos. 14-18, 23, 25-32, 35-37, 39-44, 49, and 59. The last two are classified as Geometric, the remainder Mycenaean. See also Furtwängler and Löschcke, *Mykenische Vasen* 37-39, where the description is by H. G. Lolling. He records the general shape and condition of the tombs and notes that the Geometric vases came from the same area. Most of the pieces are illustrated on their Pl. 18.
[44]*Praktika* (1880) 15-16.

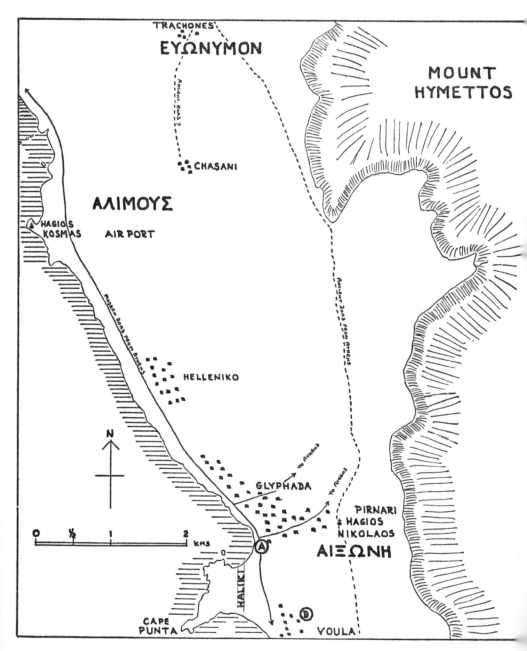

FIGURE 1. Aixone

Punta and the church of Hagios Nikolaos.[45] Around the latter he noticed, like Dodwell, sufficient signs of antiquity to describe them as "the remains of an ancient settlement." He cleared a tumulus,[46] a small structure of unknown purpose 500 metres southeast of the church, a Roman house near Cape Punta, and a circular building[47] on the shore north of Cape Punta in the bay which was and still is the harbour for this region (approximately at A on Figure 1).

In 1927, N. Kyparissis began a systematic investigation of ancient cemeteries in Attika. He did some work at Glyphada but it remains unpublished except for a note on a single marble lekythos.[48] As a result of his work there, however, an early Christian basilica was excavated and published by A. K. Orlandos.[49] This church lies on the shore of the harbour north of Cape Punta, presumably close to where Keramopoullos found the circular building (at A on Figure 1).

The latest excavations in the area were carried out by J. Papadimitriou, who since 1954 has excavated a number of late Mycenaean tombs at Voula (at B on Figure 1).[50]

A recent study by John Bradford, based on aerial photographs made during the Second World War, has revealed a system of field terracing on the slopes of Mount Hymettos, perhaps dating from classical times.

[45]Keramopoullos, "'Ανασκαφὴ ἐν Αἰξωνῇ," 32–46.

[46]This tumulus was one of the many that lie between Trachones and Vouliagmene. Travellers had taken them for burial mounds but Keramopoullos showed that the one he excavated (similar in appearance to the others) was nothing but a heap of stones. A certain amount of fragmentary pottery was found within the tumulus dating from the Mycenaean period to ca. 500 B.C. He plausibly associated these tumuli with a ground clearance scheme for agricultural purposes, such as that advocated by Peisistratos. Keramopoullos was perhaps unaware that Sir John L. Myres had opened several tumuli near Kara in 1885 and had come to the same conclusion, that they represented "heaps of stones gathered off the fields" (Gardner, "Archaeology in Greece," 58–59).

[47]The round structure is the most interesting of Keramopoullos' discoveries, especially since he would like to identify it as "the agora of the deme" and in particular "the fish-market." It must be stated, however, that there is no evidence to support this idea. Suitable as it may seem for the agora to have been on the shore near where the fish were brought in, it is even more suitable for it to have been where the larger part of public and private life was carried on, seemingly near Pirnari around the church of Hagios Nikolaos.

[48]Kyparissis, "'Εξ 'Αθηνῶν καὶ 'Αττικῆς," 55, No. 213.

[49]Orlandos, "La Basilique," 258–265. Papagiannopoulos-Palaios ("'Ενδείξεις," 131–136) believes that this church was built to mark the spot where St. Paul landed in Attika. The chain of evidence that leads to this conclusion has many weak links, not the least of which is the supposition that the altar to the unknown god mentioned by Paul is the same as the altar to the unknown gods seen by Pausanias in Phaleron.

[50]Papadimitriou, "Μυκηναϊκοὶ τάφοι (1954) 72–88 and (1955) 78–99, and Orlandos, Τὸ ἔργον κατὰ τὸ 1957 14–17.

The area of terracing stretches from Trachones to Palaiochori: between Glyphada and Hymettos the terraces are very clear both on the photographs and on the ground.[51]

To this account of published reports one can add that many of the remains recorded in the *Karten* (Sheet VIII) near the church of Hagios Nikolaos can still be seen despite the encroachments of modern building and that similar traces of houses can be made out at many places between the church and Cape Punta. Many ancient blocks have been re-used for curbs, door sills, and garden walls. On the north side of Cape Punta directly opposite the little island are remains from some hydraulic establishments of late Roman date.

IDENTIFICATION

By 1909 the two great German topographers, R. Löper and A. Milchhöfer, had agreed that the centre of the deme of Aixone should be placed near the church of Hagios Nikolaos at Pirnari.[52] Our study of the inscriptions makes the same conclusion inevitable and the actual remains justify such a position. Keramopoullos produced no evidence in 1919 to gainsay the theory of his predecessors. In 1929 A. A. Papa-giannopoulos-Palaios began his researches into the topography of Aixone with the publication of *IG* II² 3091. Without considering the finding places of the eight (at that time) Aixone decrees, and without regard for the topographic problems involved and those he was creating by his theories, he postulated that the theatre of Aixone was near Palaiochori and that therefore the centre of the deme was south of Pirnari.[53] The theory is entirely dependent upon his interpretation of *IG* II² 3091, which he insists is connected with Aixone. In our discussion of Halai Aixonides we shall demonstrate that this connection is neither necessary nor likely. For the moment it is sufficient to point out that the evidence from the authentic Aixone decrees is far too strong to be overturned by a single inscription itself unattached to any deme.

[51]Bradford, "Fieldwork on Aerial Discoveries in Attica and Rhodes," 172–180, and *Ancient Landscapes* 29–34. The possible connection between inscription No. 8 and these field systems, as well as the relation of the tumuli (Bradford does not note the works of Myres and Keramopoullos) to the agrarian policies of Peisistratos, is a subject that might be profitably studied in greater detail.

[52]Milchhöfer, *RE* 6 (1909) 1156–1158, s.v. Euonymon; W. Kolbe, *RE* 7 (1910–1912) 2226–2227, s.v. Halai (1).

[53]Papagiannopoulos-Palaios, "'Ἀττικαὶ ἐπιγραφαί 7," 161–173. The same author has published most of his researches on Aixone not only in *Polemon*, but also in a periodical called Αἰξώνη, of which I have seen volumes 1–3 (1950–1953). Since he adds nothing new in these latter studies, I have not quoted them except in one instance (see n. 49).

The only opinion offered since 1929 is that of W. Wrede, who in 1934 wrote that Glyphada was "antike" Aixone.[54]

The full history of Aixone is yet to be written. A great deal, however, can be deduced from the remains. There was a Mycenaean community in the area: one cemetery belonging to it has been discovered near Cape Punta but the settlement has not. A few Geometric graves seem to have been found along with the Mycenaean, so it is extremely likely that inhabitation of the region was continuous from the late Bronze Age. During the classical period the main centre of public and private life was near the church of Hagios Nikolaos, with cemeteries both north and south along the ancient route from Athens. By (or in) Roman times, the settlement had spread, or moved, to the shore, so that by late Roman times there was good reason to build a Christian church on the waterfront.

The extent of the territory controlled by Aixone cannot be determined with accuracy. Hymettos obviously formed its eastern limit, the sea its western. The northern boundary lay south of Hagios Kosmas and so was probably indicated by one of the large gullies that start from Hymettos near the Gyrismos and reach the sea near Helleniko. For the southern limit there is one factor that must be considered. Strabo (9.1.21) mentions that the island of Hydroussa was κατὰ τοὺς Αἰξωνέας.[55] For this statement to be true the territory of Aixone must have gone as far south as Voula. On the other hand, it is not likely that it went much further south, because then the deme of Halai Aixonides, with the centre at Palaiochori, would have controlled no land to the north of its focal point. A border running from between Voula and Ana Voula towards Hymettos, perhaps following the line of a stream bed, would satisfy both conditions.

[54]Wrede, *Attika* 30.
[55]See n. 6.

APPENDIX TO CHAPTER II

SOME FURTHER REMARKS ON FAUVEL'S LETTER

I offer a few notes on certain of the archaeological finds mentioned in the excerpt from Fauvel's letter of April 11, 1819.

LINES 11–12: "beaucoup de vases." Three large black-figured "amphorae" are now in Berlin (Furtwängler, *Beschreibung* 371–375:

nos. 1887–1889). Actually they are not amphorae but loutro-
phoroi: see Zschietzschmann, "Die Darstellungen," 41: nos.
53–55. No. 54 (= Berlin 1888) is well illustrated on his Pl. 13.
LINES 13–14: "un cipe de 12 pieds. . . ." This stele can be seen in the
background of Dupré's drawing of Fauvel sitting in his Athenian
house (Dupré, *Voyage* Pl. 19). The finial and inscription were
published by L. Vulliamy, *Ornamental Sculpture* Pl. 20, 4. The
later publications of Kinnard (in Stuart and Revett, *Supplementary Volume* 13–14) and Stackelberg (*Die Gräber der Hellenen*
41 and Pl. 6) add nothing to the record. It is not even certain that
they saw the stele; they could have made their drawings by
combining Vulliamy's description quoted by Conze (*Grabreliefs*
1.11) and Vulliamy's own drawings. Indeed, this is perhaps the
only cogent explanation of why Stackelberg both placed the
inscription about half way up the shaft and drew the shaft alone
as about 11 feet 8 inches high, thus making the whole slightly
less than 14 feet. Vulliamy's published drawings specify neither
the position of the inscription nor the height of the shaft, whereas
Dupré's drawing, reliable in other respects, shows a total height,
including finial, of apparently just under 10 feet 3 inches, and
omits the inscription, even though the central part of the shaft
is clear of foliage. It is therefore most unlikely that the inscription
was in the place noted by Vulliamy and drawn by Stackelberg. As
for the height, Fauvel's remarks favour a total of 12 feet rather
than one of over 14 feet with the finial, which was 2 feet 2½ inches
in height according to Vulliamy. There are two other reasons why
the lower figure is to be preferred. Even though Dupré's drawing
does not present a measured likeness of the stele, it is hard to believe
that he would have drawn it so small had it been in fact about
14 feet high. Secondly, if for this type of stele a standard relation
existed between width and height, we should not expect a height
of more than 12 feet; something less might be considered more
usual. Thus, we are forced to believe either that Stackelberg's
notes were in error in precisely the same places as Vulliamy's, or
that Stackelberg made use of Vulliamy's notes, even though
today we have no knowledge of their publication before 1893
by Conze.

In 1934, in that part of the Athenian Agora where Fauvel had
once lived, part of a stele was found with the retrograde inscription [Θε]ρονος. The best report is by Miss Harrison, "Archaic
Gravestones," 27 and 37–38. Its identification as the stele dis-

covered by Fauvel is made certain by the remaining letters of the name as well as the direction of the writing, the incised lines along the edge of the front face of the shaft—lines noted by Dupré—and the agreement between Vulliamy and the stele about the width at the base. The inscription is not half-way up the shaft but near the bottom, where it would have been hidden in Dupré's drawing by the plant with heavy leaves growing in front of the stele.

Miss Richter (*Archaic Gravestones* 44) publishes this fragment separately from the Theron stele but concludes that their identification as a single piece is "likely." Miss Guarducci on the other hand ("Epigraphical Appendix" in Richter, *Archaic Gravestones* 169) is not so convinced as Miss Richter and seems ready to entertain doubts about the correctness of the identification. However, most of her qualms stem from the differences between the actual stele and the drawing of the shaft by Stackelberg (which she credits to Vulliamy). I have already shown that there is no reason to put much faith in the accuracy of Stackelberg's drawing. Had Miss Guarducci been more responsive to the impressive list of similarities, she might have paid less attention to alleged discrepancies based on questionable evidence.

Finally, let us consider one difference between our sources. Fauvel shows the letters of the name on the stele as

ϾΟͶΟ𐌀𐌆⊕, Vulliamy as ϾΟͳΟϞͳ⊕.

The latter's sigma and nu when compared with those on the stone are drawn with slightly more accuracy than Fauvel's. But what of the rho? Fauvel's is angular with a pronounced tail, Vulliamy's rounded without a tail. The latter is the more likely. According to Miss Jeffery (*Local Scripts* 67) the rounded shape is one of two "normal" forms in the sixth century B.C., whereas the angular with tail "appears in the last years of the 6th c. and the early part of the 5th c." Since the stele has been dated to the third quarter of the sixth century B.C. (Harrison, "Archaic Gravestones," 38), Vulliamy's drawing is therefore more likely to be correct. Fauvel was probably careless in his transcription; perhaps he had in mind the shape of the rho on the helmet found at Olympia, bearing, according to him, the same name (see below).

LINES 15–16: "nom que j'ai lu aussi sur un casque. . . ." The name Theron has not, to my knowledge, been found on any helmet discovered at Olympia. It is, however, perfectly obvious what

Fauvel saw, and this only confirms one's suspicions that the consul's understanding of ancient Greek was limited. In 1817 a helmet dedicated by Hieron was unearthed at Olympia. It was presented to King George IV of England and by him to the British Museum. The first word of the dedication reads ΘΙΑΡΟΝ, the first letter of which Fauvel undoubtedly mistook for a theta. As a result of this misconception the names would have appeared quite similar. See Walters, *Catalogue of Bronzes* 27: No. 250.

LINE 19: "un lion." This lion is now in the Louvre: *Catalogue sommaire* 9: No. 827. See also above, n. 30.

LINE 19: "une lione." This lioness is on the Acropolis just east of the Beulé Gate where the visitor will see two marble lions: the lioness is the more southerly of the two. See also above, chap. II, n. 37.

LINES 21–24: "j'ai eu pour ma part un bas relief. . . ." I know only one bas-relief with this scene and it is now in the Musée de Mariemont (*Antiquités du Musée de Mariemont* 138 and Pl. 49: No. R. 14). Formerly it was in the Villa Altieri at Rome and seems to have been mentioned first in 1840. I do not know its history before that date. It is most unlikely that this piece is the same as that described by Fauvel, even though the sizes are approximately the same and both had four figures; "du bon tems" means very little but is not incompatible with "1er siècle avant Jésus-Christ." There are, however, a few other considerations that must be taken into account. The bas-relief in Belgium may have a respectable pedigree that makes impossible any connection with Attika in 1819. Roman collections were largely made up of finds made in Italy. Secondly, we have only Fauvel's word that the scene in fact represented the freeing of a slave. The introduction of Herakles into Olympos, a much commoner scene, might be misinterpreted as "l'affranchissement d'un esclave." The problem must be left here. We are not certain whether Fauvel correctly described his bas-relief; even if he did, there is still no compelling reason for identifying it with the Mariemont bas-relief.

III

HALAI AIXONIDES

S TRABO (9.1.21) places Halai Aixonides after Aixone but before Anagyrous. In addition, he mentions that Cape Zoster was the first cape after Aixone, by which he presumably means that Cape Zoster was in the territory of Halai Aixonides, and that off Cape Zoster lay the island of Phabra. Pausanias (1.31.1), on the other hand, numbers "Zoster by the sea" among the "small demes of Attika" and records that it had an altar to Athena, Apollo, Artemis, and Latona. Since the demotic of Zoster has not yet appeared in any official context, we must assume that Pausanias was wrong in naming Zoster a deme (in the Kleisthenic sense). The reason for his error is probably that people who lived on, or near, Cape Zoster were sometimes known as Ζωστήριοι (rather than, or in addition to, their correct demotic). The account of Stephanos clarifies the situation (s.v. Ζωστήρ): τῆς Ἀττικῆς ἰσθμός, ὅπου φασὶ τὴν Λητὼ λῦσαι τὴν ζώνην, καθεῖσαν ἐν τῇ λίμνῃ λούσασθαι. ἐνταῦθα θύουσιν Ἀλαιεῖς[1] Λητοῖ καὶ Ἀρτέμιδι καὶ Ἀπόλλωνι ζωστηρίῳ. ὁ τοπίτης Ζωστήριος.

There can be no doubt from these three references that the deme of Halai Aixonides included within its borders Cape Zoster and that the people of Halai (sometimes referred to as the people of Zoster?) had a shrine on the cape at which they worshipped.

To the above we must add a further remark by Stephanos (s.v. Ἁλαὶ Ἀραφηνίδες καὶ Ἁλαὶ Αἰξωνίδες): ἔστι δὲ ὁ δῆμος τῆς Ἀραφηνίδος μεταξὺ Φηγέως τοῦ πρὸς Μαραθῶνι καὶ Βραυρῶνος, αἱ δ᾽Αἰξωνίδες ἐγγὺς τοῦ ἄστεος· ἔστι καὶ λίμνη ἐκ θαλάσσης. Since "the lake" seems to refer

---

[1]The traditional reading is ἁλιεῖς, which Frazer (*Pausanias* 2.399) naturally translated as "fishermen." This information seems to have very little meaning and to be out of place. One would more reasonably expect the name, not the class, of the people worshipping at Zoster to be recorded. A simple emendation to Ἀλαιεῖς, Ἀλαιεῖς, or Ἀλεῖς (if we accept Stephanos' dictum that the demotic lacked the iota, s.v. Ἁλαὶ Ἀραφηνίδες καὶ Ἁλαὶ Αἰξωνίδες) recommends itself: it supplies the sentence with a proper name that is pertinent and adds a topographical detail that is quite in harmony with the other evidence. See Kourouniotes, "Τὸ ἱερόν," 12 n. 1, who gives Ἀλαεῖς as the text of Stephanos but with no explanation.

only to Halai Aixonides, it was probably not a "salt lake" that both demes possessed. It surely must have been the lake in which Leto bathed and which was, therefore, part of Cape Zoster.

The position of Cape Zoster is not disputed. It has long been recognized as the end of Hymettos that lunges into the sea at the present Vouliagmene[2] and off which is the island of Phleva. The "lake" may well be the natural pool on the eastern side of the main bay.

NAME

The name Halai Aixonides is in itself informative. It means "the Aixone salt works," thus placing the deme in close relation with Aixone. One would expect the two demes, therefore, to be neighbours, as in fact Strabo (9.1.21) indicates. From the name we also gather that in antiquity there were salt lakes in the deme.[3] The low-lying shore from Cape Punta to the church of Hagios Nikolaos near Zoster (from Voula to near Kavouri) was, until a few years ago, most suitable for the process of acquiring salt from sea water by evaporation, and two such lakes are shown in the *Karten* (Sheet VIII). These lakes are not necessarily in the same place as the ancient ones, but, since the available coast is not of great extent, the position of salt lakes at any date is more or less fixed.[4]

Finally one must consider the modern name Haliki. Recently it has been used of the area joining Cape Punta to the mainland, a waist of low land where a salt lake could easily be formed. Since this name is the modern equivalent of Ἁλαί, one is tempted to ask if there is any strong topographical connection between Haliki and the deme. Two

---

[2]The only problem not fully settled by the ancient sources is whether the name Zoster covers all three prongs of the cape, or just the central one, the only one that could be classed as ἰσθμός (see Stephanos, s.v. Ζωστήρ). Since Herodotos (8.107) describes Zoster as having ἄκραι λεπταί, it is perhaps best to consider that the name has two senses, a general one referring to the whole headland with all its promontories, and a particular one referring to a single projection. See Kourouniotes, "Τὸ ἱερόν," 9–11.

[3]Salt was not mined in Greece but acquired by the evaporation of salt water. See Forbes, *Studies in Ancient Technology* 3.170.

[4]It has been argued that there has been a change of three metres in the level of the sea about Peiraieus since classical times: see Pritchett, "Restudy of Salamis," 255–256. Pritchett is basically accepting a thesis presented by Négris in 1904. Since then more evidence has come to light and the question needs to be re-examined. That a change in the level of the sea has occurred is obvious, but it is possible that the change took place after the prehistoric and before the classical period. If that is so, the present shoreline can be taken as a good indication of the line followed by the classical shoreline.

considerations should warn against putting too much reliance on this possibility. First, the name Haliki is widely used and could be applied to any region at any time where salt is manufactured by evaporation. Secondly, the use of the name Haliki for this particular region had no long tradition. The early travellers knew it as Agiea[5] or Agyra,[6] whereas Wheler in two passages called it Zoster Halikes.[7] One cannot deny that a semantic link exists between Halai and Haliki but its use for topography is obviously too uncertain to have much value.

INSCRIPTIONS

Several decrees passed by the demesmen of Halai Aixonides have survived. Although neither IG II² 1174 nor 1175 preserves the name of the deme, A. Wilhelm clearly demonstrated with the help of IG II² 2820 that the persons appearing on the two deme inscriptions must belong to the deme of Halai.[8] The finding place of IG II² 1174 (to be discussed immediately below) makes it clear that we are dealing with Halai Aixonides rather than Halai Araphenides.

IG II² 1174

Böckh described the finding place of IG II² 1174 thus: "Ille in ruderibus Halarum (Aixonidum) repertum dicit prope Zosterem, qui etiam nunc Ἅλικες dicitur."[9] The description has been ruthlessly shortened in IG II² where we read "ad promontorium quod Haliki vocatur."[10] This is most ambiguous because Haliki is a name now applied to the region near Cape Punta and as a result Kirchner's note seems to be at variance with that of Böckh. We have already seen, however, that Wheler called Zoster "Halikes." That this equation was still true for the beginning of the nineteenth century is shown by Pittakys' description of IG II² 1356 (which might possibly be a deme inscription of Halai Aixonides): "εὑρέθησαν [i.e. the fragments] πρὶν τῆς ἐπαναστάσεως εἰς τὸ μέρος τῆς Ἀττικῆς τὸ νῦν καλούμενον Ἁλικαῖς,

[5]Dodwell, *Classical Tour* 1.525.

[6]Stuart and Revett, *Antiquities* Vol. 3, the map of Attica facing p. 1.

[7]Wheler, *Journey* 424 and 450. The first reference is straightforward except for the unexpected mention of the church of "Hagio Cosmo," which is several kilometres away; however, since Wheler repeats in a slightly different context the information that Zoster was called "Halikes," without any further troublesome phrases, we can accept it as true.

[8]Wilhelm, "Inscription attique," 94–95.

[9]*CIG* 88: 1.127. I have not been able to consult the catalogues cited by Böckh.

[10]At this point IG II² refers the reader to Milchhöfer, *AM* 13 (1888) 360, but Milchhöfer merely says "Haliki."

πλησίον τοῦ ἄκρου ζωστῆρος καὶ τοῦ δήμου ‘Αλαὶ Αἰξωνίδες.”[11] Böckh's description is, therefore, a possible one, and, lacking other evidence concerning this inscription, we should accept it as correct, and at the same time consider the citation in *IG* II² as not only inadequate but also incorrect: the verb should be in the past tense, not the present.[12]

IG II² 1175

IG II² 1175 was discovered by Abbé Fourmont and is reported to have been found "Philia in ecclesia destructa."[13] Before Wilhelm showed that this inscription was a decree of Halai Aixonides, scholars had thought that by Philia Fourmont had really meant Phyle or possibly Phlya. No good, however, is served by such suggestions, which would make the finding place quite remarkable in the light of Wilhelm's work. It is better to accept Fourmont's word and presume that here we have a comparatively rare case of a block being re-used a considerable distance from the place where it originally stood. I suggest that the Philia mentioned is the small village between Liopesi and Koropi known as Philiati, which Wheler called Fillia.[14]

[11]*ArchEph* (1839) 157: No. 118. Although Pittakys' initial description of the finding place is clear enough, his later remarks are thoroughly confused. He seems to say that this inscription was found both in the sanctuary of Hebe and in the sanctuary of Demeter that was near by. Since there were two fragments and since they were not found together, presumably this is possible. He then adds that the sanctuary of Hebe is the same as the one mentioned in *IG* II² 1199—a deme decree of Aixone. Something is wrong: it is obvious that the same sanctuary of Hebe cannot have been in both demes at the same time; also, there is nothing in the inscription to make one connect it in the first place with a sanctuary of Hebe. It is pointless to try to straighten out this problem because we have no idea where Pittakys got his information, although I think it is not unlikely that he invented most of it to fit his preconceived idea that this inscription had something to do with Hebe. These criticisms, however, do not affect the validity of his equation Zoster = Haliki, a statement based on factual topographical knowledge, not on any theory.

[12]This inscription was originally in the collection of Choiseul-Gouffier. Since his agent in Athens was Fauvel, we can assume that the latter obtained it for his patron. If so, it was acquired in all probability before September 1788, when the last shipment of antiquities for Choiseul-Gouffier was sent from Athens (Espérandieu, "Collection de Choiseul-Gouffier," 163). The finding of this inscription, therefore, has nothing to do with Fauvel's later digging in this area (cf. Wilhelm, "Inscription attique," 94 and his reference to Michon).

[13]*CIG* 89: 1.128. Böckh adds: "*Phylen* significet, ex cuius nominibus unum est *Phyla Castron*, an *Philaidas* (Philliati) nescio." I do not understand his association of Philaidas and Philliati, but I assume that he was looking for an answer somewhat similar to mine.

[14]Wheler, *Journey* 449. Fourmont does not mention Fillia in his published letters, but we know that, in the month of August 1729, he made two extensive trips within

In the excavations conducted by Kourouniotes at Vouliagmene in 1926 and 1927, one almost complete deme inscription and fragments from three others were found, all apparently passed by the demesmen of Halai Aixonides.[15] These prove—if the literary evidence had not already done so—that Cape Zoster with its shrine to Apollo was controlled by the people of Halai Aixonides and that this area lay within the confines of this deme. Little else, however, has been found in this region to suggest that the actual village was located near the sanctuary.

IG II² 3091

One further inscription must be mentioned, *IG* II² 3091. It is not a deme inscription but a monument commemorating the choregic victories of two persons, Epichares and Thrasyboulos. It was erected early in the fourth century B.C. and recorded events that took place about the middle of the fifth. As Pickard-Cambridge says, it must have been put up "either by themselves [Epichares and Thrasyboulos] in their old age or by their family or deme . . . perhaps after their deaths."[16]

The inscription was found by Papagiannopoulos-Palaios in 1929 "ἐν θέσει 'Παλαιοχώρι,' καὶ εἰδικώτερον παρά τινα αὐλὴν προβάτων, κειμένην ἐν τῷ μεταξὺ 'Βούλας' καὶ 'Βάρης' συνοικισμῷ ποιμένων." He further learnt "ὅτι τοῦτο εὑρέθη εἰς ἀπόστασιν 40–50 μέτρων ἀπὸ τῆς αὐλῆς."[17] Papagiannopoulos-Palaios immediately associated this base with the

---

Attika. The first he describes thus: "Le premier voyage a esté depuis Athènes jusqu'au cap Sunium, autrement le cap Colomnes, et de là jusques à l'ancienne Prassia, aujourd'huy le Porto Raphti. Douze jours ont esté employez dans ce voyage, parceque je n'ay voulu passer aucun buisson, aucun village, la moindre église et le plus petit débris, soit dans les montagnes, soit dans les vallées et les plaines, sans le visiter, sans y faire fouiller. J'y ay trouvé 70 inscriptions, dont une méritoit seule la peine que je me suis donnée." (Omont, *Missions archéologiques* 1.570, but see also 572 and 591.) The second trip was to Marathon and included as well "toute cette étendue de païs qui comprend les monts Pentélyens, Parnès, Corydalia, Brilessos et Gercania, enfin toute la province" (*ibid.* 1.570). Philiati lies at the foot of Mount Hymettos on its eastern side, a little to the west of the main route through the Mesogaia. Fourmont would have visited this area on his first trip: not only did he claim to have examined Mount Hymettos before he went to Marathon (*ibid.* 1.590–591), but Philiati was easily accessible to a traveller going from Porto Raphti to Athens through Markopoulo.

[15]Kourouniotes, "Τὸ ἱερόν," 40–43: nos. 4–7. See also Peek, "Attische Inschriften," 8–10.

[16]Pickard-Cambridge, *Festivals* 54.

[17]Papagiannopoulos-Palaios, "'Αττικαὶ ἐπιγραφαί 7," 161–173. The quotations are from 162.

"theatre at Aixone." The finding place, a few kilometres from that of
the Aixone deme decrees pertaining to the theatre, should have warned
him against any such conclusion. Another consideration, which later
scholars have thoroughly discussed, is whether this inscription relates
to the city Dionysia or to the rural Dionysia.[18] Whichever is the
correct answer (and I think that the city Dionysia is the more likely),[19]
there is nothing that automatically connects this inscription with
Aixone, and there is equally nothing that prevents an association with
Halai Aixonides,[20] Aixone's neighbouring deme. In fact, the finding
place is certainly more suitable for the latter than for the former:
such inscriptions were set up to be seen in public places and we have
already noticed that the public centre of Aixone was some distance
away from Palaiochori.[21]

REMAINS

The majority of early travellers paid but passing attention to the
remains between Athens and Vari other than to record that there
were many traces of ancient settlements and numerous tumuli, which
latter some took for graves. Their enthusiasm for accurate reporting
usually waned after Cape Punta, not to recover until Vari had been
reached. A typical statement is that of Chandler: "On our approach
to the shore [*sic*, the last place mentioned was Alopeke!], some vestiges
occurred, it is likely, of Aexone. We then turned, and travelled toward
Sunium, through a gap in Mount Hymettos."[22] There is just sufficient
vagueness to make it doubtful whether we can honestly insist that
Chandler saw remains near Palaiochori, where the road on which he

[18]Pickard-Cambridge, *Festivals* 52–54 with earlier bibliography on 52 n. 7. His
reference to M. Fromhold-Treu should be to *Hermes* 1934 (as in my Bibliography),
not 1936.

[19]Cf. the inscription (EM 13180) recently found near Vari and reported in *BCH* 79
(1955) 210 and *AJA* 59 (1955) 223. Again, we must believe either that great poets
"tried out" their plays in the provinces, or (and this is much more likely) that a
native son was honoured for having brought glory to his deme by acting as a successful
choregos in Athens.

[20]If we insist that this inscription refers to a local performance in a rural deme,
there is absolutely no reason why Halai Aixonides could not have provided an open
theatral area with the bare essentials necessary for a performance: cf., e.g., the in-
formal arrangement at Rhamnous.

[21]Pickard-Cambridge, *Festivals* 53, says that this inscription was found "apparently
on the site of Halai Aixonides." His source is Fromhold-Treu, "Die Telephos-
Trilogie des Sophokles," 324 n. 1, which reads "Nicht Aixone, wie eine Leipziger
Seminararbeit Werner Paesslers gezeigt hat." No additional proof is offered.

[22]Chandler, *Travels* 2.166.

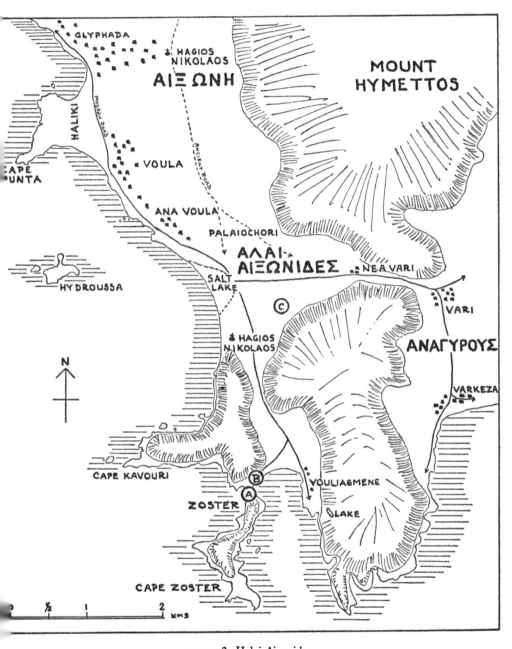

FIGURE 2. Halai Aixonides

travelled did indeed turn away from the sea. On the other hand, remains were there to be seen, because they are recorded on the *Karten* (Sheet VIII).

Modern exploration has not greatly increased our knowledge of this region except at Vouliagmene. There Kourouniotes exposed the temple of Apollo Zoster[23] (A on Figure 2) and, a few years later, P. Stauropoullos the priests' house[24] and a few other remains near by such as the foundation of a tower[25] (B on Figure 2). In the area north of Zoster only one find has been reported as far as I know. Papagian-nopoulos-Palaios considers that he has found the remains of an orchestra, which he associates with the theatre at Aixone.[26] This discovery was made in the Kanellopoulos estate, which lies south of the road running from the crossroads beyond Ana Voula to Vari (C on Figure 2). The presentation of the evidence is far from convincing; no reliable criteria for dating are established;[27] and the connection with the theatre at Aixone is non-existent. One is tempted to inquire: "Why not a threshing floor?"

On the evidence thus far presented, it would be difficult to place the deme of Halai Aixonides with any precision. Various scholars have suggested locations, and their views, up until 1912, have been ably summed up by Kolbe who agrees with Löper in placing the deme "wo der von Athen kommende Weg nach Osten umbiegt."[28] Wrede seems to agree more or less with this position.[29] Since Papagianno-poulos-Palaios places the theatre of Aixone in this same area, I presume he would disagree with both Kolbe and Wrede about the location of Halai Aixonides.

But other evidence does exist, which no previous commentators have used (except perhaps Wrede). Between Voula and Vouliagmene at the place named Palaiochori, there is a modern cemetery dating

[23]Kourouniotes, "Tò ἱερόν," 9–53.

[24]Stauropoullos, "'Ιερατικὴ οἰκία ἐν Ζωστῆρι," 1–31.

[25]The tower and the finds from within it (*ibid.* 6–7 n. 1 and figs. 6–7) deserve some attention. It is by no means a forgone conclusion that every round structure is a defensive tower. The presence of the lead weights might make one believe that this particular round building had quite a different character, one more akin to that of the most famous of all round buildings in Attika, the Tholos in the Agora where we know that official weights and measures were kept.

[26]Papagiannopoulos-Palaios, "'Αττικά· τò θέατρον Αἰξωνῆσιν," 138.

[27]The date given is "πιθανῶς" fourth century B.C.

[28]*RE* 7 (1910–1912) 2226–2227, s.v. Halai (1).

[29]Wrede, *Attika* 30. Although Wrede's description "im Walde" might imply a position closer to Vouliagmene than Kolbe's, the map (frontispiece) indicates a classical site near Voula.

from the Second World War. North and east of this cemetery towards
Hymettos is a large and reasonably level area that stretches in a
northeasterly direction as far as Hymettos' only prominent foothill
in the area. The ground is covered with sherds and it is easy to make
out the ground plans of numerous houses and buildings.[30] The limits
of this settlement can be defined on three sides. There is a road to the
northeast that passes over the shoulder of the foothill; this road
continues to Vari and was presumably in older times the main road
from Athens to Anagyrous. To the northwest is a stream bed and
quarry. The southwestern limit seems to be near the cemetery where
the ground begins to shelve quite rapidly towards the sea; on this side
there are indications of a road leading off towards Vouliagmene. The
area so defined is quite large enough to have contained a village of
moderate size.

This village was inhabited over a long period. The majority of the
sherds that we collected came from the classical and Hellenistic
periods, but there were a few from archaic as well as Roman times. In
addition, we noticed a Hellenistic pebble-mosaic floor and several
bottle-shaped cisterns. Although there seemed to be no evidence of
habitation prior to the seventh century B.C., a Mycenaean community
must have been in the vicinity, because on a knoll a little to the west
of the village were unmistakable signs of four illicitly (?) excavated
chamber tombs (1954).

IDENTIFICATION

The area controlled by the deme of Halai Aixonides is now not
difficult to establish. Its northern limit is the only one not defined by
a natural boundary, but we shall not be far wrong if we tentatively
place it on a line running in a northeasterly direction from just south
of Voula towards Hymettos, perhaps taking into account some stream
bed. The western limit is set by the sea, the eastern by Hymettos and
its spur that separates the Bay of Vari from that of Vouliagmene. In
the notch, through which the road passes to Vari, some boundary
must have been set, probably near Nea Vari.

---

[30]Most of the remains are those of small houses. Two structures, however, stood
out and caught our attention. One, a little to the southwest of the main group of
houses and on the road to Vouliagmene (?), is of considerable size with several
interior divisions as well as bases for internal supports. Perhaps it should be classed
as a public building. The other structure is set in the middle of the town and gives
the appearance of an altar cut out of the rock.

Halai Aixonides, therefore, controlled the narrow coastal plain from Voula to Vouliagmene, the easterly extension of the same plain towards Vari, and two (or perhaps two and a half) of the three prongs that constitute the Zoster of Herodotos.

The town that gave its name to this administrative unit is certainly to be placed at Palaiochori where extensive remains testify to the existence in antiquity of a large settlement. Such a position is eminently suitable for the chief village of the area, a consideration which favours the identification. Not only is the site centrally located with reference to the available arable land, but it controlled the main highway from Athens to Anagyrous at the very point where the road turned away from the coast and where also in all probability the secondary road to Vouliagmene began. It thus also commanded the route from Athens to Zoster. Its nearness to the part of the coast most naturally adapted for salt lakes makes the name perfectly understandable. Finally, we must recall the choregic dedication *IG* II^2 3091 found at Palaiochori. Such a record of honours won by native sons would surely be displayed where the majority of brother demesmen could see it and that place could hardly be any other than in the chief town of Halai Aixonides itself.

IV

ANAGYROUS

ANCIENT REFERENCES

ONCE again, the most important citation is to be found in Strabo (9.1.21). He places Anagyrous after Halai Aixonides and before Thorai. We have already noted that Halai included Zoster and so we should expect to find Anagyrous to the east (or possibly southeast) of Halai. Consequently, the area controlled by modern Vari becomes a promising candidate for the deme of Anagyrous. Other authors tell us very little about the position of this deme, even though Pausanias (1.31.1) notes one of its antiquities.

NAME

The ancient name of Anagyrous has not survived to the present in any form[1] nor has it any obvious connection with the Albanian name Vari.[2] There is no topographical information to be gained by studying the derivation of the ancient name. Two theories were current in antiquity: first, that the deme was named after a hero called Anagyros; secondly, that it took its name from a vile-smelling growth named Anagyros, a plant which at one time may have been common in the area but is not so today.[3]

[1]Sourmeles, 'Αττικὰ ἢ περὶ δήμων 'Αττικῆς 47 preserves a tradition that he rightly calls a misinterpretation: 'Ο δῆμος οὗτος παρεξηγηθεὶς ὑπὸ ἀπαιδεύτων, ὅτι δῆθεν παράγεται ἀπὸ τὸν γῦρον (στροφὴν) μετωνομάσθη ἀπλούστερον Γύρισμα, καὶ οὕτω νῦν καλεῖται.

[2]Cf. Leake, *Demi* 61 n. 1: "Vari seems to be a corruption of *Thorae*, which has *moved* into the Anagyrasia." But this suggestion is unacceptable since Vari is an Albanian word and therefore does not owe its existence to the corruption of a Greek word (Milchhöfer, *RE* 1 [1894] 2028, s.v. Anagyrus). It is interesting that the Albanian noun *varr* has the meaning "tomb" or "grave" (Mann, *Albanian and English Dictionary* 546, s.v. varr). Were those who gave the village the name of Vari the first to note the presence of the ancient cemeteries?

[3]Both theories are reported in Scholia to Aristophanes' *Lysistrata* 67–68. The ancient references to both the hero and the plant are many because of the proverb κινήσω τὸν ἀνάγυρον and one of its variants μὴ κινεῖν τὸν ἀνάγυρον. The latter might be translated today: "Don't stir up a hornets' nest."

Hanriot, *Topographie des dèmes* 72 is the only scholar to advance the theory that

INSCRIPTIONS

That there was an ancient settlement of some importance at the site of the modern village is clear from the remains of walls, fortification, and graves around Vari. This evidence is reinforced by a number of inscriptions found in the neighbourhood.

IG II² 1212

One of the inscriptions is a deme decree, *IG* II² 1212. Unfortunately there is so little remaining of the decree that it is impossible to assign it to a particular deme. Nevertheless, the very presence of a deme decree at Vari makes it highly probable that the village situated there in antiquity was the seat of local administration, the place of the agora and of the chief religious shrines.

IG II² 5642 and 5639

Two other inscriptions—*IG* II² 5642 and 5639—have received much attention because they have been frequently advanced as secondary evidence for the identification of Vari as Anagyrous.[4] Both grave monuments were found at Vari and both bear the names of members of Anagyrous. It should be noted, however, that several other grave markers with demotics have been found in, or near, Vari: *IG* II² 5522 records a man from Halai;[5] 5733, two persons, one from Aphidna, the other from Halai; 6168, a man from Euonymon; 7681, a woman from Phlya. We see at once that Anagyrous is not the only deme mentioned on the grave markers, nor is it numerically the strongest if all the references to Halai are to Halai Aixonides, Anagyrous' neighbouring deme.[6]

---

the name Anagyrous has a significant topographical meaning: "Entre le promontoire Zoster et l'Hymette-sans-eau ('Υμηττὸς ῎Ανυδρος) se trouvait le dème Anagyre, ᾽Αναγυροῦς, qui avait, à ce que je pense, pris son nom de sa position au tournant de l'Hymette (ἀνὰ-γυρόω). . . ." Ingenious though the suggestion may be, it necessitates the existence of a verb that is not to be found in classical literature (at least not cited in LSJ⁹). Even if the verb did exist, it does not seem obvious that it would have the meaning ascribed to it by Hanriot.

[4]E.g. Frazer, *Pausanias* 2.401.

[5]The reading given in the Corpus was taken from Ross's notebooks. Ross and Kirchner were both probably unaware that this inscription had been published by Leake, *Demi* 55 n. 2, who gives George Finlay the credit for its discovery.

[6]Another grave marker may possibly have come from Vari. *IG* II² 5525, which records the names of two people from the deme of Halai, has been studied by Wilhelm, "Grabgedicht aus Athen," 1008. He thinks that the Halai referred to is Halai Aixonides and that therefore the stone came from near Vouliagmene. There is,

To introduce two gravestones bearing the demotic Anagyrasios (out of a total of six stones with seven names in all) as evidence for the placing of Anagyrous is to exaggerate the information that a small number of gravestones provides.

EM 13180

One other inscription (EM 13180) remains to be discussed briefly. It was discovered at Vari in 1954, and is a choregic dedication made by a certain Sokrates, who records a victory with tragedies by Euripides.[7] Vanderpool would like to identify this man with the Sokrates who was one of the generals (441/0 and, probably, 439/8 B.C.) in the Samian War and who was from Anagyrous (Androtion, FGrH 3b, 324 F 38). If this were so, it would be a good argument for equating modern Vari with ancient Anagyrous, since it seems unlikely that, as early as ca. 440 B.C., a man would set up a dedication in a deme other than his own without adding his demotic. Vanderpool's suggested identification, however, is based on the assumption that Vari does represent Anagyrous and that Sokrates was probably a member of that deme.[8] This inscription, unfortunately, cannot be used to determine the position of the deme Anagyrous.

REMAINS

The remains from antiquity in the plain of Vari are quite extensive. We shall begin with the area around the village.

The earliest published remains are two small Mycenaean chamber

---

however, no good evidence connecting the finding place with the deme of Halai Aixonides. The demotic is not nearly enough evidence, and earlier commentators suggested other locations as far ranging as Vari and Sounion. The one clue is that it was found in the Asomatos monastery in Athens, which owned much land around both Vari and Vouliagmene. If it was found at Vari, then Halai, whichever deme is meant, appears at Vari on grave stones as often as Anagyrous.

[7]Vanderpool, "News Letter from Greece" (1955) 223. BCH 79 (1955) 210 also has a reference to this find but says that it came from Varkiza. This statement does not conflict with Vanderpool's but reflects a growing tendency to make no clear distinction between Vari and Varkiza.

[8]Otherwise one might ask why Vanderpool does not mention as a possible candidate the Sokrates of Halai Araphenides, who was General in 432/1 and 431/0 B.C. and was a contemporary of Euripides. Furthermore, since a choregos must have been a man of means and importance, both Sokrates of Anagyrous and Sokrates of Halai Araphenides would probably have qualified on these counts. Certainly they were both sufficiently important to be elected General, and the former was voted against in an ostrakophoria (Thompson, "Excavations," 337).

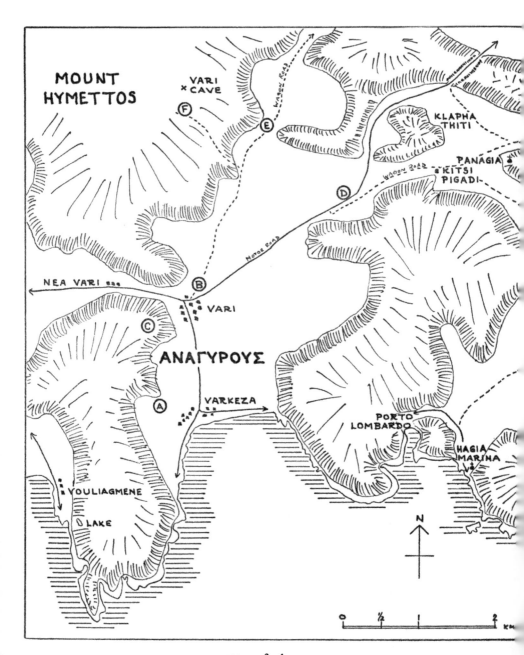

FIGURE 3. Anagyrous

tombs discovered south of Vari[9] (A on Figure 3), part of a Mycenaean cemetery largely exploited by tomb robbers towards the end of the nineteenth century. The Mycenaean settlement has not yet been located.[10]

At Vari itself, the earliest signs of habitation go back to the last years of the Geometric period.[11] The most famous remains, however, are from the succeeding archaic period. A little to the north of the village (B on Figure 3) are several walled (or partly walled) enclosures, the whole forming a large cemetery. The pottery found in the graves and offering-channels shows that the cemetery was in use from the last decades of the seventh century B.C. to the middle of the fifth century B.C.[12] The excellence and richness of the offerings made in the archaic period are perhaps best explained by the theory that a wealthy aristocratic family (or several families?) lived in Vari at that time, more or less as lords of the manor, the manor being the fertile plain.[13]

On the long spur of the hill that lies to the west of Vari and immediately south of the road through the gap in Hymettos (C on Figure 3), a small site was found and cleared under the direction of G. Oikonomos just before the beginning of the Second World War. According to the

[9]These tombs were briefly noted in the annual archaeological summaries for 1954: see, e.g., Vanderpool, "News Letter from Greece" (1954) 232. A longer report, with a full discussion of a rhyton seemingly of Cretan origin decorated with fishes and found in an unplundered niche, was published by Maria D. Theocharis, "A Knossian Vase," 266–269. Her suggestions about how this vase might have come to Attika show too great a reliance on the historicity of the Theseus-Minotaur myth. On 266 n. 4 she mentions the existence of a tomb earlier than the ones discussed above: "A L.H. II Shaft-grave has been excavated near the shore of Varkiza by D. Theocharis in February 1951 (unpublished)." For the cemetery discovered by tomb robbers, see Karo, *RE* Supplement 6 (1935) 608, s.v. Mykenische Kultur; and Stubbings, "Mycenaean Pottery," 4.

[10]There is one report suggesting that traces of a Mycenaean settlement had been found at Vari (*AA* 55 [1940] 178). This will be discussed later: it appears to be untrue.

[11]*BCH* 82 (1958) 672: eight tombs were excavated "500 mètres au Nord de la zone archéologique de Vari."

[12]Since a publication of the cemetery and its pottery has not been made, the only accounts are to be found in the various archaeological news letters. The following are the most useful: *AA* 50 (1935) 172–175; *AA* 51 (1936) 123–125; *AA* 54 (1939) 224–225; *AA* 55 (1940) 126–134 and 175–178; *BCH* 61 (1937) 450–451. The pottery and terracottas are now on view in the National Museum at Athens, and much of the former has been included by Sir John Beazley in his *Attic Black-Figure Vase-Painters*.

[13]The New York chariot stele (Richter, *Greek Sculptures in the Metropolitan* 13–14), the Boston sphinx (Chase, "Greek Sphinx in Boston," 1–5), and a fragmentary sphinx in Athens (Richter, *Archaic Gravestones* 11) perhaps also come from this archaic cemetery. If so, the impression that an important aristocratic family lived at Vari is strengthened.

only report so far published, twenty-five small houses and a sanctuary were noted and masses of offerings were collected from the sanctuary and also the houses, including thousands of terracottas, and bracelets, earrings, and fibulae of various metals.[14] The excavators announced that the settlement covered the same period as the cemetery mentioned above, that is, from the seventh to the fifth century B.C.

A settlement of the archaic period represents a unique find in Attika. I therefore visited the site and offer a brief description of the remains now visible. The buildings fall into groups owing to the contours of the spur. There are two main groups, one lying on the highest part of the ridge and the other partly down the slope to the south. These two are linked by a number of houses that are poorly preserved. The houses were of various shapes: circular, rectangular, and apsidal. Some contained low benches. The little extant chronological evidence on the site supports the dates for the period of use proposed by the excavators. There is nothing that would suggest inhabitation or use in the late classical or Hellenistic periods.

A settlement of this kind is certainly not to be recognized as general living quarters: it is not big enough; in addition, the nature of the finds makes it clear that many of the buildings were used for cult purposes. The excavators, in fact, called one of the buildings a sanctuary.[15]

To suggest any interpretation at this moment is to anticipate the full record of the excavation. Thus I make the following remarks with some hesitation. The settlement appears to be a sanctuary area in which various gods and heroes were worshipped. Just as the Acropolis was the sacred place *par excellence* for the Athenians, so this area probably served the religious needs of the people who inhabited the plain below. Some of the houses with the low benches may have been the shrines themselves, the offerings being placed on the benches.[16] It is unlikely that all the buildings were shrines; some may have served secular needs, while yet others may have been storerooms for either religious or secular objects.[17]

---

[14] *AA* 55 (1940) 177–178. Gardikas ("Δῆμοι Ἀττικῆς," 41) was perhaps the first to report the existence of these remains.

[15] I was unable to decide which building they had in mind as the sanctuary. The report in *AA* makes it appear that the sanctuary and the houses were together. If this is a misunderstanding, then it is possible that the excavators meant a small sanctuary on the northern side of the hill at about the same level as the settlement, which seems to have been excavated. This sanctuary will be noted later.

[16] Some of the boundary walls of the archaic cemetery have low benches along the inner face. These benches, however, were used for burned, not dry, offerings.

[17] Divine protection was considered important in Athens for certain secular objects;

Whatever the final interpretation, this can be considered certain: the masses of offerings, some expensive, some of little value, testify to the importance of this area in the archaic period not only to the people of wealth but also to those of little means. This must have been one of the main places of religious worship for the local inhabitants.[18]

Other remains are still visible on this hill. On the northern side at the same level as the settlement are the foundations and lowest wall courses of a small temple with cella and pronaos. The building looks as if it had been partially cleared at some time. The sherds found in the area immediately around it are classical.[19]

Another group of remains lies at, and around, the peak of the hill. The top is ringed on three sides by a low defensive wall, which in places stands more than a metre high; the fourth side needed no wall to protect it as the rock there drops sheer and presents an adequate defence in itself. The wall, which has at least one projecting tower and one gateway, encloses an area about thirty metres square. Within this area at the very peak are a well-preserved altar of stone, the scanty remains of a building that might be a temple, and a rock-cut inscription of late date that seems to read as follows:[20]

I offer no explanation of it other than that it appears to be a marker of

for example, the Mother of the Gods watched over the civic archives. Consequently, the juxtaposition of the religious and secular is quite normal, especially where state and religion were bound so closely together.

[18]There is no visible evidence that would explain the apparent abandonment of this site during the fifth century B.C. Without full knowledge of what was observed by the excavators, any such explanation as fire or invasion is entirely hypothetical. On the other hand, some may wonder whether the fact that the archaic cemetery and the settlement seem to have gone out of use at the same time is to be regarded as other than coincidental. One might argue that both belonged to a small group—a family, a *genos*, or an association with restricted membership—and that the group went out of existence or moved away during the fifth century B.C. Attractive as this explanation may seem—and it does take into account the suggestion that an aristo- cratic family lived at Vari—it does not satisfactorily explain the great quantity of offerings, both rich and poor, and the large number of buildings. Both these observa- tions hint at a wider use of the settlement than that which a small restricted group would provide.

[19]The clearing (see n. 15 above) may have been done by Oikonomos.

[20]The letters have the following approximate heights: line 1, 0.08 m.; line 2, 0.14 m.; line 3, 0.08 m. The signs placed at the beginning and end of line 2 probably mark divisions between abbreviated words or phrases.

some limited area.[21] The structures were noted by the excavators of the sanctuary area on the lower slopes of the hill and reported as probably from a Mycenaean settlement.[22] There must have been a mistake in the reporting because the surrounding wall is undeniably classical, as can be seen from the use of stacking to fill the interstices between large stones.[23] Both the altar and what pottery I noticed would fit a context of either the fifth or the fourth century B.C., some of the pottery being undoubtedly of the fifth century B.C.

The simplest explanation of this little walled acropolis is that the inhabitants of the area wanted a defended height to which they could retire in time of stress. The need for such hideouts would have been increased by the Second Peloponnesian War. Several *Fluchtburgen* have been noted in other parts of Attika,[24] but despite these other examples I am not convinced that this little fortress at Vari should be placed in the same category. It has one great disadvantage as a place of refuge: the amount of space enclosed within the walls is small and hardly sufficient for the needs of a town. A better explanation is that it was an observation post maintained by a small detachment for the purpose of watching the movement of ships between capes Zoster and Astypalaia and of reporting to Athens any hostile action or landing in this area. It could have been used also as a relay station for messages between Athens and Sounion. These considerations will be examined further under Atene in chapter XI. For the moment it is sufficient to note that the acropolis at Vari is well suited for either operation. The surrounding wall could have prevented "unauthorized persons" from entering, and in time of emergency supplied some measure of protection to the garrison (a duty perhaps shared by the divinity worshipped at the summit).

So far we have described only the remains that lie on the upper part of the hill. There are also many traces of ancient construction on its

[21]I think we can assume that these abbreviations would have been easily understood. Thus, in the geographical context of Cape Zoster, one possible interpretation of the first line might be that it represented the name Zoster, the expanded form being either nominal or adjectival.

[22]*AA* 55 (1940) 178.

[23]"Stacking" was a technique used frequently during the fifth century B.C. It first appears at the end of the sixth century B.C. and can still be seen in Attika as late as the second half of the fourth century B.C. After that it seems to have been given up. See Jones, Sackett, and Eliot, "TO ΔEMA," 182 with references.

[24]Wrede (*Attika* 30) lists several *Fluchtburgen* in various parts of Attika, and Vanderpool and I have noticed several others that clearly resemble those listed by Wrede. All seem to date from classical times, though not all from the fifth century B.C.

lower slopes and at the base, on both the north and the east. The remains on the north lie alongside the road leading through the gap in Hymettos. They combine with similar remains on the northern side of the road to form an extensive cemetery of the classical period, presumably the successor to the archaic cemetery, since the latter went out of use ca. 450 B.C. The most prominent structures are large rectangular grave terraces: the walls are made of big stones which in many places are laid in the artificially polygonal technique frequently used for graves during the fourth century B.C.[25] Behind these terraces one can find less elaborate graves, some merely cysts cut in the earth. Since the whole cemetery has been ruthlessly pillaged by robbers, only a very few finds have been reported from these graves, but the fragments of pottery left by the despoilers testify to the cemetery's use in the fifth and fourth centuries B.C.[26]

On the eastern lower slopes of the hill already described, just above the last houses of Vari, one can see copious traces of an ancient settlement. There are remains of many walls, some of which appear in the *Karten* (Sheet VIII), as well as ancient building blocks built into modern structures. The fields are strewn with pottery from the classical, Hellenistic, and Roman periods. Milchhöfer succinctly describes these remains and adds that they represent "das Centrum eines alten Demos."[27] He also notes that southeast of Vari at the chapel of Hagioi Pantes are further traces of antiquity, including column drums. This last site has been suggested as a possible location for the temple of the Mother of the Gods mentioned by Pausanias (1.31.1).[28]

To complete our description of the ancient remains lying in the plain of Vari we must mention three small sites, all of which seem to have been overlooked by previous explorers. The first lies beside the road that skirts the western side of Kiapha Thiti (D on Figure 3) and is thus very close to the northern limit of the plain. The remains might be interpreted as a substantial and well-built farmstead with a large walled area behind it. The whole complex has been almost denuded of stone through the clearing of the fields for ploughing, but the general

---

[25]See Scranton, *Greek Walls* 48–50 and 166.

[26]Staïs ("περὶ τῶν ἐν Βάρῃ ἀνασκαφῶν," 28–32) did a little excavating along the road in 1891 and cleared a few graves of the classical cemetery. One group that had not been pillaged was of seven graves surrounded by a low circular terrace. The pottery belonged to the fifth century B.C.

[27]Milchhöfer, *Erläuternder Text* 3–6.15.

[28]Chandler, *Travels* 2.166, and Frazer, *Pausanias* 2.401, but there is no evidence to prove it.

outlines remain clear. A cistern within the enclosed area suggests by its shape that occupation began during Greek times. The pottery that we saw was largely Roman but there were a few pieces of the Hellenistic period.

The second site (E on Figure 3) is beside the road that leads to Lambrika through the foothills of Hymettos. Again, one notes that it is placed very near the northern edge of the plain. Here, the scanty remains were probably from a house complex of moderate size, occupied in the late Roman period.

The third site lies on the low spur of a hill (F on Figure 3) on the higher slopes of which is the Cave of the Nymphs. It is approached from the plain along a small narrow valley. The remains, which are marked on the *Karten* (Sheet VIII) but not discussed in the text, are those of a small rectangular enclosure made of rough stones with a room at one corner. The sherds lying around when I visited the place were of the classical period, including some that were black-glazed.

All three appear to have been farmhouses.[29] Although the distances from the ancient settlement at Vari to these houses are not great, they are enough to have caused considerable loss of time, especially during harvesting, if the workers had to commute from the village to the fields lying at the extreme edge of the plain. Complexes such as these would not only provide shelter for those working the farms but also a safe place to store the produce until harvesting was over or the yield had been taken to market. Today the same system is employed whether the farm be for grain or grape. Most of the farmers live in the centrally placed village and throughout most of the year commute to their fields. But at harvesting time they live in small shacks on their fields and so can guard their harvest until the work is over and the produce taken to the near-by community pool, either for thrashing or for pressing.

IDENTIFICATION

Since Chandler's visit to the Cave of the Nymphs, Vari has been identified as ancient Anagyrous.[30] Our examination of the available evidence has shown that the only real basis for this identification is the

[29]See J. H. Young, "Studies in South Attika," 133–139 for a general discussion of country estates and their plans. Our third site is similar in ground plan to Young's Thasos 5.

[30]Chandler, *Travels* 2.166. This view has been held by every scholar whose works I have consulted. To Frazer's bibliography (*Pausanias* 2.402) can be added Philippson, *Attika und Megaris* 811 n. 1 where the recent writings on Anagyrous are listed.

evidence from Strabo. The argument runs thus: since Strabo mentions all the demes on the coast from Peiraieus to Sounion and since Anagyrous is placed after Halai Aixonides, then the settlement that comes next after Cape Zoster (a part of Halai) must be Anagyrous. Since the settlement at Vari is without doubt the next immediately after Zoster, it must be identified as Anagyrous. The level plain, naturally bounded on all sides, is then the area controlled by the deme of Anagyrous.

Such is the positive evidence for the identification of Anagyrous, and, if one had complete faith in Strabo's accuracy, there would be no grounds for further discussion. But complete faith is not possible when one is concerned with Strabo's account of Greece. It is necessary, therefore, to confirm the witness of Strabo, and, in the case of Anagyrous, this can be done only with evidence that is by and large negative.

First, there is no evidence that contradicts the proposed identification. Secondly, where was Anagyrous if it was not at Vari? Thirdly, what is the correct identification of Vari if it is not to be Anagyrous? One question has already been answered: since we have no candidates other than Anagyrous, Vari would remain unidentified and Strabo would be accused of omitting an important deme from his list. As for the second question, if Anagyrous was not at Vari, then it must have been further down the coast. But I shall show in the next chapter that the coastal settlement immediately after Vari was in ancient times Lamptrai Paralia, and, in succeeding chapters, that all suitable coastal sites from Lamptrai to Sounion have been identified. The adjective "suitable" demands explanation. Since we know that the bouleutic representation of Anagyrous during the fourth century B.C. was five or six members,[31] we can be certain that we are looking for a deme of relatively large size,[32] similar to Aixone or Halai Aixonides. Obviously, then, a site of little extent commanding only a small area is unsuitable.

This process of elimination leaves little doubt that Anagyrous must have been at Vari and that Strabo is to be trusted in this instance.

Our knowledge of this deme and the area it controlled is remarkably full. Its boundaries are clearly defined. The fertile plain, the source of

---

[31]These figures are based on Agora I 3812 (Pritchett, "Greek Inscriptions," 231-239), a recently published bouleutic list (Charitonides, "First Half of a Bouleutai List," 30-57), and an unpublished inscription, Agora I 3400.

[32]Milchhöfer (Die Demenordnung 9) concluded on the basis of the number of names from each deme preserved on the gravestones that Anagyrous was one of the "mittelgrosse Demen."

the deme's wealth, is limited to north, east, and west by hills: to the
west by Hymettos, to the east by Karamoti, and to the north, partially
filling the gap between the two other hills, by Kiapha Thiti. To the
south lies the sea, a gentle bay with sandy beach between the most
easterly of Zoster's prongs and Karamoti. Despite these hills and the
sea, the plain is not landlocked. The main route from Athens to
Sounion entered the plain through a definite break in Hymettos and
communication east and north was secured by routes that left the
plain at its northern end. The settlement was well placed, being
astride the Athens–Sounion highway at the place where it entered the
plain and with its back against a lightly fortified hill. It was also
sufficiently removed from the sea to be both centrally located within
its territory and safe from sudden attack by sea raiders. At the village
itself, we can follow the history of its cemeteries during the Geometric, archaic, and classical periods; and, from the evidence of the
archaic cemetery, we can imagine an aristocratic family with large
estates living in the area. Finally, there are the remains of houses and
sanctuaries in which the people of Anagyrous lived and worshipped.
This mass of material makes one wish for more, especially if more
material would elucidate what we already have but do not clearly
understand. Perhaps, however, we should remember that no deme,
except Rhamnous, has yielded such a good account of itself, an
account moreover based only in small part on written records.

V

LAMPTRAI

STRABO (9.1.21) records the demes from Anagyrous to Anaphlystos in the following order: Anagyrous, Thorai, Lamptrai,
Aigilia, Anaphlystos. The position of Anagyrous at Vari has
been established (chapter IV) and there is adequate evidence, independent of Strabo, to show that Anaphlystos was in the neighbourhood
of the modern Anavyssos and thus controlled an area lying immediately
west of the Laureion hills (chapter VIII). The remaining three demes
must therefore be placed between these fixed points. Since Strabo's
statement constitutes our only literary evidence for the location of
two of the three demes involved, we must examine it with care,
especially as it has been much discussed by Löper and Milchhöfer.
Both these scholars recognized that the order Thorai-Lamptrai-
Aigilia presented a difficulty. Since Lamptrai belonged to the phyle
Erechtheis (I) while Thorai and Aigilia were parts of Antiochis (X),
a literal interpretation of Strabo's account would make both Lamptrai
and Thorai enclaves and therefore exceptions to the principle that
demes of an inland or coastal trittys were contiguous, a principle
vigourously advocated by both Löper and Milchhöfer and widely
accepted at present.[1] The two scholars did not agree, however, on the
method of eliminating the problem. Milchhöfer decided that the
received text was incorrect and that the names Thorai and Lamptrai
were reversed, the original and proper order being Lamptrai-Thorai-
Aigilia. He accordingly proposed this simple emendation, which
resulted in the avoidance of both enclaves, Lamptrai (I) being thus
adjacent to Anagyrous (I), and Thorai (X) to Aigilia (X).[2]

Löper did not accept this solution: he did not approve of emending
the text of Strabo. His own answer to the problem was much more
complicated. From Strabo's description of Boeotia, Löper saw that
the geographer's method was to enumerate the towns along one

---

[1]See e.g. Pritchett, *The Five Attic Tribes* 27–28 n. 56, and Bradeen, "The Trittyes
in Cleisthenes' Reforms," 23.

[2]Milchhöfer, *Die Demenordnung* 38.

section of the coast and then, before proceeding to the next coastal section, to mention important settlements lying inland near those towns that he had noted. Löper suggested that the same method was used in the description of Attika, that some of the demes mentioned by Strabo were not actually on the coast but lay inland. Upper Lamptrai, with its centre at modern Lambrika, was according to Löper, a sufficiently important deme to merit enumeration, but, because it lay back from the coast, it had to be listed after the demes that lay along the coast in front of it. Lower Lamptrai, on the other hand, was too small to be recorded. In this way, Löper came to the same conclusion as Milchhöfer regarding the positions of Upper Lamptrai, Thorai, and Aigilia: he also avoided the two enclaves, but found it unnecessary to emend the text of Strabo.[3]

Löper's arguments are not convincing. Strabo's method of describing Boeotia cannot be applied to Attika. When dealing with the former, Strabo notes towns both on the coast and in the interior; but in his description of the latter he avoids all mention of inland towns and villages (except Athens).[4] This method is clearly brought out by his own statement in 9.1.22: ἀλλὰ περὶ Εὐβοίας μὲν εἰρήσεται ὕστερον, τοὺς δ' ἐν τῇ μεσογαίᾳ δήμους τῆς Ἀττικῆς μακρὸν εἰπεῖν διὰ τὸ πλῆθος. This strong implication that he has not yet described any of the interior demes is in keeping with the equally strong implication in 9.1.21 that he has enumerated in order (ἐφεξῆς) only the demes on the coast (ἐν τῇ παραλίᾳ). We should therefore not expect him to mention an inland deme however important.

This conclusion suggests a further criticism of Löper's position. A prytany list of the phyle Erechtheis makes it clear that, of the two demes of Lamptrai, Lower Lamptrai was considerably larger than Upper Lamptrai: the former sent nine members to the Boule, the latter five.[5] Even if Strabo did depart from his intended purpose, it is hardly likely that he would have done so to record the less important (at any rate, the smaller) of two demes with the same name in the same general area. Finally, one should note that Lower Lamptrai was also called Lamptrai Paralia,[6] a sure indication that it was on the coast. Since there is no compelling reason why the Lamptrai mentioned by Strabo should be identified as Upper Lamptrai, it seems more reasonable to

---

[3]Löper, "Die Trittyen," 328–333.

[4]Strabo mentions the names of a few demes in 9.1.17, and in 9.1.20 lists the twelve cities. In neither case does he describe their locations.

[5]Pritchett, "Greek Inscriptions," 231–239.

[6]E.g. Harpokration, s.v. Λαμπτρεῖς.

consider that it was the Lamptrai "by the sea." Such being the case, Löper's whole argument dissolves, as it is based on the assumption that Strabo's reference to a deme of Lamptrai was to a deme set back from the coast. Milchhöfer's suggestion of emending the text is obviously to be preferred. It does not make Strabo mention demes other than those on the coast, it avoids enclaves, and it admits of a Lamptrai "by the sea."

Having discussed and criticized these two proposals, I now turn to the two assumptions which Löper and Milchhöfer held in common and which prompted their close examination of Strabo's text: first, that Upper Lamptrai was at Lambrika; secondly, that enclaves were exceedingly rare in the Kleisthenic arrangement of demes (except those in the city). Milchhöfer made such assumptions when he wrote:

Vorher nennt er (rückwärts gezählt) Aigilia, Lamptrai, Thorai. Hier ist zweifellos ein Versehen zu berichtigen. Lamptrai (Erechtheis) grenzte unmittelbar an Anagyrus aus derselben Phyle, da letzterer Demos nur bei Vari angesetzt werden kann (wo ein grosser Demos erfordert wird, die Reste und Inschriftfunde aber zustimmen), während wir die Stätte Ober-Lamptrai = Lambrika nordöstlich benachbart wissen."[7]

The first assumption is a strong one, but, as was pointed out above, it is not proved that Strabo was in fact referring to Upper Lamptrai. The second is not so strong: that enclaves were, or were not, entertained in the Kleisthenic system can be proved only by first locating the demes, not by first deciding the question of enclaves and then locating the demes on the basis of that decision. Even today, with more material available than at the close of the nineteenth century, we can only say that, although the great majority of trittyes were composed of contiguous demes, a few exceptions seem to have been allowed. Obviously, therefore, criticism of Strabo's order of the three demes, Thorai-Lamptrai-Aigilia, would be more telling if not based on the second assumption.

What Löper and Milchhöfer overlooked in their examination of Strabo's description is that it can be questioned without making these two assumptions. After noting the coastal demes from Peiraieus to Sounion, Strabo (9.1.21) then enumerates the capes and the islands μεταξὺ δὲ τῶν λεχθέντων δήμων. First there is Cape Zoster and the island of Phabra, which are both placed "after Aixone." Then comes Cape Astypalaia with the island of Eleoussa "after Thorai." There can be no doubt about the identification of Astypalaia and Eleoussa: the former can only be the large projection forming the northern side of

[7]Milchhöfer, *Die Demenordnung* 38.

the Bay of Hagios Nikolaos, the latter the island of Arsida.[8] With Astypalaia securely located, we must place Thorai immediately before it, that is, to the north of Mount Olympos (which actually forms the cape) in the neighbourhood of the present Phoinikia (where there are classical remains), if we accept Strabo's statement concerning the relation of the cape to Thorai. If Strabo's order Thorai-Lamptrai-Aigilia is correct, it then follows that there were no coastal demes between Vari and Phoinikia and two (probably three, since logically Upper and Lower Lamptrai should be contiguous) between Phoinikia and Anavyssos. But neither contention is likely: there is hardly enough room between Phoinikia and Anavyssos for two important demes, whereas there are far too many remains, with far too much good land, between Vari and Phoinikia to justify the conclusion that the area contained no demes. The simplest remedy is to reverse the order of Thorai and Lamptrai as Milchhöfer proposed so as to obtain the sequence Lamptrai-Thorai-Aigilia. This sequence would allow one deme (perhaps two demes) between Vari and Phoinikia and one deme between Phoinikia and Anavyssos, conclusions that both the topography and the remains suggest.

The above argument is based on one assumption: that Strabo was right when he said that Cape Astypalaia was after Thorai. If Strabo was wrong, the possible choices for Thorai in this context are surely limited to Lamptrai and Aigilia. If we substitute the former, then we are forced to change the received order of these three demes to Thorai-Aigilia-Lamptrai; if the latter, then the order as given in the text stays unchanged. The first proposal, demanding two crucial emendations of the text, is neither satisfactory nor likely; it merely suggests that Strabo's evidence is worthless without presenting any good reasons for so thinking. The other proposal, emending Thorai to read Aigilia vis-à-vis Cape Astypalaia, has the advantage of keeping the number of emendations to a minimum. On the other hand, it leaves the order Thorai-Lamptrai-Aigilia unchanged and therefore still open to the criticisms brought against such an order by Milchhöfer and Löper. It is better to accept Strabo's statement that Cape Astypalaia came after Thorai.

Since the received text cannot stand as it is, the two statements

[8]This identification has been questioned by Hammond, "The Battle of Salamis," 48 n. 65. Similar doubts had been expressed earlier by Kastromenos, *Die Demen* 47–48. But the positions of Cape Kolias at Hagios Kosmas and Cape Zoster near the modern village of Vouliagmene make it clear that Cape Anavyso was the ancient Astypalaia. There is no other promontory between Vari and Anavyssos that could possibly have merited Strabo's (or his source's) attention. Furthermore, Strabo's evidence demands that Astypalaia be near the deme of Anaphlystos.

about the position of Thorai being contradictory, some change must be made. The change that appears to be the best, without involving too much external or dubious evidence, is to reverse the order of Thorai and Lamptrai. The resulting order, Lamptrai-Thorai-Aigilia, is not only compatible with Strabo's other reference to Thorai, but, as we shall see later, agrees with the remaining evidence for the location of Lamptrai.

This examination of Strabo's text leads us, in common with Milch-höfer and Löper, to believe that Lamptrai followed Anagyrous with no other deme (or demes) intervening between them.[9]

NAME

"For there was another *Lampra*, called Καθύπερθεν, or *Superior*: which without doubt was the ruin'd Town, about three or four Miles more towards the Midland, called yet *Lambra*: for so the *Greeks* pronounce Λαμπρά, that is, π after μ as we do *b*. At this last we sate down, and dined: and after Dinner we kept on something North-Westwards. . . ."[10] This was the opinion of Sir George Wheler in 1676, an opinion that has been accepted by all scholars from his time to our own: that the mediaeval and modern village known now as Lambrika has preserved with little change the ancient deme name of Lamptrai. There is no reason to doubt this view: the present name is certainly not due to any modern antiquarian interest. On the other hand, there is no need to jump to the conclusion that because Lambrika has inherited an earlier place name it has also preserved the actual location of that earlier village. It is, however, a very good indication that the ancient village of Lamptrai (and for the moment I assume it to be Upper Lamptrai) was situated somewhere in the neighbourhood of Lambrika.

INSCRIPTIONS

There are two inscriptions of importance for our study.

IG II[2] 2967

The first, *IG* II[2] 2967, was discovered by A. Milchhöfer at Lambrika "unter dem Kuppeldach der Kapelle H. Lukas (östl. von Triada), an

---

[9]One should note one other literary reference to Lamptrai. Pausanias (1.31.3) numbers it among the small rural demes that have interesting monuments. Lamptrai's claim was the tomb of Kranaos, which was still in existence in Pausanias' time. Unfortunately, we have no way of knowing to which of the two demes he was referring, nor does his description give us any topographical clues. If the tomb were found, then Pausanias' information would have value.

[10]Wheler, *Journey* 449.

der Südseite vermauert."[11] The heading of the inscription reads]τρεῖς τῷ 'Απόλλωνι τῷ [and below this is a list of at least thirty-seven names arranged in four columns, twelve in each of the first three and a single name in the fourth. Clearly we have the record of a dedication to Apollo made by the persons enumerated, all of whom are recorded without patronymic or demotic. The lack of the demotics implies that all the persons involved in making the dedication were from the same deme.[12] Since there can be no doubt that [– – –]τρεῖς is a collective noun applicable to all the dedicators, the supplement [Λαμπ]τρεῖς has obvious advantages. Not only does it fill the available space but it also agrees with the traces of two letters preserved before τ. No one has suggested any other restoration and it should be noted that no other demotic in the plural has the ending τρεῖς. Once this supplement has been made, it is possible to identify a number of the persons listed with members of the deme Lamptrai who are known from other sources.[13]

Since a dedication to Apollo made by so many members of the deme of Lamptrai would be most unlikely anywhere other than in the deme of Lamptrai (or possibly at one of the shrines of Apollo in Athens), it is clear that the finding place of this inscription provides evidence for the location of Lamptrai, evidence that is in agreement with that from the name Lambrika. The ancient deme of Lamptrai must have been either at, or very near, modern Lambrika.

IG II² 1204

The second inscription, IG II² 1204, is a decree passed by the demesmen of Lamptrai honouring Philokedes of Acharnai. It was first published in 1872 by S. A. Koumanoudes who wrote that it was found "'ς τοῦ Κίτση τὸ πηγάδι, μίαν ὥραν ἀνατολικῶς τῆς Βάρης (τῆς 'Αττικῆς), ὅπου καὶ Εἰσοδίων Παναγίας ἐκκλησία," καθὼς εἶπεν ὁ πωλήσας τὸν λίθον. . . ."[14] This statement on the place of finding is a little ambiguous since there is a distance of about eight hundred metres separating the two places named.[15] It is possible, however, that the

[11]Milchhöfer, "Antikenbericht" (1887) 102-103.

[12]Another possibility might be that none of the persons concerned in the dedication enjoyed civil rights (cf. IG II² 2934). A study of the names, however, makes this extremely unlikely.

[13]J. Kirchner in his commentary to IG II² 2967 has related six of the names to previously known demesmen of Lamptrai.

[14]Koumanoudes, "'Αττικῆς ἐπιγραφαὶ ἀνέκδοτοι," 17-19, the quotation coming from 18.

[15]The church was at a village named Thiti, now in ruins. Kitsi Pigadi, which lies west of Thiti, is today a collection of two or three houses near a well. The houses do not appear on the Karten (Sheet VIII) but the well is marked where the road from Vari divides (the road that goes to the east of the hill Kiapha Thiti).

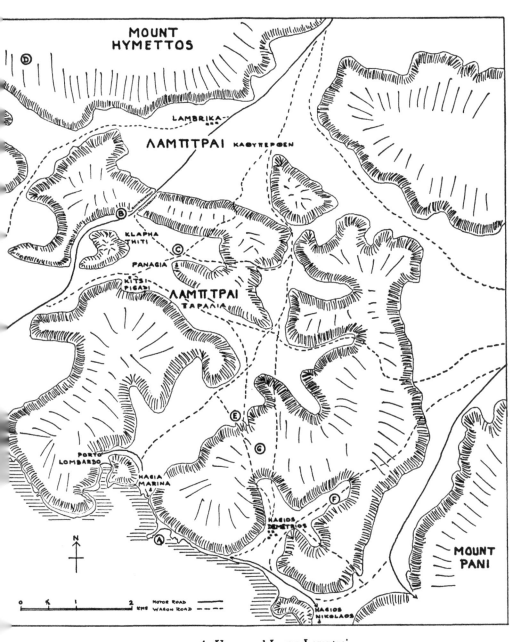

FIGURE 4. Upper and Lower Lamptrai

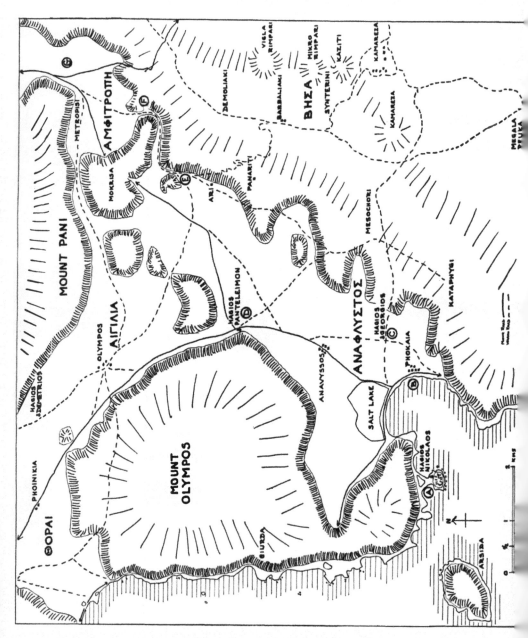

FIGURE 7. Aigilia, Anaphlystos, Amphitrope, and Besa

reference to the church was added merely because it was a well-known landmark, standing as it does on a knoll. Nevertheless, the general location is securely established and perhaps we should assume with Milchhöfer that the inscription was found at the hamlet of Kitsi.[16]

The inscription, unfortunately, is not complete and the preserved portion does not record where the stele was to be erected. We should expect from the nature of the decree that it was set up in a place frequented by the public, either in the agora or possibly in a sanctuary. We can be certain, therefore, that the finding of this decree near Kitsi indicates that the centre of the deme of Lamptrai was near by.[17]

These two inscriptions reveal that there were two centres for the demesmen of Lamptrai, one near Lambrika, another near Kitsi Pigadi. This is as it should be, since it is known that Lamptrai was a split deme, one part called Upper Lamptrai, the other part Lower Lamptrai or "Lamptrai by the sea." Lambrika should be identified with the former, Kitsi the latter, since the latter was not only closer to the sea, but also, as we shall see later, controlled an area that included part of the coast.

One might wonder why the two inscriptions examined above did not make it clear which part of Lamptrai was involved either in the dedication to Apollo or in the honours voted to a non-demesman. However useful such an indication might have been, it is clear that a distinction was rarely made between the two parts of a split deme. Except in the prytany and bouleutic lists and in a few other isolated instances, a man was never named as belonging to the upper or lower part of a deme, merely to the deme. Even in the lists mentioned, the practice of enumerating divided demes is not consistent.

Other inscriptions have been found both at Lambrika and at Kitsi. They are of no special import for our study but they do show that these two places were inhabited centres.[18]

REMAINS

The earliest remains in the area covered by Figure 4 are at A, a rocky islet divided from the mainland by a narrow strip of water. The

[16]Milchhöfer, "Antikenbericht" (1887) 104.

[17]One should perhaps ask whether the inscription might have come originally from Lambrika. Inscriptions have been known to move and so anything is possible. However, I think it fair to suggest that had it been placed originally near Lambrika it probably would have stayed there and been used in the building of one of the numerous stone structures of the later village. If one is prepared to argue that this decree came from Lambrika, perhaps one should also be prepared to argue that the other ancient but uninscribed blocks near Kitsi came from the same place.

[18]Mitsos and Vanderpool, "Inscriptions" (1953) 181.

islet was inhabited during Early Helladic times. Slight indications of walls can still be made out and there is considerable pottery on the surface.[19] No later pottery was found here and we must assume that this very small village went out of existence perhaps at the end of the Early Helladic period and was never reinhabited.[20]

One other site preserves clear evidence of habitation during the pre-classical period. On the top of the hill called Kiapha Thiti there are many sherds, some decorated and of good quality, of the Late Helladic period (Mycenaean). Although this hill seems impregnable for most of its circumference, it is easily climbed if one approaches from the west. Near the top there is a considerable area made level by terracing and thus suitable for buildings. Indeed, one can still see the ruins of a Byzantine church, testifying to the hill's use in post-classical times. No sherds of the classical period were found. Those from the pre-classical period show that habitation began in the Middle Helladic period, possibly even earlier. Some Mycenaean graves have been excavated at B (Figure 4), Vourvatsi, and they surely must be connected with the settlement on Kiapha Thiti.[21]

No other Mycenaean sites have been noted in this area. It is therefore possible that those who lived at Kiapha Thiti controlled (or farmed) the plain lying to the south and east and its continuation southwestwards to the sea as well as the plain lying to the north around the modern Lambrika. Communication between Kiapha Thiti and Lambrika must always have been as easy as it is today. The motor road passes through a natural gap in the low range dividing these two plains and beside the road are considerable traces of earlier roads. If this conclusion is sound—that ease of communication made it feasible

[19]Various trips to the site have been made by members of the American School since its discovery in 1955. A selection of the pottery found has been placed in the sherd collection at the School.

[20]The phenomenon of a village going out of existence at the end of the Early Helladic period finds a parallel in the settlement of Hagios Kosmas where the Early Helladic village was destroyed and reinhabited only in Late Helladic times (see Mylonas, *Aghios Kosmas* 162 and 164).

[21]Kyparissis, "'Εξ 'Αθηνῶν καὶ 'Αττικῆς," 65–66. He notes the presence of a hill on which are the traces of an acropolis. He refers the reader to fig. 19 (p. 61) in the background of which is supposed to be the hill with the remains. In actual fact, the hill appearing in the photograph is part of Hymettos, not Kiapha Thiti. We carefully examined all the hills in the neighbourhood of Vourvatsi and none of them had Mycenaean remains except Kiapha Thiti. We conclude that Kyparissis' reference to fig. 19 is incorrect. A proper publication of the pottery from this excavation was made by Stubbings in his article "Mycenaean Pottery," 1–75. The index, 73–75, makes it possible to sort out the material from Vourvatsi.

for these two districts to be controlled from Kiapha Thiti—it suggests
a possible reason why in the classical period they should both have
borne the same name, Lamptrai, a name perhaps handed down from
a time when a single settlement dominated the whole area.

Remains from the classical period are concentrated around two
places, Lambrika and Kitsi Pigadi. We have already noticed that
inscriptions have been found at both. Of the area around Lambrika,
Milchhöfer wrote that the ancient remains "finden sich nicht so wohl
in situ als verbaut vor."[22] Lambrika was a large Byzantine village and
today one can see the remains of four churches as well as many houses.
For over a kilometre large piles of stone line the wagon road that goes
west from Lambrika and these piles represent houses torn down in
order to free the land for ploughing. This mediaeval village is presumed
to have been built over the small classical settlement. Blocks from
classical times appear in the churches and houses still standing;
other blocks can be seen in the piles of stone. Strangely enough, we
have found no classical pottery despite many trips to Lambrika. In
most places this would be sufficiently compelling negative evidence to
consider that the site had not been inhabited during classical times. At
Lambrika, however, one cannot come to that conclusion. Not only
do we have the inscription discussed above, but we have also other
inscriptions as well as important sculptural remains,[23] sure indications
of a classical settlement. The lack of pottery is embarrassing, especially
as pottery is practically indestructible, has a habit of coming to the
surface, and is a necessary concomitant of normal existence. One could
argue that the mediaeval village so completely covers the ancient one
that the remains of pottery of the latter are far below the surface and
therefore not readily accessible. This may indeed be the correct
explanation, since the area covered by the mediaeval village is flat,
not mound-shaped,[24] and since not all the area has been subjected to
deep ploughing. Another explanation is that we have not yet found the
exact location of the ancient village. I prefer to think this possi-

[22]Milchhöfer, *Erläuternder Text* 3–6.14.

[23]Milchhöfer, "Antikenbericht" (1887) 102–104; Winter, "Grabmal von Lamptrae,"
105–118; Reisch, "Heraklesrelief," 118–130. The Herakles base has been the subject
of two recent articles: Wrede, "Heraklesbasis," 160–165, and Walter, "Heraklesbasis," 139–147. The most recent description of the gravestone first seen by Abbé
Fourmont is in Richter, *Archaic Gravestones* 18–19. Conze, *Grabreliefs* 1.9 does not
make it clear whether Fourmont saw this gravestone at Lambrika or Vari. In my
opinion Fourmont's description is more applicable to Lambrika than to Vari.

[24]Were it mound-shaped, there would be every chance of finding the classical
sherds on the slopes where the classical strata break the surface.

bility unlikely, for we searched the area with great care because of the peculiar circumstance of there being no classical sherds visible at Lambrika.

In the region of Kitsi Pigadi there is no such lack of pottery. At Kitsi itself, a few ancient blocks are built into the farmhouses but they may have been moved from further east; no ancient pottery has been found in the immediate vicinity. A few hundred metres to the east, however, pottery of the classical period can be picked up in abundance and the slight walls of a few houses can be made out. These remains are located on both sides of the wagon road leading east from Kitsi and they stretch for a kilometre and a quarter.[25] The fields are lined with stones, many of which are cut blocks coming from ancient buildings. These traces of an ancient settlement are undoubtedly all that are left of the antiquities noted by Sir William Gell in the early years of the nineteenth century.[26] Such remains can represent only a community of considerable size that flourished in the classical period. We need have no hesitation in identifying the community as Lamptrai Paralia.

The hill on which the Church of the Panagia stands is also covered with ruins. On the slopes are broken-down houses from a recent period, but on the top, where the church is situated, we found remains from the classical period. Built into the church are various ancient blocks but these may have come from the settlement in the plain below. The church is placed in a level area, a scarp of rock rising above it to the south and the hillside falling away to the north. On the southern scarp we found carved into the rock in two places the letters HO. Two other rock-cut inscriptions with the same letters were discovered to the north (Figure 5).[27] These inscriptions served as markers of some *temenos*, HO standing for HOPOΣ.[28] One or two classical sherds were

[25]We noted that the modern village of Koropi stretches for exactly the same length along both sides of the main road. This gives a good indication of the physical size of the village near Kitsi.

[26]Gell, *Itinerary of Greece* 87. See Appendix 1 to this chapter for Gell's remarks. Milchhöfer (*Erläuternder Text* 3–6.15) noted that the remains seen by Gell could no longer be identified. The same is true today if one is strictly literal about the meaning of "identify." Nevertheless, it is certain from the distance covered by Gell in his journey from Olympos to Vari that he was very close to Kitsi when he saw all these remains.

[27]All the letters are a foot high.

[28]Cf. *IG* II² 2524. Rangabé (*Antiquités helléniques* 2.587) originally published this inscription as No. 891 d. He does not give the dimensions of the letters, but states only that they are "très-grandes." He adds that the inscription is "peut-être de l'époque d'Hérode Atticus, qui affectait l'archaïsme." Archaic traits connected with

THE CHURCH OF THE PANAGIA AT THITI

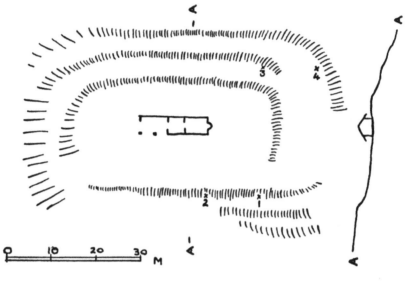

ROCK-CUT INSCRIPTIONS NEAR THITI

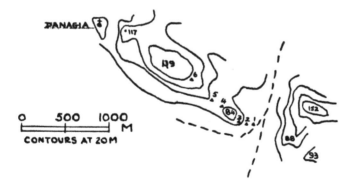

FIGURE 5. The Church of the Panagia at Thiti and rock-cut inscriptions near Thiti

noticed in the level area to the south of the church. We presume that in classical times this area, its boundaries marked by four inscriptions, was sacred and that some building, a temple perhaps, or an altar, was erected on the level ground enclosed by the markers. An inscription recently found at the church might be used to connect the sanctuary with Dionysos.[29]

Two other places where classical material has been found should be noted. At C (Figure 4) we discovered classical sherds concentrated in an area so small that the remains must represent nothing more than a few houses. The second place is Porto Lombardo where an inscription honouring the Nymphs was discovered.[30] Probably there was a small sanctuary near the spring that bubbles forth in the marshes.

No other traces of classical settlements were found either in the plain leading eastwards from Kitsi or in its continuation southwestwards to the sea. I conclude that this whole area was farmed and administered from the centre near Kitsi. Although the position of the settlement is somewhat removed from the sea, the land it controlled went as far as the sea and had a reasonably wide sea frontage. The name Lamptrai Paralia (sometimes used instead of Lower Lamptrai) is, therefore, appropriate.

Remains from the late Roman or early Byzantine periods have been noted at a few places. At D (Figure 4) there are house remains, a ruined church of Hagios Nikolaos, and pottery. This area interested us greatly because it seemed cut off from Upper Lamptrai as well as from Anagyrous and might have supported a small independent community such as Kedoi or Pambotadai which are usually assigned to this trittys.[31] The remains, however, give no evidence for habitation

---

boundary stones are not however a good indication of age since the "*spiritus asper* in certain conventional formulae did not disappear with the archonship of Eukleides" (Fine, *Horoi* 49).

[29]For the inscription see Mitsos, "'Επιγραφαὶ ἐξ 'Αθηνῶν," 47–49, and Lang, "Epigraphical Note," 62, both of whom make it clear that the document is personal and obscene or at best, Lang says, "a scurrilous joke on a lady." Mitsos dates the inscription to the first half of the third century B.C. and says (p. 49) of the rock-cut letters marking the boundaries of the sanctuary that they are of the fifth century B.C. To Mitsos' suggestion that the sanctuary might have been attributed to Dionysos, I think we may add that Aphrodite too makes a good candidate.

[30]Vanderpool, "News Letter from Greece" (1955) 223. See also *BCH* 79 (1955) 210.

[31]E.g. Gomme, *Population* 56 but with a question mark after Pambotadai. Both Milchhöfer (*Die Demenordnung* 13) and Löper ("Die Trittyen," 341) attribute these two demes to the coastal trittys but they are too confident in view of the meagre evidence. Milchhöfer points out that in various lists Kedoi is regularly (*regelmässig*) found with Lamptrai. Whatever the reason for this order, it should be remembered that, from these same lists and because of a repeatedly found order, Löper assumed

in the classical period, and for the moment at least it is better to consider this hamlet as a manifestation of the late Roman period when people no longer found it necessary to live in a single centre and when small villas and large farm estates became common.

Remains of a similar type and probably demanding a similar explanation were found at E and F (Figure 4), the former of which is marked on the *Karten* (Sheet XIII).

Two purely Byzantine sites have been known in this area for many years. The first is at G (Figure 4), the second at Hagios Demetrios. Much of the former still stands in ruins and it must have been a medium-sized village in the Middle Ages. There are remains of at least two churches. No classical sherds were noticed, nor any other signs suggesting earlier inhabitation.[32] The same is true of Hagios Demetrios where a Byzantine church in honour of that saint is well preserved. Again, we noticed nothing from the classical period and came to the conclusion that this valley was uninhabited until the late Roman period. Of course, it may have been farmed at an earlier date since it is accessible from both west and east, but the centre from which it was worked must have been outside the valley.[33]

IDENTIFICATION

I have already commented on the identification of Lambrika as Upper Lamptrai. This identification has been accepted by all topographers and there is no reason to doubt it. The evidence is certainly in its favour.

---

that Euonymon could be placed between Anagyrous and Lamptrai, whereas we know that Euonymon was a city deme. In these various lists there is no discernible geographical order for the enumeration of demes. The only evidence for the approximate location of Kedoi that is of any importance is the grave marker *IG* II² 6383 found in Lambrika. It records the names of two persons of the same family from the deme of Kedoi. However, no conclusions should be drawn about the location of Kedoi on the basis of a single grave marker when there is no other evidence to connect Kedoi with Lambrika other than that Kedoi was in the same phyle as Lamptrai and so might have been in the same trittys. Similarly, the finding of a grave marker with the name of a person from Pambotadai in the village of Chasani (?), *IG* II² 7141, is not evidence that Pambotadai should be placed in the city trittys near Euonymon. There is no evidence as yet that enables us to determine in what trittys (or trittyes) these two demes were located.

[32]Milchhöfer (*Erläuternder Text* 3-6.14) noted these remains and identified them "als Spuren mittelalterlicher Ansiedlung."

[33]In order to make this record of finds as complete as possible, I include in Appendix 2 to this chapter a description of a series of rock-cut inscriptions recently found by Mitsos and Vanderpool.

Upper Lamptrai controlled the plain which lies to the south, east, and west of it. We have noted above the question whether Upper Lamptrai's authority stretched as far west as the small valley nestling beneath Hymettos. Topographically this valley seems quite separate from the plain near Lambrika but, since no classical settlement has been found in the valley,[34] one should assume perhaps that the area was worked from Upper Lamptrai. Otherwise, the limits are clear, even to the north where it appears on the map as if the plain around Lambrika joined the Mesogaia without any break, for there is a watershed a few hundred metres north of Lambrika, which doubtless formed the boundary.

The position of Lower Lamptrai (or Lamptrai Paralia) has never before been fixed with certainty. Löper and Kock are both vague on this point and suggest a general location near the coast between Anagyrous and Thorai.[35] Milchhöfer was more specific and assigned to Lower Lamptrai the lands on either side of the hill west of Hagios Demetrios, that is, the valley in which Hagios Demetrios is situated and the plain which runs southwestwards to the sea ending between Porto Lombardo and Hagia Marina.[36] As for Kitsi, he tentatively suggested that it might have been Kedoi.[37] Frazer, on the other hand, without committing himself to a positive identification, seemed to favour the area around Kitsi as the site of Lower Lamptrai.[38] Vanderpool and Mitsos also believe that this area contained Lower Lamptrai and they note the finding of the decree discussed above as a good indication in favour of such an identification.[39]

In my opinion there can be no doubt that the extensive remains lying east of Kitsi and between Kitsi and Thiti are the remains of the ancient settlement of Lower Lamptrai. The deme decree is excellent evidence for this identification. Milchhöfer's suggestion is unconvincing because there are no traces of a village in the area where he would locate Lower Lamptrai. Both he and Löper were under the impression that this deme was small. Perhaps Milchhöfer might have argued that the smallness of the village made it unlikely that it would be found except by a thorough search and that even then its slight remains might be overlooked. However, such an argument has little meaning following the discovery of the prytany list of the phyle

[34]Our examination of this valley was not conducted in sufficient detail to allow anything but a tentative conclusion.

[35]Löper, "Die Trittyen," 332; Kock, RE 12 (1924-1925) 593, s.v. Lamptrai.

[36]Milchhöfer, Die Demenordnung 38. On the map at the end of his book the site of Lower Lamptrai is placed very near Porto Lombardo.

[37]Ibid. 13.   [38]Frazer, Pausanias 2.406-407.

[39]Mitsos and Vanderpool, "Inscriptions" (1950) 28 n. 4.

Erechtheis noted above.[40] This new evidence makes it certain that Lower Lamptrai was a large deme, the remains of which should reflect its size.

The remains near Kitsi are large and entirely appropriate for a deme that was represented by nine bouleutai. To look for something small in the face of the evidence of the prytany list would be to deny that the figures have any validity in determining the approximate sizes of the demes. Similarly, the area controlled by the deme should be quite extensive. Lower Lamptrai administered two large plains that lie approximately at right angles to each other. Nature provided clear-cut boundaries except to the east where uncertainties exist. The valley of Hagios Demetrios is cut off from Lower Lamptrai by a long range that runs to the sea. The hills are not so high nor so steep that communication across them is difficult. To the east of Hagios Demetrios another long hill divides the valley from the large coastal plain beginning near Phoinikia. It was our impression, and Milchhöfer apparently had the same impression,[41] that the hills to the west of Hagios Demetrios constituted less of a barrier than those to the east. We have included Hagios Demetrios, therefore, in the area controlled by Lower Lamptrai. By this we mean that, since it possessed no centre of its own in classical times, it was farmed (unless it lay unworked) by people who commuted from Lower Lamptrai.

To conclude: the location of Lower Lamptrai near Kitsi is in accord with the epigraphic evidence, relates the extensive remains there to a large deme, makes the epithet Paralia appropriate, and thereby defends Strabo's naming of Lamptrai as a deme on the coast.

[40]See p. 48 and n. 5.

[41]This is indicated by Milchhöfer's belief that Lower Lamptrai controlled an area from Porto Lombardo to Hagios Demetrios.

APPENDIX I TO CHAPTER V

THE REMAINS SEEN BY GELL NEAR THITI*

Elympo to Vari

H   M

From Elympo the road turns to the west, or left, between two hills.

*Gell, *Itinerary of Greece* 86–88. H = hours, M = minutes.

— 12 R. a little mount, with ruins; and more distant, another, with a church.

— 18 A tower l. Woods of cedar.

— 4 A little insulated rock l., 100 yards distant. All these seem to have had towers on their summits. Other vestiges near.

— 20 A bushy plain. Two other insulated rocks left.

— 8 Ascend in a glen, covered with pretty pines.

— 7 Descend.

— 8 An opening l. to the sea. Another r. to the Mt. of Kerratia or Elympo. L. a church and garden. Ascend.

— 15 A tumulus or an anathema of stones l. The country consists of pretty insulated elevations, separated by little plains, and the whole is well shaded by pines.

— 13 A plain with pines. The sea is visible l.

— 12 Enter a glen. Beautiful scenery. L. rocks of white marble and quarries. See in the road the traces of wheels in the rocks.

— 3 Cross a wall. Another wall r. of the road, and a triangular plain.

— 3 Cross a wall. An Attic demos.

— 4 Another wall near a brick kiln. The site of a considerable ancient town.

— 2 Cross other walls. R. observe a hollow like a stadium. The rock cut for the road.

— 2 Walls continued. A tower in the road.

— 2 R., 100 yards, ruins, perhaps a temple. Cross a strong wall.

— 3 More walls.

— 2 Walls.

— 3 A well. The plain is very pretty, and toward Hymettus is bounded by a beautiful, bold, and well wooded insulated hill, which seems to have been the acropolis of the city below.

— 15 The ruins of modern walls l.

— 9 Three great heaps, or tumuli, r. and l. Hymettus, or rather a branch of it, often called Anudros, seen finely clothed in forests of pine r.

— 11 Three more heaps, perhaps only made by clearing the soil for culture.

— 2 Bari, pronounced Vari, a little metochi, the property of the monastery of Asomatos, under Anchesmus. Possibly the Hegumenos, or Superior, may only reside here during the harvest. The country is in general more deserted than any other part of Greece, so that it is difficult to learn the names of places as they occur in the journey. Eastward, and directly opposite Bari, are several rocky islets in the sea.

— —
2 58

APPENDIX II TO CHAPTER V

ROCK-CUT INSCRIPTIONS NEAR THITI

The Church of the Panagia, Thiti, stands on the western end of a ridge that runs eastwards for about two kilometres. After rising to a high point of 139 metres above sea level, this ridge ends some five hundred metres short of the next one, there admitting the passage of a stream and a road.

On the ridge's eastern half, M. T. Mitsos and Eugene Vanderpool found a series of at least six rock-cut inscriptions. The first was seen by Mitsos in 1958; two more were noticed in the same year; the remainder were discovered in 1961.[1]

The six inscriptions have identical texts:

ΟΡΣΠΜ

They differ only in certain dimensions and in the precise character of the third letter. All the letters are carved on the horizontal surface of the native rock with strokes about two centimetres wide and as much as one centimetre deep. The over-all height varies from 0.13 m. to 0.27 m., the length from 0.68 m. to 0.87 m. On two of the inscriptions the third letter is only about half as high as the surrounding letters, while all are level at the top. This third letter, perhaps better called a symbol, also shows slight variations in shape. Nevertheless, the general appearance remains the same and such differences as can be detected should not be considered meaningful.

The inscriptions run along the crest of the ridge, in so far as there is a distinct crest, and the bottoms of the letters are always to the south. On Figure 5, lower half, they are numbered from one to six and

[1] I have not seen these inscriptions and my knowledge of them is entirely derived from letters written to me by E. Vanderpool. I am therefore grateful to him and to M. T. Mitsos for allowing me to publish them. The description and interpretation presented here are mostly taken from an account written by Vanderpool and dated August 19, 1961. I have made no special attempt to paraphrase his material and much of it is as he wrote it. Mabel Lang has also contributed to the discussion of the date and interpretation.

from east to west. The first is at the foot of the ridge, five or six paces
west of an old wagon road that runs along the west side of the stream
bed. The second is about a hundred paces up the slope, the third a
hundred and twenty paces beyond that. From the third inscription to
the top of the hill marked with an altitude of 84 metres is a distance
of about a hundred and thirty paces. On the top of the hill there
appears to have been a small mound of stones, now ruinous, probably
the remains of a cairn. No inscription was found here, and perhaps we
may assume that the cairn took its place (see LSJ⁹ 2057, s.v. βολεός).
The fourth inscription is in the saddle about a hundred and twenty
paces west of Hill 84, the fifth about two hundred paces farther west.
Between the fifth and sixth inscriptions the distance is about four
hundred paces, but it may be that other inscriptions are still to be
found between them. From the sixth inscription to the edge of the
plateau forming the top of the hill marked with an altitude of 139
metres the distance may be from fifty to a hundred metres.

The top of Hill 139 does not have a surface suitable for the carving
of inscriptions, and this may explain why none were found. The highest
point, however, was marked by a ruined cairn. Even though the area
was searched as far west as the church, no other inscriptions were
discovered. These inscriptions were carved in Greek times, perhaps
during the fourth century B.C. The omission of the initial H rules out
an earlier date, and, although the third letter tends to be a little
cursive, the shape of the pi does not encourage a later date.

So much is reasonably certain. Regarding the interpretation, only
the significance of the first two letters is obvious: an abbreviated form
of ὅρος. The third letter has the shape of a stigma. It may indicate that
the first word has been abbreviated or that there is a break between the
first pair of letters and the second, or perhaps both. The second pair
of letters, if an abbreviation, can hardly be one consisting of the
opening letters of a single word. Rather, it must represent a phrase of
two words and have been so formulaic in character that its meaning
was unambiguous.

Vanderpool makes the attractive suggestion that, if the second pair
of letters is an abbreviated form of a phrase, then the letters might be
expanded thus: π(ρὸς) μ(εσημβρίαν). Even if other inscriptions turn up
bearing ΠΑ, ΠΒ, or ΠΔ in the appropriate quarters, it may still remain
a mystery what it was that needed such frequent and public notices
of a line of demarcation.

VI

THORAI

ANCIENT REFERENCES

STRABO'S two references, which we have considered in our
discussion of Lamptrai, constitute the sole evidence for the
position of Thorai. In 9.1.21 he places Thorai after Anagyrous
and before Lamptrai. I have argued above, however, that this order is
incorrect and that Thorai should be placed after Lamptrai and before
Aigilia.

Strabo's second comment about Thorai is that Cape Astypalaia was
"after Thorai." Assuming this statement to be correct and accepting
the identification of Cape Astypalaia as the headland immediately
north of the bay of Anavyssos, we must place Thorai after Hagios
Demetrios but before Olympos, in the plain that today has its
administrative centre at Phoinikia.

NAME

The name Thorai does not seem to have survived in any form.[1]

INSCRIPTIONS

No inscriptions have been found that provide any evidence for the
location of Thorai. Not even the ubiquitous grave marker is of any
help. In *IG* the two markers whose provenience is known and which
bear names of demesmen of Thorai were found in Athens and so have
no topographical significance (*IG* II² 6211, 6213).

In 334/3 B.C. Thorai was represented in the Council of Five Hundred
by four members, according to *IG* II² 1750.

REMAINS

The remains appearing in the area covered by Figure 6 have been
described in general by Milchhöfer.[2] They are marked in red on the

[1] But see above, chap. IV, p. 35, n. 2.
[2] *Erläuternder Text* 3–6.19.

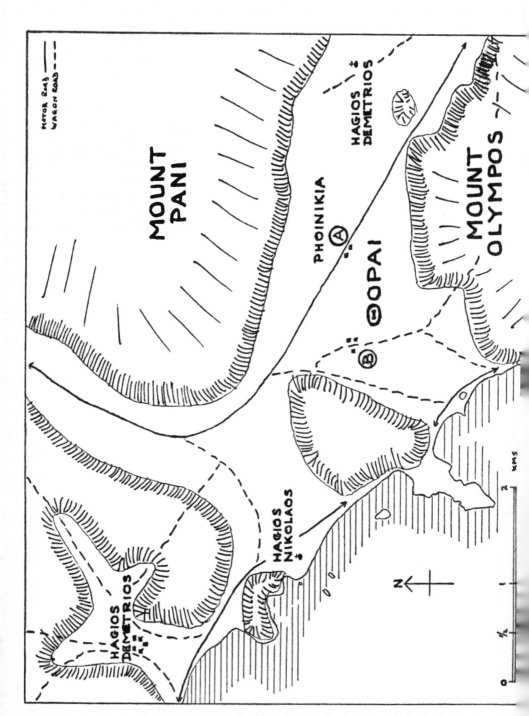

FIGURE 6. Thorai

Karten (Sheet XVII). I have looked at most of them and have little additional material to present. Today, owing to an increase in farming activity, the remains are far less extensive than they were at the close of the nineteenth century.

The greatest concentration of traces of an ancient settlement occurs around Phoinikia, which is not so much a village as a manorial estate established about the house owned by Elias Melissourgos (A on Figure 6). Traces of walls can still be seen, ancient blocks are plentiful (the majority re-used), and some marble blocks, including columns, capitals, and other architectural members, are gathered together in Mr. Melissourgos' private garden. In addition, Mr. Melissourgos has presented the shaft of an archaic stele from Phoinikia to the National Museum at Athens.[3] Pottery fragments lie on the surface in quantity. The majority seem to be from the late Roman and Byzantine times. (The latter period is also represented by the ruins of a small chapel.) But there are a sufficient number of pieces from the classical and Hellenistic periods to show that a large village existed on the same site from classical times to the Middle Ages. We did not find pottery of the early Iron Age, but this site has such obvious advantages because of its central location within a rich plain that we should expect some settlement to have existed during that early period. Further and more intensive exploration may yet reveal it.

West and a little south of the centre of the estate of Melissourgos is a group of several houses forming a small village (B on Figure 6). Here too were quite extensive traces of an ancient settlement (also shown on the *Karten*). The pottery suggested that this settlement had flourished during the same periods as had the larger one discussed above. There is very little distance between the two villages and it may be that they were really parts of a single settlement.

Milchhöfer noted considerable remains at the shore.[4] Although we did not find the system of fortifications that he described, we did see traces of a small community, presumably a little harbour village. This settlement seems to have existed in late Roman times.[5]

[3] Richter, *Archaic Gravestones* 21–22.

[4] *Erläuternder Text* 3–6.19.

[5] I add the following notice in order to make this record of the remains as full as possible. In August 1958, Vanderpool found remains of a settlement in the valley that ends at the sea at Hagios Nikolaos. He reports that all the pottery and tiles he inspected were late Roman or Byzantine. Since there is no evidence as yet to suggest that a settlement existed here in classical times, and since we know the position (if at times only approximately) of all the demes usually ascribed to this trittys, I think we can assume that this village played no part in the Kleisthenic system of demes.

IDENTIFICATION

Milchhöfer,[6] Löper,[7] and Wrede[8] all agree in identifying the present Phoinikia with the ancient Thorai. The only evidence suggesting this identification is the text of Strabo. The problems concerned with this passage have already been discussed (see chapter v). If one accepts the emendation that results in the order Lamptrai-Thorai-Aigilia, then the identification seems certain, despite the lack of definite corroborative material. As we have mentioned, from Strabo's emended text we can establish the limits within which Thorai must have been situated. Within that area the only site with remains indicating a settlement of sufficient size[9] and antiquity is at Phoinikia. Its identification as Thorai follows automatically.

The limits of the area controlled by Thorai are easily established. The plain in which Thorai was situated is bounded on the north by Mount Panion, on the southwest by the sea, on the southeast by Mount Olympos. Directly to the east, where the lowest slopes of Panion and Olympos almost meet, the plain narrows appreciably, a phenomenon obvious to a viewer on the terrain but not brought out by a map (for instance Figure 6). A border just west of Hagios Demetrios (near Olympos) would be a natural one. The western boundary of the deme was probably formed by the hills lying immediately east of the valley which contains the community clustered around the Byzantine church of Hagios Demetrios (discussed in chapter v above). If this boundary is accurate, then Thorai controlled the narrow belt of land lying between Panion and the range east of Hagios Demetrios, a valley which reaches the sea at Hagios Nikolaos. This western boundary constitutes a natural border because the spur of Panion that seems to divide the plain around Thorai from the valley to the north of Hagios Nikolaos is not very high and would not have provided such a definite limit as the range further west.

[6]*Die Demenordnung* 38; and *RE* 1 (1894) 962, s.v. Aigilia.

[7]"Die Trittyen," 421. Although Löper does not mention Phoinikia, it is clear that he placed Thorai in this area.

[8]*RE* 6 (1936–1937) 331; s.v. Thorai.

[9]On the basis of prytany representation, Thorai ought to be the equal in size of Upper Lamptrai.

VII

AIGILIA

ANCIENT REFERENCES

THE most important reference to Aigilia is in the passage of Strabo that I have already discussed. He places Aigilia after Thorai but before Anaphlystos (9.1.21). Thorai has been identified as Phoinikia, while the modern Anavyssos is clearly a corruption of Anaphlystos and thus indicates the approximate location of that deme. Aigilia, therefore, should be situated between these two fixed points.

One other piece of information about Aigilia can be extracted from literary sources. It was famous in antiquity for its figs, which were considered the finest in Attika and highly esteemed by the Romans.[1] Milchhöfer saw in these references to the production of figs a clue to the topography of Aigilia: "Aigilia, the next deme according to Strabo, which had a great reputation for its figs, therefore requires a location not far from the sea, yet sunny and protected."[2] If indeed these are the only requirements necessary for the growing of excellent figs, then the knowledge that Aigilia was the centre of such an industry is of little help topographically, since the description "not far from the sea, sunny and protected" might well be applied to almost all the coastal demes that we have so far discussed.

NAME

The name Aigilia does not seem to have survived in any form. Stuart perhaps saw a connection between the names Ialou and Aigilia, but there is nothing to support this.[3]

INSCRIPTIONS

In this section I shall consider only those inscriptions that are now independent of sculpture. There are no inscriptions such as those from

[1]Theokritos 1.147–148 and *Scholia* (ed. Wendel) 75, s.v. ἀπ᾽Αἰγίλω; and Athenaios 14.652 E. [2]*Die Demenordnung* 38. [3]Stuart and Revett, *Antiquities* 3.xi.

Lamptrai to supply evidence for the identification of a particular place as the deme of Aigilia. A few inscriptions have been found, however, in the neighbourhood of Olympos, proving that Olympos was inhabited at least as early as the archaic period.

SEG X 326

One such inscription, perhaps a dedication, is dated in the second half of the sixth century B.C. It was published by Miss L. H. Jeffery, who states that the inscription was found "on the east side of the main road about half-way between Anavyssos and Phoinike, in the ancient deme of Anaphlystos."[4] It is clear from this account that the stone was found near Olympos, perhaps slightly south and east of the houses that today constitute this village, but the statement that this place was in the deme of Anaphlystos is a most unlikely assumption.

SEG XV 30 and IG II² 4954/5

Another inscription of the same period, SEG XV 30, was found in the remains of the basilica at Olympos. It appears to be part of a dedication.[5] Milchhöfer[6] records the finding of yet another dedication, though of later date, at Olympos, IG II² 4954/5.

IG II² 1750

According to IG II² 1750, Aigilia was represented by six councillors in the Boule of 334/3 B.C. It must have been, therefore, a good-sized deme.

REMAINS

First I shall discuss the important sculptural finds, five large works, which probably came from near Olympos. They range in date from the end of the seventh century B.C. to the very beginning of the fifth. The evidence for their provenience is, although incomplete and vague, nevertheless consistent.

We shall begin with the New York kouros and the Anavyssos

[4]"Sixth-Century Poros Inscription," 90.

[5]This inscription was first published by Kotzias, "'Ανασκαφαὶ τῆς βασιλικῆς," 107 and 120.

[6]"Antikenbericht" (1887) 304: No. 305. Kahrstedt (Das wirtschaftliche Gesicht Griechenlands in der Kaiserzeit 72 and 76) lists some other inscriptions as found at Olympos. In every case, however, the evidence for the finding place is exceedingly vague and one cannot honestly say that they were found at Olympos unless one accepts a very wide topographical interpretation of that name.

kouros. The latter kouros has now been mounted on the Kroisos base,[7] and this disposition seems in accord with the evidence.[8] Despite the conflicting testimony of unreliable witnesses[9] concerning the relation between these two kouroi and the base, it seems clear that all three were found at about the same time and all near one another. Thus, I think we can be certain that, if the provenience of one can be established, it will hold true for the other two pieces. Today, there is a remarkably consistent tradition held by those who live near Olympos and Anavyssos that the Anavyssos kouros was unearthed near Olympos and, like the first inscription noted, probably a little east and south of the village.

The third work is the impressive grave stele shared by New York and Berlin. Miss Richter says that the stele is "said to have been found in Attica,"[10] a phrase she uses several times of other pieces. The Berlin catalogue is not so vague, and Carl Blümel writes: "Angeblich bei Athen gefunden, nach einer anderen Mitteilung in der Gegend des Olympos in Südattika."[11] Miss Richter does not challenge Blümel's second suggestion, perhaps for the reason that it is correct. Indeed, I have been told that the authorities at the Metropolitan Museum agree with Blümel. What evidence there is, then, suggests that the stele was found near Olympos.

This conclusion is of importance when the provenience of the Munich kouros is considered, for, although no finding place is given in the principal publication,[12] there is, I am informed, evidence that it and the New York–Berlin stele were found in the same neighbourhood, if not together, and I know no reason to doubt this. Consequently I am prepared to believe that the Munich kouros also came from the region around Olympos.

Finally, there is the Aristodikos kouros. Karouzos has recently made it clear that this statue was discovered near Olympos.[13]

[7]Arvanitopoulos, "'Αττικαὶ ἐπιγραφαί 14," 81–88; Stevens and Vanderpool, "An Inscribed Kouros Base," 361–364.

[8]Karouzos (*Aristodikos* 63) considers the connection between the statue and the base to be "most likely." This mounting had already been suggested as a possibility by Arvanitopoulos ("'Αττικαὶ ἐπιγραφαί 14") and Richter (*Kouroi* 115 and 119).

[9]Cf. e.g. Arvanitopoulos, "'Αττικαὶ ἐπιγραφαί 14," 81–82.

[10]*Greek Sculptures in the Metropolitan* 12.

[11]*Katalog der Sammlung antiker Skulpturen* 8.

[12]P. Wolters in *Brunn-Bruckmann's Denkmäler* pls. 661 and 662.

[13]*Aristodikos* 3. Karouzos is not certain what deme is involved. He suggests either Aigilia or Amphitrope, but his description rules out the latter, if we assume Amphitrope to have had the boundaries I claim for it in chapter ix.

As I said above, the evidence about these five sculptural finds is vague, annoyingly incomplete, yet remarkably consistent. The consistency is not so obvious that one feels it to be the result of a plot to fabricate a provenience. Rather, it is a consistency that points to the truth, making justifiable, I think, a claim that these five grave monuments were all set up in the neighbourhood of Olympos, presumably in cemeteries attached to some archaic settlement.

Just as sculptural remains are plentiful, so are the remains from ancient settlements. From Milchhöfer's description of the area east of Phoinikia, it is clear that two places demand special attention, Trapuria and Pherisa, the former near Hagios Demetrios, the latter east of Olympos (Figure 7).[14]

The place known as Hagios Demetrios lies at the base of a hill, near a chapel which contains worked blocks originally intended for other positions. The most interesting remains are those on the hill. As one ascends from the east, in places by man-made steps, one passes extensive cuttings in the rock, among which is a cistern roofed with large slabs of stone. Traces of the two walls described by Milchhöfer can still be made out at the summit. Although some of the remains are of the Byzantine period, there are sections of terrace walls that appear to be Greek. From other blocks and roof tiles, it is certain that there was a building on the summit. There is no question that the hill was in use during classical times: in addition to the cistern, which is lined with waterproof cement typical of late classical or Hellenistic workmanship, we found fragments of black-glazed pottery of the fifth or fourth century B.C.

The history of Hagios Demetrios might be reconstructed as follows: in antiquity the summit was made reasonably level by terraces and in the flat area so formed a sanctuary was established. This sanctuary was used in Greek and Roman times, but in the Byzantine period a Christian chapel replaced the pagan shrine. This in turn disappeared and its place is now taken by the chapel at the foot of the rocky hill. Hagios Demetrios seems never to have been a settlement but always a rural shrine established on the one craggy outcrop in an otherwise even plain.

Near Olympos the remains are very extensive, as can be seen in the *Karten* (Sheet XVII). Most of the remains, however, are of chapels, "at least seven" according to Milchhöfer,[15] and houses from the Middle Ages. A large settlement also existed in the early Christian

[14]*Erläuternder Text* 3–6.19–20.
[15]*Ibid.* 20.

period, as the ruins of a basilica help to show.[16] The remains from these post-classical villages extend over a distance of more than one kilometre. The fields are full of pottery, worked stones are a common sight, and blocks *in situ* still break the surface in many places.

But what of a classical settlement? The traces are few. Some of the worked blocks look as if they might have come from that period, and I have picked up pottery of unmistakably classical date. It cannot be doubted that, if there was a classical settlement, its remains must lie beneath those of the later villages.[17]

IDENTIFICATION

Milchhöfer places Aigilia near Olympos,[18] and Löper locates it at either Trapuria or Pherisa.[19] I have not come across any other different opinion.[20]

According to Strabo, Aigilia (as already mentioned) was situated between Thorai and Anaphlystos, that is, between Phoinikia and Anavyssos. Within this area there are remains of a classical settlement at Hagios Demetrios and there are definite indications of a settlement of greater antiquity near Olympos. Aigilia must have been at one of these two sites.

Despite the lack of house remains and the small amount of classical pottery, I am convinced that the village of Aigilia was a little to the east of Olympos. The traces of a settlement at Hagios Demetrios suggest that it was small and during Christian times certainly no rival to the village near Olympos. If there was a settlement at Hagios Demetrios during the time of Kleisthenes, I imagine that its relation to the village near Olympos was the same. For even if we lack certain types of evidence for the size and age of this settlement, we still have the five works of sculpture and the dedications from the seventh and sixth centuries B.C. These remains demand the presence near Olympos of an archaic settlement and its cemeteries. And among the inhabitants of this village we can assume the members of at least one aristocratic

[16]Kotzias, "'Ανασκαφαὶ τῆς βασιλικῆς," 92–128.

[17]If I understand Kirsten correctly (Philippson, *Attika und Megaris* 831 n. 2), he assumes the existence of a Mycenaean settlement on this same site. I do not know the source of his evidence. There is no reference in Stubbings ("Mycenaean Pottery," 2–9) nor in Wrede (*Attika* frontispiece) to any prehistoric site at Olympos.

[18]*Die Demenordnung* 38 and map facing 48; and *RE* 1 (1894) 962, s.v. Aigilia.

[19]"Die Trittyen," 421.

[20]Kirsten (in Philippson, *Attika und Megaris* 831 n. 2) seems to support Milchhöfer's view.

and wealthy family.[21] No such remains have been found at Hagios
Demetrios, and so it cannot claim an importance and an antiquity
greater than those of the settlement near Olympos. I think we must
conclude that Aigilia was situated east of Olympos: no other conclusion
is consistent with the available evidence.

The limits of the deme of Aigilia are easily established. To the north
was Mount Panion, to the south Mount Olympos,[22] and to the east a
low group of hills dividing the area around Olympos from the northern
end of the plain of Anavyssos. To the west the limit is less obvious
but no less real. Immediately west of Hagios Demetrios the slopes of
Panion and Olympos almost come together, and the width of the plain
is greatly reduced. A border at this point would have been natural and
easily understood.

The plain between Panion and Olympos was limited both to the
west and to the east. From the archaic period to the Middle Ages it
had its most important settlement a little east of Olympos. This
settlement was once called Aigilia.

[21] I intend to publish in the near future an article setting out the theory, admittedly
speculative, that one of the aristocratic families that lived at Aigilia was the
Alkmaionidai. My case is based largely on the identification of Kroisos as a member
of that family.

[22] Mount Olympos must have made it impossible for the deme of Aigilia to have
direct access to the sea, unless the small coastal plain at Giurda was considered
part of Aigilia. This little plain (noted by Milchhöfer, *Erläuternder Text* 3–6.21) was
inhabited, though very thinly, in Roman times. Although it is cut off from both
Thorai and Anaphlystos, it is even more definitely separated from Aigilia. If the
plain was indeed considered part of Aigilia, then Aigilia was literally a coastal deme.
But then why did Strabo (9.1.21) record that Astypalaia was after Thorai? It should
have been after Aigilia under these circumstances. It is better, I think, to consider
this plain part of Thorai—certainly the easiest of the three demes from which to
administer it—and assume that Strabo listed Aigilia as a coastal deme because it
had always been thought of as such owing to its position in a coastal plain with
coastal demes on either side.

VIII

ANAPHLYSTOS

INTRODUCTION

S TRABO (9.1.21) places Anaphlystos and Atene[1] between Aigilia and Sounion, and in so doing he is following his practice of noting the demes that controlled the coast. However, in addition to Thorai, Aigilia, Anaphlystos, and Atene, the coastal trittys of the phyle Antiochis contained Amphitrope and Besa, and I have included these last two among the demes to be discussed (see chapters IX and X) since there is information about their location.

As part of the evidence for the location and extent of the individual demes from Aixone to Aigilia, I have tried to give an account of all the archaeological remains that have come to my attention, whether published, unpublished, or newly discovered. When dealing with Anaphlystos and the demes set in the Laureion hills—Amphitrope and Besa—I shall have to proceed differently. The reasons are obvious from a glance at the *Karten*: the remains are too numerous. In addition, many of the sites were studied in the late nineteenth century by those engaged in mining operations, but, because the results of the studies were not published, the evidence has not come down to us. It is therefore difficult to come to firm conclusions.

This abundance of remains from centres of habitation brings to the fore a problem that complicates any discussion of the demes of Laureion. The Kleisthenic demes in this area were not administrative divisions each containing a single village and perhaps a few isolated farmsteads. Rather, they were divisions containing several villages. Of these one was pre-eminent, the "capital" of the deme, and gave its name to the administrative unit. The problem is easily stated: how are the "capital" villages to be distinguished from ordinary villages?

This situation is not created by a superfluity of agrarian communities. It is the peculiar circumstance that the Laureion hills were rich in silver and therefore capable of attracting and maintaining large

---

[1]The problem whether the text is secure and whether one should read Azenia or Atene will be examined later.

groups of people who neither owned nor farmed extensive tracts of land. Thus villages were established by people other than farmers and, since these inhabitants were not interested in working the land about them, communities could be located at no great distance from one another.

Undoubtedly the first settlers in the Laureion hills were primarily concerned with agriculture, for Laureion and its foothills are not utterly barren and would have supported, though precariously, a limited number of farmers. The oldest villages, therefore, would have been founded by farmers, and the villages established by those engaged in mining activities would have been accordingly later.[2] If the second group could be shown to be post-Kleisthenic, then we should look for the "capital" demes among the villages situated in basically agrarian environments.

This easy method is not open to us. The exploitation of the mineral resources of Laureion clearly began before Kleisthenes and activities during his time must have been on no small scale. By the end of the sixth century B.C., villages entirely dependent upon mining must have been in existence.

That mining communities existed so early would be hard to prove from surface finds alone. The great majority of the artefacts from classical times found in the Laureion area are dated in the fifth and fourth centuries B.C. I have discovered little from the sixth century B.C. This lack, however, is not surprising: legitimate excavation has been negligible and the early remains undoubtedly lie beneath the later and now visible remains. Fortunately, literary evidence and evidence from the mines themselves make it clear that Laureion was the scene of extensive mining before the Persian Wars.

The first great strike recorded in Laureion is that which occurred at Maroneia either in, or a few years before, 483/2 B.C.[3] Large quantities of silver became available, sufficient to be described a few years later by Aischylos as ἀργύρου πηγή τις and θησαυρὸς χθονός.[4] There can be no doubt that the silver at Maroneia came from the "third contact," and that the continuing success of the Laureion mines during the following centuries was due to the ability of the miners to exploit this particular fault.

---

[2]There is always the possibility that some of the agrarian villages were so situated that discovery of mines did not entail separate communities but merely an enlargement of the earlier settlements.

[3]Aristotle, *Ath. Pol.* 22.7.

[4]*Persians* 238.

The Laureion hills are divided horizontally into five strata, three of limestone and two of schist in alternating layers, the highest, of limestone, being found in very few places. Theoretically there are four contacts, but the topmost is of such slight extent that it has become customary to ignore its presence and to call the contact between the first layer of schist and the second bed of limestone the "first" contact. This contact is in many places above ground and visible, and even where underground is very close to the surface. On the other hand, the lowest stratum of limestone breaks the surface only near the coast and at the bottom of the Legrana Valley, and so the "third" contact, between the second layer of schist and the third of limestone, is for the most part deep beneath the surface, in some cases more than a hundred metres.

The workable silver deposits are in the first and third contacts. The earliest workings were in the first, which could be tapped by simple caves and primitive horizontal passages, of which there are many examples. The third contact necessitated deep shafts connected with well-constructed passages, the building of which demanded knowledge and practice, not to mention an accurate understanding of the geology of Laureion. Such knowledge and experience were not gained overnight and the fumbling efforts to draw silver from the first contact are testimony of a long period of experiment and self-education in mining methods.[5]

By 483/2 B.C. this knowledge had been not only gained but put into effect. Assuming that Maroneia was near the present Kamareza,[6] we must imagine shafts between seventy and one hundred metres deep, complicated galleries following the line of the contact, washing and milling establishments, and furnaces—in fact, all the signs of an established industry. That the Athenian state could benefit so greatly in 483/2 B.C. means that the first plans to exploit the third contact had been put into operation several years, perhaps several decades, before. The task of excavating a shaft a hundred metres deep would alone have taken at least a year and a half.[7]

It cannot be doubted that interest and activity in the mining district

[5]Ardaillon, *Les Mines* 136: "Il est en effet hors de doute que la prospérité des mines du Laurion avant les guerres médiques, ne fut que la récompense de longs efforts et le résultat des progrès décisifs précédemment accomplis." Most of my technical information about mining in the Laureion district comes from this book, still the best work on the subject.

[6]This assumption is not made by all scholars: see, e.g., LaBarbe, *La Loi navale* 34–35.

[7]Ardaillon, *Les Mines* 31.

must have been strong for many years before 483/2 B.C. Xenophon says (περὶ πόρων 4.2): οὐκοῦν ὅτι μὲν πάνυ πάλαι ἐνεργά ἐστι, πᾶσι σαφές· οὐδεὶς γοῦν οὐδὲ πειρᾶται λέγειν ἀπὸ ποίου χρόνου ἐπεχειρήθη. This somewhat vague assertion of the antiquity of the Laureion mines is made much more explicit by a remark of Herodotos (1.64.1): "and so Peisistratos gained mastery of Athens for the third time and made firm his tyranny with many mercenaries and revenues derived from both Attika and the Strymon River." Revenues from the Strymon, in particular from Mount Pangaios, were the result of Peisistratos' mining interests. From Herodotos' statement we can infer that Peisistratos had similar interests in Attika, indeed received income from the operation of mines in Laureion.[8] This inference need not be extended to mean that the third contact had been reached by the middle of the sixth century B.C., but only that by then the first contact was being systematically attacked.

It is generally agreed that silver was first extracted from Laureion in the eighth or seventh century B.C.[9] The great incentive to increase the scope of silver mining must have been given by the appearance and adoption of silver coinage in Attika. If this stimulus was applied between 600 and 550 B.C. the science of mining had time to develop to such an extent that a century later the third contact could be worked with profit.

This sketch of the early history of the mining industry in Laureion is sufficient to show that mining villages must have been established in the area before the constitutional changes of Kleisthenes, even if the archaeological remains from the period are so far slight.

Our purpose, therefore, when dealing with Anaphlystos, Amphitrope, and Besa, will be to try to locate the villages that were known by these names. We must assume that the Kleisthenic deme had its "capital" at the village from which the deme took its name and that in any one deme it was not customary for two villages, otherwise separate, to bear the same name.

[8] The full evidence can be seen best in Ure, *The Origin of Tyranny* 37–51 (esp. from 46) and 54–56, and Seltman, *Athens* 39–41 and 65–70. Svoronos' theory, accepted by Seltman, that Peisistratos established a mint at Sounion is difficult to maintain: see J. H. Young, "Epigram at Sunium," 355–356.

[9] See, e.g., Davies, "Ancient Mines of Laurium," 6: "It has often been supposed that the mines of Laurium go back to Mycenaean times, and are connected with the prehistoric site of Thoricus. . . . As Thoricus is eminently a position chosen for defence, and as no slag apparently has been found there, it is probable that the working of the mines did not start till the late eighth or seventh century B.C."

ANCIENT REFERENCES

Strabo, as we have noted, places Anaphlystos after the deme of Aigilia and before that of Azenia, which in turn is before Cape Sounion. The positions of Aigilia and Sounion thus determined, Anaphlystos must have been situated immediately west of the Laureion hills, there being insufficient room for two demes in the coastal region between the bays of Hagios Nikolaos and Legrana.

Anaphlystos is classified as πόλις by Ptolemy[10] and Skylax.[11] The latter also notes that Anaphlystos had a harbour and fortification. Both writers consider Anaphlystos to be one of the leading towns of Attika. Herodotos (4.99) implies that Anaphlystos and Thorikos were by the sea. But we cannot be certain whether he is referring to the village of Anaphlystos or to the deme of the same name, even though he uses the expression 'Αναφλύστου δήμου. When Herodotos uses the term δῆμος he usually means "a village" rather than a political division.[12]

The most interesting reference to Anaphlystos is that given by Xenophon (περὶ πόρων 4.43):

Λογίζομαι δ' ἔγωγε καὶ πολέμου γιγνομένου οἷόν τ'εἶναι μὴ ἐκλείπεσθαι τὰ ἀργύρεια. ἔστι μὲν γὰρ δήπου περὶ τὰ μέταλλα ἐν τῇ πρὸς μεσημβρίαν θαλάττῃ τεῖχος ἐν 'Αναφλύστῳ, ἔστι δ' ἐν τῇ πρὸς ἄρκτον τεῖχος ἐν Θορικῷ. ἀπέχει δὲ ταῦτα ἀπ' ἀλλήλων ἀμφὶ τὰ ἑξήκοντα στάδια.

The word θαλάττῃ has been bracketed in recent texts on the authority of Theodor Bergk, who offers no reason for this deletion other than that "ist θαλάσσῃ ein ganz abgeschmackten Zusatz."[13] It is a pity that his suggestion has been so widely adopted, because the reason given is far from adequate and in no way justifies the removal. In place of the eliminated θαλάττῃ, Bergk presumably supplied χώρᾳ or γῇ as the implied noun to which τῇ refers. The omission of the substantive is normal with such nouns when the meaning is clear and

[10]Geographia 3.15.22.
[11]Periplus 57.
[12]This certainly seems to be the case in 5.74 and 5.81. One of the most interesting uses of δῆμος is in 1.62: while Peisistratos was at Marathon οἵ τε ἐκ τοῦ ἄστεος στασιῶται ἀπίκοντο ἄλλοι τε ἐκ τῶν δήμων προσέρρεον. The meaning is strikingly clear: Herodotos is contrasting the men from the city with those from the country. There is no suggestion of political divisions, and ἐκ τῶν δήμων means "from the villages." For a discussion of this problem see Jacoby, Atthis 367–368.
[13]" 'Kritische Bemerkungen' I Xenophon," 432.

when they are used along with attributives. But why remove θαλάττῃ? There is considerable difference in meaning between "a fortification in the land towards the south (or north)" and "a fortification on the south (or north) coast." Since we have already seen that the deme of Anaphlystos had a fortification (presumably) at the coast and since there was a similarly placed fort at Thorikos,[14] Xenophon's unemended description appears entirely apt. But perhaps Bergk was not concerned with this geographical aspect and took exception to the phrase ἐν . . . θαλάττῃ τεῖχος. If he assumed that this meant "a fortification in the sea," a location certainly hard to credit, then he was being too restrictive in his interpretation of ἐν followed by the dative. Xenophon (*Anabasis* 4.8.22) has the phrase πόλιν Ἑλληνίδα οἰκουμένην ἐν τῷ Εὐξείνῳ πόντῳ, which obviously means "a city built on the banks (or shore) of the Euxine sea." In both cases the preposition ἐν has a force similar to ἐπί with the dative[15] or even παρά with the dative,[16] the prevailing idea being one of proximity. Bergk's emendation should be ignored and the text retained as all recorded manuscripts present it. If one wanted to take exception to the text, criticism would be better directed against the points of the compass mentioned. West and east would be more accurate than south and north. Nevertheless, the meaning is clear: south refers to the Saronic Gulf, north to the Aegean Sea or the Euboean Strait.

These references in Xenophon's περὶ πόρων to Anaphlystos and Thorikos are to the demes.[17] This is made clear in the next sentence where Xenophon refers to the "highest point of Besa." The only possible interpretation here is that Besa was a district. We can now translate the whole passage:

I for my part consider that it is possible not to abandon the silver mines in the event of war. Indeed, for the protection of the mines there is a fortification on the south coast in the deme of Anaphlystos, and one on the north coast in the deme of Thorikos. These are separated from each other by about sixty stades.

---

[14]Cf. e.g. Skylax, *Periplus* 57:Θορικὸς τεῖχος καὶ λιμένες δύο.

[15]E.g. Thucydides 7.4.2:τὸ ἐπὶ θαλάσσῃ τεῖχος. At least one critic has advocated emending ἐν to ἐπί but his reasons are not convincing. See Herwerden, "Lectiones Xenophonteae," 21: "Bis pro ἐν requiro ἐπί, cui praepositioni exitiosa fuisse videtur alterius vicinitas. Praepositio EN sic usurpata procul dubio aliena est a pedestri oratione Atheniensium."

[16]E.g. Xenophon, *Anabasis* 7.2.25: τὰ παρὰ θαλάττῃ . . . χωρία.

[17]ἐν followed by a place name in the dative is normal Attic for "in the district of," according to LSJ⁹ 551 (s.v. ἐν, A.I.1). There are, however, many examples of the locatival dative used for the same purpose with names of demes, and it is therefore impossible to establish a firm rule.

A circle with a radius of sixty stades and with its centre at the fortification at Thorikos crosses the southern coastline within the Bay of Hagios Nikolaos.

The literary evidence for Anaphlystos presents a remarkably consistent picture. The deme of Anaphlystos lay west of the Laureion hills and controlled at least part of the Bay of Hagios Nikolaos, on the shore of which the Anaphlystioi maintained a harbour and fortification.[18]

NAME

The name Anaphlystos survives as Anavyso (or Anavysso) or, more formally, Anavyssos. Not only are the names similar but the accent is on the second syllable of all these words.[19] The present village is situated about one kilometre from the shore; it dates from the last years of the nineteenth century, but its present size is a direct result of the transference of nationals after 1922.[20] North of this village and about three kilometres from the shore was the metochi of Anavyso, a monastic settlement surrounding a church dedicated to Hagios Panteleimon; this centre of habitation was noticed by several early travellers and we can be certain that the monastery was in existence during the eighteenth century.[21] Near the bay is a little settlement surrounding a church dedicated to Hagios Georgios; Milchhöfer reports that this church and a few barracks are the sole remains of an earlier village of Anavyso.[22] Yet a fourth place seems to have been known by this name: the travellers report that there was a harbour of Anavyso,[23] but today the village on the shore is named Nea Phokaia, the name recalling the cause of its founding. This widespread use of a single name is not perhaps surprising. In the past few centuries the position (and indeed the fate) of the leading village seems to have been anything but settled. "In the Middle Ages the inhabitants appear to have withdrawn to the easterly hills where have been found a ruined castle and abandoned villages, one of which has the informative name Kataphygi ('Place of refuge'). In the Turkish period the region was quite deserted, but it has somewhat revived during the present."[24]

[18]The deme of Anaphlystos is also mentioned by Pausanias (2.30.9) and Harpokration (s.v. Ἀναφλύστιοι), but neither reference gives us any additional information.
[19]E.g. see Leake, *Demi* 59 and n. 1.
[20]See the figures in Philippson, *Attika und Megaris* 832–833.
[21]Stuart and Revett, *Antiquities* 3.vii.
[22]*Erläuternder Text* 3–6.21.
[23]Stuart and Revett, *Antiquities* 3.vii and the map of Attika facing p. 1.
[24]Philippson, *Attika und Megaris* 832.

Even though we cannot trace the use of the name Anavyso back
beyond a few centuries, I think it certain that the present use is not
due to any modern revival of the ancient name with a change of the
form. On the contrary, it is surely due to the name Anaphlystos and
its derivatives having remained in use over a long period of time,
perhaps even in constant use from classical times, thereby achieving
for themselves a traditional quality that made it proper for them to be
employed many times over for centres of habitation.

Continuity of use, however, is one thing, continuity of position
another, and the former does not necessarily indicate the latter, as
can be seen here where we have established that the name Anavyso
has been applied to several distinct localities in the same district. From
the survival of the name Anaphlystos we cannot state exactly where
the classical village of that name was located. We can with reason,
however, expect ancient Anaphlystos to have been in the same general
area as modern Anavyssos, perhaps further north near the metochi
that took the same name, perhaps further south near the harbour
that may have been used for millennia, perhaps further east near
Hagios Georgios.

INSCRIPTIONS

The lists published by the poletai recording the leasing of mining
properties supply topographical evidence for Anaphlystos, Amphitrope,
and Besa, as well as for other demes. Excavations in the Athenian
Agora have brought to light a great many fragments of such lists, and
these, along with others previously known, have been published by
Margaret Crosby.[25] All the known records come from the fourth
century B.C. and the scheme employed for presenting the information
that the poletai wanted inscribed is approximately the same for all.[26]
The leases contain the following facts: name of registrant, name of
lessee, category of mine, price, location.[27]

[25]"Leases" and "Fragments." When citing the inscriptions published in these
two articles, I use the system of abbreviation already accepted by some scholars:
inscriptions from the first article are numbered Crosby 1–38, from the second article
Crosby S 1–S 8. Miss Crosby's publications are concerned primarily with establishing
the texts. She does, however, provide a very useful introduction to the whole problem
of the leases in "Leases," 189–205. The contents of the leases have been more fully
discussed (based on Miss Crosby's texts) by Hopper, "Silver Mines."

[26]See Crosby, "Leases," 192–193 for an example of a "typical lease." Only Crosby
1 shows marked differences from the others, perhaps to be explained because it is
the earliest we have.

[27]Not all leases contained all these facts. Certain types did not name both a regist-

It is the locations of the mines that are of special importance for this study. The position of each mine is first described generally, for example ἐπὶ Σουνίωι, ἐν Νάπηι, Θορικοῖ, then located accurately by boundaries north, south, east, and west. The boundaries are given in relation to neighbouring mines, workshops, estates, buildings, sanctuaries, geographical features, roads, etc.[28] Place names are mentioned in connection with roads and gullies, for instance "the road from Amphitrope to Besa," "the gully from Laureion to Thalinos (?)." It seems clear that in the case of roads the named reference points are villages, not demes or districts. A road going from the deme of Amphitrope to the deme of Besa would have little meaning as a specific limit, whereas a road from the village of Amphitrope to the village of Besa would be readily understood as a particular road, not one of several possible routes.[29]

The same is perhaps not true of place names used with gullies. The example given above is difficult to understand if the reference to Laureion is to a village. Since Laureion was near the coast, the gully mentioned would have been extremely short, unless we assume that Laureion was at the foot of the gully and Thalinos (?) at the head, in which case the directions noted in the Greek are surely misleading.

rant and a lessee, and in Crosby 1 the registrant and the category of the mine are not included.

[28]Crosby, "Leases," 194-196 and Hopper, "Silver Mines," 217-224.

[29]This point is not discussed by either Crosby or Hopper, although the former assumes that the names refer to villages ("Leases," 193-194). LaBarbe, *La Loi navale* 28 n. 3 is of the opinion that when Laureion is noted as the beginning or end of a road it must in these instances be a village (*une localité*), not a district as it sometimes is.

If the method of describing roads is to show any consistency, then the place names must all refer either to districts (including demes) or to actual localities such as towns and villages. In the case of a small district there would be little ambiguity whichever system was used. But the same would not be true of a large area such as the deme of Anaphlystos. A road labelled "to the deme of Anaphlystos" might be heading towards one of several small villages, none of which was actually called Anaphlystos. I am convinced, therefore, that these roads were named in relation to the towns or villages which they joined. Any other system would have allowed doubt in the very part of the lease where accuracy was demanded. (Modern analogy has little weight in such an argument, but it is perhaps worth mentioning that we speak of the Athens–Salonika highway, not the Attika–Makedonia highway.) This insistence upon accuracy, however, should not be carried too far. It is clear from some of the leases that the boundaries were recorded, not so that the poletai (or anyone else) in Athens could make detailed maps of the holdings, but so that the limits of a property could be readily established by anyone who went to that property. Thus, it was not always necessary to record that a "road going from A to B" formed the southern boundary of a mine but merely a "road going to B." Nor was it essential to identify every gully. χαράδρα appears unqualified as a boundary several times.

In this instance it is preferable to understand Laureion as a district.[30] A similar meaning is presumably attached to the phrase ἡ χαράδρα ἡ Θορικίων, where again, had the reference been to a "gully from Thorikos," we should have had to explain it as a reference to a district, in this case a deme.[31]

Some commentators think that where a name carried by a deme appears in the general location the reference is to the village of that name, as in the case of roads.[32] This view may be right of some places but it is not applicable to all. For instance, if it is assumed that the village of Anaphlystos was near the shore, then the location Ἀναφλυστοῖ cannot mean "at the village of Anaphlystos" (even if we allow the term to refer to a limited area around Anaphlystos) because the nearest mines were more than five kilometres away.[33] The term Θορικοῖ perhaps admits of a wider meaning than just "at the village of Thorikos." Although there were some mines near the settlement, there was a much larger group approximately three kilometres west of the village of Thorikos in land that was within the deme of Thorikos.[34]

The methods of locating mines need further study. Mines are given

---

[30]LaBarbe, *La Loi navale* 29 n. 3.

[31]*Ibid.* 29–30 n. 2 indicates that LaBarbe would probably agree with this. He remarks of this ravine that it got its name "apparemment par référence à son origine." J. H. Young ("Greek Inscriptions," 30 n. 26) takes a similar view and says that "the Θορίκιοι must be the demesmen of Thorikos."

Two other named gullies are preserved in the leases, the one "from Nape," the other "flowing to Anaphlystos." Nape was probably a district, not a village, and Anaphlystos here refers to the deme since there is no gully near the village of Anaphlystos.

[32]This view is most forcefully expounded by J. H. Young, "Greek Inscriptions," 30: "The explanation is clear and certain: the sites here recorded are mining towns or mining regions; each one of five such towns gave its name to the deme surrounding it, the others did not. But in no case do the mining leases give locations by demes, or otherwise refer to demes except in the demotics." Crosby, "Leases," 193–194 supports this contention and adds, by way of proof, "inasmuch as no one of the demes in the district (notably Φρέαρροι) which did not have a corresponding town name is ever given as the location of a mine." Crosby's case has been weakened by the subsequent discovery of a lease in which the location of a mine is given as Φρεαρροῖ (Crosby S 2.36 and Crosby, "Fragments," 8). Hopper ("Silver Mines," 217) does not commit himself on this issue. LaBarbe, on the other hand, believes that the general locations refer to districts, which may coincide with demes (*La Loi navale* 28 n. 3).

[33]I should have preferred to take another example. In the case of Anaphlystos, however, its approximate position can be established without the evidence from these inscriptions.

[34]To the few mines found near the settlement, we must now add another discovered recently on the southern slope of the hill forming the acropolis. The entrance to the mine came to light in quarrying operations.

a general location in three ways: (*a*) place name in the locative; (*b*) ἐπί followed by a place name in the dative; (*c*) ἐν followed by a place name in the dative. For the most part the reference is held to a single place name, although occasionally two are employed.

Place Names in the Locative

The following names are used in the locative: Amphitrope, Anaphlystos, Besa, Phrearrhos, and Thorikos.[35] Miss Crosby also records locatives for Maroneia and Thalinos. With the exception of these last two, the locative is used exclusively with names that are common to villages and demes, that is, demes named after their chief village.

The evidence for the appearance of Maroneia and Thalinos in the locative is not satisfactory and should be reviewed in light of the above. In Crosby 19.18, Μαρωνεί[α]⟨ι⟩ has been restored where the stone reads Μαρωνει.ν.[36] In lines 23–24 of the same inscription ἐ]ν Μαρ[ωνείαι has been rightly restored and the same phrase appears in two other inscriptions.[37] I do not feel we are justified in believing that the locative was intended in Crosby 19.18. Rather I should assume the accidental omission of ἐν before Miss Crosby's Μαρωνεί[α]⟨ι⟩;[38] otherwise Maroneia would constitute the sole example of a place name being referred to in the general location by more than one of the three methods mentioned above.[39] Miss Crosby restores the locatival form of Maroneia in two other inscriptions, Crosby 5.54 and 14.4. In neither case is the supplement mandatory, there being no letters preserved.[40]

[35]For statistical information of this kind, I have relied on the comprehensive indices prepared by Miss Crosby, to be found in "Leases," 293–312 and "Fragments," 20–23.

[36]Crosby, "Leases," 262 points out that "the last letter ... most resembles a nu or kappa. I have assumed that a nu was written by mistake for an iota." After looking at the stone I am convinced that here Miss Crosby is too cautious. The final letter is certainly a nu.

[37]Crosby 1.59 and 2.17.

[38]To assume a mistake is not as arbitrary a method of getting out of this difficulty as it might appear. That there is a mistake in the line as inscribed is obvious, and whatever solution is suggested will have to be imputed to the engraver. The same is true of the next line where Miss Crosby has had to emend στήλης to στήλην.

[39]There is one doubtful exception to this statement. When Thrasymos is given as the general location of a mine, the phrase denoting this location is ἐπὶ Θρασύμωι. In one instance, Crosby 37.2, Miss Crosby has restored ἐν Θρ[ασύμωι. However, she has herself questioned the restoration ("Leases," 285) because it constitutes a unique departure from standard practice.

[40]The restorations in these leases are dependent upon each other, there being sufficient similarity in the preserved portions to admit the suggestion that both leases are concerned with the same concession. Miss Crosby gives no reason for

The other name, Thalinos (?), presents different problems. Θαλινοῖ has been restored as the general location of a mine in one instance, Crosby 20.6. ἐπὶ Θάλινον has been restored in two places as a feature of a particular boundary, Crosby 16 (Face A, Col. II) 54–55 and Crosby S 5.7. ἐπὶ Θαλιν – – has been restored once, Crosby 16.76–77. In the first example θαλινο appears on the stone but there is no accurate control over the length of the word. In the second and fourth, θαλ remains, and again there is no control over the length. In the third instance, nothing remains, but the phrase has been restored on the basis of Crosby 16.54–55, because in both cases a boundary is given in relation to "a gully from Laureion to – – –."

In Crosby 16.53–55 (to take the second example first), a mine is described having as its eastern boundary "the road from Laureion to Thrasymos" and as its western boundary "the gully from Laureion to Thalinos (?)." If we assume that all three place names refer to villages and that the gully is described "from top to bottom" and not vice versa, then the two boundaries are almost mutually exclusive, there being reasonable evidence for placing Thrasymos in the hills and Laureion near the coast. If, however, the second mention of Laureion is of Laureion as a district, then the double reference makes sense. In fact, we can place the mine within close limits. The gully mentioned is in all probability the ravine noted on Ardaillon's map as the "Ravin de Camaréza," which runs between Kamareza and Ergastiria.[41] Today a motor road follows this ravine, as it affords the only method of easy access from coast to highland. A few mines lie to one side or other of the ravine and in at least two places it runs north–south despite its prevailing west–east direction. This identification of the ravine is even more credible when we recall that Thrasymos is generally placed near Kamareza, and Laureion near

restoring Maroneia (both times with question marks) but the reason is evident: in both cases there is space for a location with nine letters, and no other known location, either in the locative or in the dative preceded by a preposition, has this number of letters. The argument is not as strong as it may appear. First, there is always the possibility that there were place names used that are not preserved in our incomplete records. Secondly, it must be remembered that abbreviations were common in the mining leases. The abbreviation for Amphitrope was ᾽Αμφιτροπ, eight letters, but since abbreviations were frequently followed by interpuncts one would have to allow nine spaces for the name and sign. Crosby 14 contains many abbreviations, Crosby 5 is not free of them. I am not suggesting that ᾽Αμφιτροπ: is the correct supplement. It is, however, a possible supplement and one that does not entail the use of a place name in an unusual form. In this respect, I consider it a better supplement than that suggested by Miss Crosby.

[41]Ardaillon, *Les Mines* endpiece.

Ergastiria.[42] What then of Thalinos? It too should be placed, presumably, near Ergastiria and in the district of Laureion.

This same general area is perhaps indicated for the mine in Crosby 16.75–80 (the fourth example). Line 75 ends with a reference to ἐπὶ θρα, clearly to be restored as ἐπὶ Θρα|[σύμωι.

Miss Crosby has restored Thalinos in Crosby S 5.7 (the third example). Two of the boundaries of a mine are given as follows (restored): "On the north, the gully from Laureion to Thalinos; to the east, the same." The gully obviously makes a right-angled bend, in the crook of which is the mine. The character of the gully is quite in accord with the "Ravin de Camaréza." This mine will have been south of the ravine, the one described above, north. The restoration is entirely plausible if we assume the other restorations involving Thalinos to be correct.

Now we must look at the first example, Crosby 20.6, where the letters θαλινο are preserved, which Miss Crosby restores (with a question mark) as the locative Θαλινο[ῖ, the name indicating the general location of a mine. A further indication of the mine's position is given two lines later as ἐν [Νάπ]ηι. One of the boundaries confirms this relation to Nape: part of the northern boundary of the mine is "the gully running from Nape." Whatever the true interpretation of a double location, in this instance it certainly suggests the proximity of Thalinos and Nape. But the name of the latter implies a position in the hills, and we have already seen that the former should be placed near Ergastiria, where, it must be noted, there are no mines. The mention of a gully other than "the gully from Laureion" does nothing to strengthen the idea of closeness. Although I cannot prove that Thalinos and Nape were not closely connected in some way, I can find nothing to suggest it except this inscription. In addition to the difficulties mentioned above, we must remember that Θαλινοῖ would constitute the only locative used of a name other than of a deme name.

Because of these objections I think we are justified in looking for

---

[42]See LaBarbe, *La Loi navale* 27 (map), 29 (re Laureion), 35 (re Thrasymos). While I believe LaBarbe's conclusions to be correct, the method by which he establishes the position of places is open to some question. To assume that A was north of B because, when a road from A to B passed a certain mine it constituted the mine's western boundary and therefore was oriented north–south at that particular section, is to assume that the road formed an undeviating straight line from A to B. The assumption is unwarranted. Evidence from the supposed direction of roads and gullies must be used with great care and in most cases will provide only corroborative evidence for the position of places already located (or merely indicated) by other means.

other supplements. In the *Corpus*, Crosby 16.54–55 and 76–77 are both restored with θάλ[ατταν.[43] Since we have already come to the conclusion that Thalinos (if so restored) must be placed near the sea, this supplement is entirely satisfactory and can also be restored in Crosby S 5.7 without any difficulty. "The gully going from Laureion to the sea" would adequately describe the "Ravin de Camaréza." This supplement, however, would neither fit, nor be suitable for, Crosby 20.6. Since we have one general location for the mine being leased, we might expect the full name of the registrant to be a more appropriate beginning. After Θαλινο[ῖ Miss Crosby has restored Thoutimides of Sounion as registrant on the ground that in a lease of an ergasimon mine the registrant and lessee are usually the same. However, were we to restore the name of a person, we should have to assume that the registrant and lessee were different men, that the name of the former began with Θαλινο, and that the rest of the available space contained the conclusion of his name, his patronymic, and his demotic.[44] But are we yet in a position to state that registrant and lessee were "normally" the same in this type of lease? Not only have we an insufficient number of fully preserved leases to warrant anything more than a general hypothesis,[45] but also there is an exception to this general rule.[46] (As to the coincidence of a place name and a personal name with the same beginning, one need only note Θράσυμος and Θράσιππος or Θρασύλοχος.)

Although an overwhelming case for either retaining Thalinos (in any form) or rejecting it cannot be made, I am quite persuaded that rejection answers more questions and poses fewer than retention. Accordingly I do not accept Thalinos as a place name in the form of either ἐπὶ Θάλινον or Θαλινοῖ.

Our first category, then, consists entirely of place names that are (also) names of demes. All are given in the locative.

[43]*IG* II² 1582.

[44]Miss Crosby's restoration contains no patronymic owing to requirements of space. Such a supplement is entirely possible in this lease because there is no established way of naming citizens: some appear with patronymics, others without.

[45]Cf. Hopper, "Silver Mines," 233: "The position of *ergasima* is not clear beyond doubt because of the limited number of such leases, and the defective state of available examples."

[46]Miss Crosby ("Leases," 197, 201, 257, 258) notes that Crosby 18.18–22 provides an exception, but she suggests that this abnormality hides an unusual situation. Hopper ("Silver Mines," 233) says that Crosby 16.76–83 constitutes a second exception. Certainly this lease does not conform to the pattern; nevertheless, registrant and lessee were the same person. For further discussion see Hopper, "Silver Mines," 233–234.

Place Names in the Dative Preceded by ἐπί

The following place names appear in the dative preceded by the preposition ἐπί: Laureion, Skopia, Sounion, and Thrasymos. There is no unrestored instance of the use of these names in the leases as a general location either in the locative or with a preposition other than ἐπί.[47]

Place Names in the Dative Preceded by ἐν

The third method of indicating a general location is the use of ἐν followed by a place name in the dative. The following place names are used in this way: Aulon, Bambideion Hill, Maroneia,[48] Nape, Pangaion, and Philomelidon.[49] It appears that this group embraces at least villages (or mining centres), hills, and an estate.

Differences in Methods of Location

Before considering the final group, that of double locations, let us look briefly at the three categories to see if we can establish any essential differences among them. It is hardly likely that three methods of expressing location would be employed if there were not differences. The first group, place names in the locative, is made up of names that can be used equally well both for villages and for the demes called after those villages. In the context of the mining leases, however, I think the point of reference is the deme, not the village. Ἀναφλυστοῖ, as has already been said, must refer to an Anaphlystos larger in area than the village of that name: therefore it must mean "in the deme of Anaphlystos." It is probably best if Θορικοῖ be understood in the same way. Since there is no compulsion to interpret otherwise the remaining names in this group, I assume that, even as these names are all used in the same manner and are all of the same group, so they all refer to demes.[50] It is relevant to note that this use of the locative

[47]But see Crosby 37.2 and n. 39 above, where the restoration ἐν Θρ[ασύμωι is considered.

[48]See above, this chapter, for a discussion of alleged uses of Maroneia in the locative.

[49]For completeness we should add a name partly preserved in Crosby 20.13: [ἐν. . . . .]μηι.

[50]My main concern is to show that the location of a place name is in fact the locative of a deme name and not a village name. This does not mean, however, that the Athenian of the fourth century B.C. could not localize the reference and immediately understand that the mine was in a particular part of that deme. I should go further: it is possible that in a given deme there might be two or more distinct centres of mining. The centre first exploited might be referred to by the deme name, the later centres by other names (not in the locative). I suggest an example: "in the deme of Besa" might describe mines near Synterini, while another name might describe mines at Demoliaki, even though the latter was technically within the deme of Besa.

is a normal one for expressing *place where* within an Attic deme.[51]

The second group, ἐπί followed by a place name in the dative, is discussed by LaBarbe. He writes: "le type 'ἐπί + datif' ne désigne pas des localités . . . , mais bien . . . des *districts* 'sur le territoire desquels' elles [sc. the mines] étaient établies."[52] His case rests largely on his proof that the word Laureion was used not only of a town and of the mining district as a whole, but also of a particular part of the mining district. The arguments are convincing, but it should be pointed out that the district of Laureion was undoubtedly centred around the town of Laureion, otherwise the appellation would have had little meaning. The name Sounion also had more than one meaning. There were a deme and a town of Sounion, and the name was also applied to the whole promontory thrusting south from between Anaphlystos and Thorikos.[53] If we have assessed the significance of the first group correctly, then ἐπί Σουνίωι is not a reference to the deme (otherwise it would have been in the locative) but to the village and, following LaBarbe, to the district around the village. Since the village of Sounion was near Agrileza, and thus in the heart of one of the mining areas, this interpretation is apposite. But why refer to the district around the village of Sounion and not to the deme of Sounion, when one refers to the deme of Anaphlystos and yet not to the district around the village of Anaphlystos? I think the answer is obvious. A reference to mines in the demes of Anaphlystos, Amphitrope, and Besa would not constitute a vague indication of location. The mines in these demes were for the most part together,[54] so that a reference to the deme would focus immediate attention on one particular part of that deme. This was not true of the deme of Sounion, which not only was a large deme but also embraced within its borders several distinct areas of mining operations.[55] A reference to the deme of Sounion would have given little information, whereas a reference to the districts around the villages of Sounion or Laureion would have been as precise as a reference to the deme of Amphitrope.

Thrasymos, also found as a place name in the dative with ἐπί, was a village, and presumably the phrase ἐπί Θρασύμωι has the meaning "in the district around the village of Thrasymos." LaBarbe would

[51]See Smyth, *Greek Grammar* 351 (section 1534).

[52]*La Loi navale* 28 n. 3.

[53]Herodotos 4.99.

[54]Mines in Anaphlystos were near Ari, in Amphitrope near the "col de Metropisi" (see Ardaillon's map), and in Besa between Demoliaki and Synterini.

[55]E.g. the area around the village of Sounion near Agrileza and the district around Kamareza.

exempt Thrasymos from this category but his objections are without basis.[56] On the other hand, I feel considerable hesitation in admitting that ἐπὶ Σκοπιᾶι has the meaning "in the district around Skopia." It appears only once, in Crosby 1.41, where it is the second element of a double location, ἐν Νάπηι ἐπὶ Σκοπιᾶι. σκοπιά has the basic meaning "a place to keep watch" and therefore is used of "watchtower," "lookout," or "peak." It is surely conceivable, if not probable, that in the above context σκοπιά is not a placename at all and that the phrase merely indicates the proximity of a mine in Nape to a prominent watchtower.[57]

There can be little doubt that the villages of Sounion, Laureion, and Thrasymos and their surrounding lands were within the deme of Sounion.[58] This observation suggests an explanation for the use of

[56]LaBarbe (La Loi navale 35–36 n. 2) believes that Thrasymos was a small area centred around a stele or small building. He bases his belief on a statement found in the lexicographers elucidating the phrase ἐπὶ Θρασύλλῳ of Demosthenes 37.25, the reading in Demosthenes being an obvious mistake for ἐπὶ Θρασύμῳ. Harpokration gives the following explanation (s.v. ἐπὶ Θρασύλλῳ): Δημοσθένης ἐν τῇ πρὸς Πανταίνετον παραγραφῇ φησὶ "τὸ ἐπὶ Θρασύλλῳ," 'Αττικὸν ἔθος ἀντὶ τοῦ ἐπὶ τῷ Θρασύλλου μνήματι. LaBarbe assumes that even as we change Thrasyllos to Thrasymos in the text of Demosthenes so we must read "the monument of Thrasymos" instead of "the monument of Thrasyllos" in the lexicographer's text. This would indeed be logical if the latter had been trying to explain ἐπὶ Θρασύμῳ. Unfortunately, it is all too clear that the lexicographers were unaware of the mistake in Demosthenes' text and that they offered the only explanation they knew for the phrase ἐπὶ Θρασύλλῳ. "Near (or at) the monument of Thrasyllos" is quite intelligible when one recalls that a certain Thrasyllos built a choregic monument on the south slope of the Acropolis directly above the theatre of Dionysos, a position that ensured notice as long as the monument survived. Under these circumstances it is unjustifiable to conclude that there was a monument of Thrasymos in the mining district to which ἐπὶ Θρασύμῳ refers.

[57]Remains of watchtowers have been noticed in the mining districts. See J. H. Young, "Studies in South Attica," 131–132.

[58]The full extent of the deme of Sounion is a problem owing to our lack of knowledge of the position of the deme of Phrearrhos. In fact, this whole coastal trittys is troublesome because it appears to be divided, one part north, one south, of Thorikos. Phrearrhos is normally placed south of Thorikos and north of Sounion, and thus would contain Laureion within its boundaries. Two considerations militate against this view. First, Phrearrhos is used as the general location of only one mine in the preserved leases (see n. 32 above). The deme therefore seems to have had comparatively few mining interests. This would not be true of a deme that included Laureion. Secondly, if Phrearrhos was between Sounion and Thorikos, then it was a coastal deme in the full physical sense. Yet it is overlooked by Strabo in his list of such demes. He names Sounion, then Thorikos, Potamos, Prasia, etc (9.1.22). Phrearrhos would constitute his one important omission. The evidence against placing Phrearrhos between Sounion and Thorikos is very great and cannot be

these names with ἐπί and the dative. They described the three major districts into which the deme of Sounion was divided for the purposes of mining.

Finally, there are the place names that are preceded by ἐν. Two names, Bambideion Hill and Philomelidon, must refer to definite places, surely of no great extent. Maroneia and Pangaion, names that were clearly given after the finding of silver,[59] need be no more than two small areas containing several mines, the former perhaps a village, the latter a hill. There is no evidence for supposing that Nape and Aulon were large centres; in fact, the former may have been nothing more than a certain glen.[60] Our knowledge is obviously insufficient to come to a firm conclusion about these six place names. There is created, however, a general impression that we are dealing with small places, certainly smaller than "the district around the village of Sounion," etc. In other words, there appears to be an appreciable difference in size between those places with ἐπί and those with ἐν, a distinction easily understandable.

Double Locations

Let us now look at the instances of double locations. The following combinations are well attested: in Crosby 1, ἐν Νάπηι ἐπὶ Σκοπιᾶι,[61]

---

ignored. Phrearrhos should be placed elsewhere. Sounion thus seems to extend northwards as far as Thorikos. The boundary between these two demes is the hilly spur running west–east from the main mountain mass, a spur that reaches the sea just north of Ergastiria. The general position of the north–south boundary is easily determined. The southern half of the Laureotike is divided longitudinally by a valley that runs from just south of Kamareza to the coast at Legrana. In places this valley is quite broad, but at its southern end, where it nears Legrana, it becomes exceedingly narrow and is bordered by precipitous cliffs. The deme of Sounion either controlled the whole of this valley or was limited by the hills to the east of the valley. If the latter was the case, then the valley belonged to another deme, perhaps Besa. In point of fact, I am confident that this valley belonged to Sounion. At its northern end it is cut off from contact with Synterini (and thus Besa) but naturally joins Kamareza, and the latter was surely part of the deme of Sounion. If this analysis is correct, the deme of Sounion certainly included Thrasymos (at Kamareza) and Laureion (near Ergastiria).

[59]Both names were used in the mining areas of Thrace. Is this further evidence for a Peisistratid exploitation of the Attic silver mines?

[60]No roads are recorded going to or from Nape, an indication perhaps that it was not a settlement. On the other hand, Aulon is mentioned in connection with roads and very probably was, therefore, a small community (see Crosby, "Leases," 194 n. 17).

[61]See above, this chapter, for a discussion of this location. In Crosby 1, there is no established spelling for Νάπηι: it also appears as Νάπει.

ἐπὶ Σουνίωι Βήσησι,⁶² ἐπὶ Σουνίωι ἐν Νάπηι (twice), ἐπὶ Σουνίωι ἐπὶ Θρασύμωι; in Crosby 16, Θορικοῖ ἐμ Φιλομηλιδῶν; in Crosby 18, Βήσησι ἐμ Παγγαί(ωι);⁶³ in Crosby 20, Θορικοῖ [ἐν. . . . .]μηι.⁶⁴

It is generally assumed that in these combinations the second element is situated within the first element, with the exception of ἐπὶ Σουνίωι Βήσησι. This exception had to be admitted because on no interpretation of the place names could Besa be considered part of Sounion.⁶⁵ On the other hand, if my interpretation of place names with ἐπί is correct, then ἐπὶ Σουνίωι ἐπὶ Θρασύμωι should also be excepted, since Sounion and Thrasymos were two separate districts. In addition, it has already been argued that ἐν Νάπηι ἐπὶ Σκοπιᾶι may not represent two place names but only one, that is, Nape.

One other fact should be noted before any explanation of these double locations is attempted. In Crosby 1, we find mines located at Nape and at Sounion, as well as the two mines ἐπὶ Σουνίωι ἐν Νάπηι. Sounion, Thrasymos, and Maroneia are also given as single locations on other leases. The same may be true of Besa and Pangaion.⁶⁶ As for Thorikos and Philomelidon, both names appear together once, Thorikos

---

⁶²The two elements of this location are separated by five words: ἐπὶ Σουνίωι τῶν ἐκ τῆς στήλης Λευκίππειον Βήσησι.

⁶³Miss Crosby's restoration of Βήσησι appears sound. Certainly I can think of nothing as suitable to fit the traces of letters, and Vanderpool tells me (by letter) that he can see what Miss Crosby saw, although he admits that the remains are "all a bit hazy."

⁶⁴The position of the word ending -μηι makes it clear that it qualifies either the location of the mine or the description of the mine. The datival ending is applicable only to the former. Miss Crosby's suggestion that the lacuna be filled with a place name is therefore unavoidable.

To this group we should perhaps add a workshop described by Demosthenes as situated both ἐν Μαρωνείᾳ (37.4) and ἐπὶ Θρασύλλῳ, usually emended to read Θρασύμῳ (37.25). This may constitute a double location. On the other hand, the first reference occurs in Nikoboulos' general introduction to his plea, the second in the official ἔγκλημα. If the latter is authentic (see Hopper, "Silver Mines," 217 n. 124 and LaBarbe, La Loi navale 35–36 n. 2), then the location ἐπὶ Θρασύμῳ is probably accurate and to be trusted, and the first reference may have been used more in the interests of effect than of strict truth. Maroneia, even in the fourth century B.C., may still have been more famous than other mining centres, and a reference to it might have elicited from the jurors a more immediate response than a reference to Thrasymos.

⁶⁵There is one interpretation of the term Sounion which would include Besa, that used by Herodotos (4.99). But this usage is impossibly general for the leases.

⁶⁶Besa appears often singly. Pangaion, on the other hand, is found unrestored only twice, in Crosby 18.6–7. In the first instance it is the second half of a general location of a mine, Βήσησι ἐμ Παγγαί(ωι). In the second the phrase ἐμ Παγγαίωι describes another mine. Unfortunately there are no letters preserved to the left of ἐμ and so

alone frequently, but we lack other information about Philomelidon.[67]

Let us consider ἐπὶ Σουνίωι Βήσησι. It has already been pointed out that the two terms appear to be mutually exclusive. I know of three explanations that have been suggested. The first is that the stonecutter made a mistake and copied ἐπὶ Σουνίωι from the preceding lease, and

we do not have overwhelming evidence that the phrase was used by itself. However, there is very strong circumstantial evidence that this was indeed the case.

This lease is the last of four abbreviated leases that head Crosby 18. Miss Crosby published lines 6–7 as follows: [........................Βήσ]ησι ἐμ Παγγαί: ὠνή: Γλαυκ|[.....................μέταλλον] ἐμ Παγγαίωι ὃ ἠργαζ:|. The beginning of line 7 must contain the end of the purchaser's name, his patronymic, his demotic—this last abbreviated—and the price. It is hard to imagine all these (and interpuncts) taking fewer than fifteen letters. This leaves a maximum of fifteen letters for whatever is ἐμ Παγγαίωι and was worked by someone whose name is lost at the beginning of line 8. Miss Crosby supplies μέταλλον: there are many examples of μέταλλον as the antecedent of a relative clause that contains some form of the verb ἐργάζομαι. But in every case, as far as I know, the μέταλλον is not the mine being leased but a mine named as one of the boundaries; and in no case is there any indication of the general location of the mine so named. In line 7 there is clearly no room for naming the boundaries of the leased mine. Instead, the phrase ὃ ἠργαζ: presumably introduces the name of the previous lessee (the registrant). The mine being leased is probably therefore of the category anasaximon (Hopper, "Silver Mines," 234 says the same thing but adds a question mark in 234 n. 263) or palaion anasaximon. Because of the brevity of the lease and the lack of available space I doubt whether the classification was mentioned. On the other hand, the name of the mine should have been included: a name is preserved in the second of the four leases. The shortest name recorded has six letters, but the majority have closer to ten. Since I am not persuaded that μέταλλον is a necessary supplement, especially since its inclusion virtually excludes the name of the mine, I believe that of the thirty spaces before ἐμ Παγγαίωι the first twenty approximately completed the previous lease, and the last ten contained the name of the mine being leased in lines 7–8. Under these circumstances, I should argue that we have here almost unimpeachable evidence for the use of ἐμ Παγγαίωι by itself. (Miss Crosby has restored the same phrase in Crosby 2.17–18 where there is no indication of what preceded.)

[67]In Crosby 20.40 and 44, ἐμ Φιλομηλιδῶν has been restored by Miss Crosby. In the second instance the whole name is preserved, but we do not know what came before and so we cannot assume evidence for the use of this phrase by itself. In fact, lines 43–44 can be easily restored as follows: [.........]ι: μέταλλον ἀπεγρ[άψατο παλαιὸν ἀνασάξιμον Θ]|[ορικοῖ ἐμ] Φιλομηλιδῶν στήλη[ν ἔχον ὧι γεί: βορρᾶ: ......]. This supplement makes it clear that a double location must be considered a strong possibility.

In line 40, only –ιδων is preserved. Miss Crosby's restoration is tempting but I am not convinced that it is correct. The name of the mine is preserved to the left of the centre of line 39. Between the end of Ἑρμαικόν and the beginning of the standard phrase στήλην ἔχον there are forty-one letter spaces. Much of this space must have been used by noting that the mine was "in the property of so-and-so." If this mention were then followed by ἐμ Φιλομηλιδῶν, such a postponement of the general location,

that therefore the phrase has no place in the lease under discussion.[68] The second is that Sounion in this instance represents a place of registration.[69] I can see no virtue in this. Why should one particular mine have to be registered at Sounion? Another mine at Besa appears on the same stele but did not demand this special treatment. This explanation asks more questions that it solves, and, in addition, fails to provide an answer that one would apply willingly to other cases of double locations. The third suggestion is LaBarbe's—that the mine so located straddled the boundary between Sounion and Besa and was therefore correctly described as being in both districts (or demes).[70] I think it extremely unlikely that LaBarbe's explanation is correct. In order for it to be so, the deme of Besa and the district of Sounion (unless we assume that ἐπὶ Σουνίωι has a wider meaning in this lease than in others) must have shared a border, if only for a short distance. There is no evidence to support such contiguity, while there are several observations that warn against it.[71]

What then of the double location ἐπὶ Σουνίωι Βήσησι? I see no other

which in leases of this kind is usually near the beginning or no later than immediately after the name of the mine, would be, I think, unique. Under these circumstances I suggest the following restoration exempli gratia: [. . . . .]Ἑρμα⟨α⟩ι[κ]ὸ[ν Θορικοῖ ἐν τοῖς ἐδάφεσιν τοῖς]|[. . . . . πα]ίδων στήλ[η]ν [ἔχον etc.

[68]Crosby, "Greek Inscriptions," 25 and "Leases," 194 n. 16, where the explanation is given little prominence. Of the three proposed solutions, it will be seen later that I think this one the most likely to be correct.

[69]J. H. Young, "Greek Inscriptions," 29.

[70]La Loi navale 29 n. 3.

[71]A common border, however small, between the deme of Besa and the "district around Sounion" could have come about only if the deme of Besa included within its limits the valley near the base of which is Megala Peuka. If, on the other hand, the deme of Besa or the "district of Besa" as understood in the leases (see n. 50 above) did not continue south much beyond Synterini, then I think it impossible for Besa and Sounion—the former with a centre at Synterini, the latter with its centre at Agrileza—to have shared a boundary. That the second possibility is the more likely is indicated by two geographic considerations: the valley with Megala Peuka is naturally part of the deme of Sounion (see n. 58 above); the deme of Besa is naturally limited by a range of hills south of Synterini (see below, chap. x, p. 124). Thus the "district around Sounion" and the deme of Besa seem quite divorced from each other. LaBarbe (ibid. 29 n 3) nevertheless writes: "Car rien ne s'oppose à ce que Sounion et Bésa, dèmes et districts, aient eu une frontière commune—peut-être Thrasymos." But LaBarbe believes that Thrasymos was part of Sounion (ibid. 35 n. 1), whereas I believe that Thrasymos and Sounion were distinct areas with a common border. LaBarbe also believes, as do I, that Besa and Thrasymos may have shared a border. But as long as Thrasymos and Sounion are considered separate areas, then Besa and Sounion cannot be credited with a common border on the basis of this second belief alone.

course than to accept the first explanation and suppose the entry in Crosby 1 to be in error. LaBarbe has emphasized that the two elements of this location are separated by several words, while other examples show both elements together. Perhaps this peculiarity is better explained by considering that the stonecutter mistakenly copied ἐπὶ Σουνίωι from the preceding two leases rather than that the exception once again proves the rule. It is, I think, easier to believe that this mine was located in Besa alone, and that the phrase ἐπὶ Σουνίωι should be bracketed, than to assume either a common boundary between "the deme of Besa" and "the district of Sounion" or some condition involving Sounion that was peculiar to this one mine in Besa.

LaBarbe applies his theory of mines straddling boundaries to one other case. He considers the mine situated Θαλινοῖ . . . ἐν Νάπηι (Crosby 20.6–8) to be in two localities. But I have argued above that Θαλινοῖ is an improbable restoration and that the mine was in Nape alone. This second example, like the first, does nothing to prove LaBarbe's thesis.

Nevertheless, the theory is attractive, particularly as it involves a phenomenon that seems so natural. There must have been some (though not necessarily many) mines so situated that they fell between two localities. Such mines might have had their position described by a double location. This would explain why on a single stele mines are described as "at Nape," "at Sounion at Nape," and "at Sounion." Mines in the first and third category were within their respective districts; mines in the second were between two districts, straddling a border that was either clearly defined or vaguely plotted.

Let us take the remaining cases of double locations in Crosby 1 and see whether LaBarbe's thesis can be applied to them. I have already indicated my feelings about ἐν Νάπηι ἐπὶ Σκοπιᾶι and nothing can be proved from this entry until the full meaning of σκοπιά has been ascertained. The two mines ἐπὶ Σουνίωι ἐν Νάπηι are more interesting. The first (Crosby 1.62–65) was bounded on the east by the property of Nikias of Kydantidai, and leased by Kallias of Sphettos; Nikias, son of Nikeratos and grandson of Nikias the General, is known to have owned property of perhaps large extent in Nape,[72] and Kallias held the

---

[72]Crosby 1.41–42 and 58. Nikias' son, Nikeratos, perhaps also owned property in Nape: see Crosby, "Leases," 244. Hopper ("Silver Mines," 243) says that Nikeratos owned land "at Anaphlystos (?)." This statement is supposedly based on Crosby 15.46, but Hopper ignores the commentary, where it is noted that either Thorikos or Nape can be restored as the location of the mine. Miss Crosby allows only seven spaces for the name.

lease of another mine as well as property in Nape.[73] The second mine (Crosby 1.79–81) was in the property of the sons of Charmylos and was bounded on the south by the property of Leukios of Sounion and on the north by the property of Pyrrhakos of Aigilia. The same stele (Crosby 1.44–47) bears the lease of another mine in the property of the sons of Charmylos bounded on the south by the property of Leukios of Sounion but on the north by the property of Kleokritos of Aigilia; and, like the second mine ἐπὶ Σουνίωι ἐν Νάπηι, it was leased by Pheidippos of Pithos. Clearly the two mines leased by Pheidippos were not in the same holding but in holdings that were adjacent.[74] Yet one was located ἐπὶ Σουνίωι ἐν Νάπηι, the other ἐπὶ Σουνίωι. Finally we should note that the widow of Charmylos held property in Sounion.[75]

If we assume for the moment that ἐπὶ Σουνίωι ἐν Νάπηι indicates a location in Nape, and that Nape itself lay within Sounion, then the boundary (or whatever it was that distinguished Sounion from Nape) came between the two adjacent fields owned by the sons of Charmylos. One field would have been in Sounion (ἐπὶ Σουνίωι), the other in Nape (ἐπὶ Σουνίωι ἐν Νάπηι). And there would be one further corollary: the designation ἐν Νάπηι would be equivalent to ἐπὶ Σουνίωι ἐν Νάπηι. This last I cannot accept, if we are to believe that there was some logic behind these varied locations. The basic assumption is therefore best rejected.

Since the boundary between Sounion and Nape did not pass between the two adjacent fields (otherwise one field would have been ἐπὶ Σουνίωι, the other ἐν Νάπηι), it must have passed through the field labelled ἐπὶ Σουνίωι ἐν Νάπηι, because, if not, both fields would have been ἐπὶ Σουνίωι or ἐν Νάπηι. The phrase ἐπὶ Σουνίωι ἐν Νάπηι is obviously used, therefore, to indicate a position neither wholly in Sounion nor wholly in Nape but one straddling both. We can perhaps go further and say this of Kallias of Sphettos, Nikias, the family of Charmylos, and Pheidippos: that the first two had their major interests centred in Nape, but had acquired holdings where Nape met Sounion; and that the rest were primarily interested in Sounion but held properties or leases on the fringe of Sounion next to Nape.

We have shown that the expression ἐπὶ Σουνίωι ἐν Νάπηι is not used

---

[73]Crosby 1.42 and 48.

[74]In theory, of course, one must admit that the coincidence of two quite separate properties having the same owner, lessee, and property owner to the south is possible, but I think it fair to assume it a remote possibility. Miss Crosby shares my feelings: she too calls them adjacent ("Greek Inscriptions," 26).

[75]Crosby 1.68.

to indicate a mine situated within a locality which in turn was situated within another locality, but in fact describes a mine situated *between* two localities. However, this demonstration is not formal proof that Nape lay outside Sounion: logically, a mine could be located between Sounion and Nape whether Nape was within or adjacent to Sounion. Yet if we were right in believing that Sounion, Laureion, and Thrasymos were the major mining districts of the deme Sounion, and that each of the three got its name from the community on which it was centred, it is surely most unlikely that these districts had within them other localities of such independence that we can postulate boundaries between these other localities and the three major districts. Rather, it appears that the deme Sounion may have contained a number of minor units as well as the three major districts.

Nothing can be gained from the remaining example of a double location in Crosby 1. However, if we may press the argument from ἐπὶ Σουνίωι ἐν Νάπηι, this mine should be placed between the districts of Thrasymos and Sounion with a part in each.[76]

The remaining examples of double locations are rather different in character. The first member of the group is a deme; the second is not usually found except in the context of a double location. The example of ἐμ Παγγαίωι in Crosby 18.7 does not constitute a true exception[77] because the lease is very abbreviated and we should perhaps understand Βήσησι from the preceding lease. Moreover, these double locations with a deme are similar to the references in *IG* II² 1594 to certain properties located Ἀφίδνησι ἐν Πεταλιδῶν and Ἀφίδνησι ἐν Ὑπωρείαι, where there is no doubt that the second member in both locations is a district or community within the deme of Aphidna.[78] The same relation must be assumed, I think, for the localities in the mining leases that are named along with a deme in a double location. These localities are within their respective demes. The evidence available does not permit us either to ignore the exact parallel of the references in *IG* II² 1594 or to grant to these localities the measure of independence needed for them to exist apart from, even outside of, the demes, just as Nape is apart from, and probably outside of, the mining district of Sounion.

We must therefore recognize two different types of double locations,

---

[76]The workshop of Demosthenes 37.4 and 25 might be similarly explained as being in either Maroneia, or Thrasymos, or both (see n. 64 above), but I somehow doubt the need.

[77]See p. 93 and nn. 66 and 67 above.

[78]See below, Appendix to chap. xii, pp. 152–153, for a discussion of these double locations connected with Aphidna.

those that occur in Crosby 1 and are concerned only with the various districts and localities within the deme of Sounion, and those that occur elsewhere than in Crosby 1, in which the first element of the double location is a deme other than Sounion. In the first group the double location indicates a mine straddling a boundary between two distinct localities, in the second a mine located in a specific locality within a certain deme.[79]

We must now summarize the results of this long digression. In the leases the position of a mine is given in two ways, first by a general location, secondly by a specific location. The place names used in the general location are names of districts, those in the locative being demes, those preceded by ἐπί being (large) areas surrounding the most important towns in the deme of Sounion, and those preceded by ἐν being (small) areas surrounding villages or notable geographical features. In every case, however, the references are to districts, large or small, and not to towns or villages alone. But place names used in the specific locations refer for the most part to the actual towns and villages and not to the areas. This multiple use of the same place name may seem confusing to us, but the practice exists today and the context usually makes clear in what sense the name is being used. The name London can be cited as an example: it may mean the square mile of the City, the larger area of the Administrative County of London, or even the area known as Greater London,[80] depending on the context. And so in the mining leases: what was probably immediately apparent to the Athenians of the fourth century B.C. can frequently become equally clear to us by a close study of the context.

Anaphlystos

Let us now turn to the problem of Anaphlystos. In the preserved leases six mines are recorded with a general location 'Αναφλυστοῖ, "in the deme of Anaphlystos." Five of these are in Crosby 16 and of these five, three, perhaps four, appear to be grouped near one another. These mines must have been in the district northeast and east of Ari, for that is where the only mines are that are close to the Bay of

---

[79]Since the first system of double locations is found only in Crosby 1, perhaps it should be thought of as an experimental method of describing locations which was later discarded as unnecessary (or even impractical).

[80]Greater London is the district of the Metropolitan and City Police. "The area within the jurisdiction of the Central Criminal Court, the Metropolitan Water-Area, the Main Drainage Area, and the London postal district form four other 'Londons,' all differing in size and population" (Baedeker, *London and Its Environs* xxx).

Hagios Nikolaos[81] and in an area with an easily discernible relation to the territory immediately north of the bay. Among the boundaries that are featured in these leases the following seem important: the road to Thrasymos, a gully (unqualified), and the ὁδὸς ἀστική. If our suggested location is correct, it should be possible to identify these landmarks.

The road to Thrasymos clearly leads to the centre of the mining district at Kamareza. Immediately north and east of Ari there is a road that climbs up the western slopes of the hills of Laureion and at Barbaliaki joins the road from Plaka to Kamareza. This was one of the major roads in the nineteenth century when the slag heaps were being worked and the only one of importance giving direct access from the plain of Anavyssos to the highlands of Laureion. I suggest that its route and function had been established in the classical period. The unnamed gully is perhaps the branch of the large "revma d'Ari," which flows from the valley north of Ari and which runs close to several mines. The ὁδὸς ἀστική seems at first glance an inadequate notice. The same adjective is found in Crosby 4.24 where a road is described as ἡ ὁδὸς ἡ] ἀστικὴ Βήσαζε [φέρουσα. Most roads are named "from A to B," and so I assume that ἀστική represents the place where these two roads originated. That place can hardly be any other than Athens. In the one instance we have "the road from Athens," in the other "the road from Athens to Besa." Both, I think, were parts of the Athens–Sounion highway,[82] one of the major Attic arteries. The former must have been a road that, at Ari, was instantly recognized as the road from (or to) the city. Such a road must have come through Aigilia, crossed eastwards to the plain near Metropisi, then turned south to pass through Besa. From Aigilia to Metropisi there are two natural ways, one going south, one north, of the ridge blocking the gap between Mount Panion and the hills of Laureion. The southerly route would have crossed the upper end of the Anavyso plain, and passed through the gap east of Lulje Kuki (*Karten* Sheet XVI); thus it would have followed the valley from which flowed the gully we have already mentioned. A road goes by this route today and north of Ari passes

[81]The mines at Ari that are closest to the sea are about six kilometres from the bay. Those at Synterini are about 5.2 kilometres from the sea as the crow flies, but they clearly have no association with Anaphlystos and are in fact within the deme of Besa.

[82]See also J. H. Young, "Greek Roads in South Attica," 97 and fig. 2 on 96. Young and I are not in complete agreement: he says of "the principal ancient road leading from Sunium" that "we should probably identify [it] with the ἀστικὴ ὁδὸς mentioned in the *poletai* lists." He has in mind the reference in *IG* II[2] 1582: he is not certain of the reference in Crosby 4. I feel the reverse to be more likely.

many remains of mining installations, but there is no way of estimating the road's age.

The northerly route keeps to the foot of the southern side of Mount Panion and passes north of the hill called Mokrisa (*Karten* Sheet XVII).[83] This route does not come near the mining operations, no disadvantage today, but in classical times a serious one surely. Given a choice between these two natural routes, the Athenians of the fifth century B.C. or later would have picked the one that went nearest to the mines had they kept in mind considerations of economic importance. Therefore I judge the southern route to be "the city road."

The above discussion is enough to show that the identification of the area near Ari as the mining district within the deme of Anaphlystos is not contradicted by other indications in the leases. In fact, the ease with which we can suggest identifications of important landmarks provides our thesis with some corroboration.

Besides being used as a general location, Anaphlystos is used in a specific location three times, one of which is restored. Crosby 21.14–15 reads, when restored: βορρᾶ: ἡ]|[χαράδ]ρα ἡ εἰς Ἀνά[φ]λυ[στον] φ[ἑρου]σα, and Crosby 7.20 has the following, the supplements being based on Crosby 21: ἡ χ]αράδρα εἰς [Ἀνάφλυστον(?) φέρου:. Despite the latter's uncertainty, the former contains a clear reference to a gully that went to Anaphlystos. I take this to be the deme of Anaphlystos,[84] and the gully to flow into the deme from outside it. Where this mine was located is not preserved. Miss Crosby suggests Anaphlystos, Besa, or Amphitrope on the basis of this reference to a gully.[85] I should exempt Anaphlystos: were the mine in Anaphlystos, the gully would have required some other qualification. I doubt very much whether there was any mine in the deme of Besa that could have been bordered by a gully leading to Anaphlystos;[86] this would have necessitated too westerly a location. Amphitrope is certainly a possibility, and we shall see that this deme lay north of Anaphlystos. The gully near Ari that we have already discussed has its origin just south of Lulje Kuki in territory I judge to be outside the deme of Anaphlystos. There are

[83]Today this route is used by motor traffic and is without any doubt the more important, whereas the other is less formal, yet easily passable in a jeep.

[84]See above, n. 31.

[85]"Leases," 269.

[86]Most of the mines in Besa seem to have been located near the centre of the narrow upland plain between Demoliaki and Synterini. The watershed between the demes of Besa and Anaphlystos ran along the extreme western edge of this plain.

mines near by, and the gully would serve as a distinct boundary. To describe such a gully as leading to Anaphlystos would be apt.[87]

The third mention is in Crosby 8.3–5. The pertinent line in the *Corpus* appears thus: πρὸ[s ἡλίου ἀνιόντος ἡ ὁδὸs ἡ ἀπὸ Θρασύμ]ου εἰς Ἀνάφλ[υστον φέρουσα. This restoration is based on a line of thirty-nine letters. Miss Crosby says of this inscription[88] that "the length of line cannot be established with any certainty, but was probably either of 37 or 39 letters." She offers no new restorations nor does she comment on the readings of the *Corpus*. Yet in her geographical index she includes this restored reference to Thrasymos but with the reading ἀπὸ Θρασύ]μου.[89] Vanderpool and Mitsos have studied this line at my request (November 1958). They report that Miss Crosby was quite right to move the bracket because there is clearly part of an inscribed letter in the space before –ου. The trace is that of "the lower end of a hasta." Vanderpool writes: "It looks to me as if it *could* be from a M, but need not be absolutely. Mitsos says he would never have read it as M. Nor would I, I think, have *read* it so." It appears that whatever letter is read it should be dotted.[90] So we must admit two areas of doubt when considering the number of supplements possible for the phrase ending –ου: the preceding letter is not firmly established, nor the length of line. If the preceding letter is μ, then the place name must be either Thrasymos or (less) possibly Panormos.[91] But if we allow other possibilities for the letter (for example a dotted iota), then the following must be considered candidates: ἀπὸ Λαυρε]ίου, eleven letters, is epigraphically sound; ἀπὸ Σουν]ίου, ten letters, is possible but unlikely.[92]

---

[87]According to Miss Crosby the next lease (Crosby 21.17–23) is of a mine either in Amphitrope or in Besa. Frequently several mines are recorded consecutively from a single area. Could it be shown that this mine was at Amphitrope, the chances that the previous mine was in the same place would be increased. In connection with the lease of the mine called Eudoteion in lines 17–23, Miss Crosby draws attention to *IG* II² 1583.21 in which a mine also called Eudoteion is named as one of the boundaries of another mine. She points out that these mines may be identical. I notice in this latter inscription that in line 24 the next mine is recorded at Amphitrope, which, if nothing else, makes it entirely possible that the previous mine (and therefore the mine Eudoteion) was in the same district. Such arguments, however, can never prove that the mines in Crosby 21 were at Amphitrope.

[88]"Leases," 222.   [89]*Ibid.* 309.

[90]The letter is certainly incomplete and therefore covered by Woodhead's clear dictum: "Any imperfect letter should be distinguished by its dot, even if its identity can be regarded as to all intents and purposes certain" (*Study of Greek Inscriptions* 9).

[91]There is no mention in the leases of a road "from Panormos," only "to Panormos."

[92]So far no road is recorded coming "from Sounion"; there are references to roads

Geographic considerations can be used to limit the number of candidates. I imagine that roads were usually named in the following way when they were used as boundaries for mines. Let us take a road passing through towns A, B, and C. If a mine is located between A and B, so that the road forms one of its boundaries, the road is not named "the road from A to C," but "the road from A to B"; and if the mine is located between B and C, the road is named "the road from B to C." Anaphlystos was in all probability almost ten kilometres from Laureion, Panormos, or Sounion. Roads joining these places with Anaphlystos would certainly have gone through other towns. A road from Anaphlystos to Panormos, for example, would be like "a road from A to C," whereas in the leases we expect to find roads named A to B, or B to C. Thrasymos presents quite a different picture: lying in the centre of the mining area, it was so placed that roads from both east and west converged upon it. A road from Thrasymos to Anaphlystos would seem therefore the most likely; such a supplement is both epigraphically and geographically acceptable. And, in addition, the road, I think, can be identified. Less than a kilometre from the shore of the Bay of Hagios Nikolaos there is a meeting of roads at a church of Hagios Georgios. From there—a location I take to be near the village of Anaphlystos—one road went due east and, passing south of Mesochori, made its way into the Laureion hills, finally arriving at Kamareza (*Karten* sheets XVI and XVII). Between Hagios Georgios and Kamareza this road does not go through any villages. As for mines, just before reaching Kamareza the road passes through an area which is full of shafts. The road could have formed the boundary of a mine with no difficulty.

Such is the evidence for Anaphlystos from the mining leases. We are really no wiser about the location of the village of Anaphlystos, although we can say that a location near the bay would suit Crosby 8.3–5. Of much more importance, we now know that the deme of Anaphlystos included the mining area north of Ari within its limits. This knowledge will help us when we try to set out the boundaries of this deme.

Finally we should note that the deme of Anaphlystos supplied ten bouleutai in the fourth century B.C. (*IG* II² 1750). If the deme had only one centre of habitation, then we ought to find the remains of a

---

going "to Sounion." Two improbable supplements are noted: ἐκ Θορι]κοῦ, nine letters (we could assume a line of thirty-seven letters here), is unlikely because of the kappa; ἀπὸ Μαρωνε]ίου, twelve letters, is a most unusual form but one that has been found (Crosby, "Leases," 239).

large village. But such centralization is unlikely for two reasons: first, the deme was too long (at least six kilometres) to be adequately served by a single centre, which would have been too far from the harbour for effective use of the natural bay, a point which will be discussed below; secondly, the deme had at least two major interests— agriculture and mining—and the needs of the one were not necessarily the same as the needs of the other. We must be prepared therefore to find not one large community but several villages within the borders of this single deme.

REMAINS

There are many remains in the plain of Anavyssos, and they cover a great range of time from the Middle Helladic period to the present day. We were unable to look at all of them and so concentrated our attention on two areas, the one bordering the sea, the other about Ari. We thought that the village of Anaphlystos would be either at the foot of the plain or at the head. The reasoning was simple: literary sources suggested the coast, but the mining leases recorded mines "at Anaphlystos." It was only later that I considered the phrase "at Anaphlystos" to be a reference to the deme.

Remains in five locations proved of special interest: (1) about Hagios Nikolaos on the western side of the bay (A on Figure 7); (2) at the modern harbour village of Nea Phokaia (B on Figure 7); (3) about Hagios Georgios, a little over a kilometre northeast of Nea Phokaia (C on Figure 7); (4) about Hagios Panteleimon, almost two kilometres north of Hagios Georgios (D on Figure 7); (5) about Ari (E on Figure 7).

1. On entering the Bay of Hagios Nikolaos, one sees on the northern side the promontory on which the church of Hagios Nikolaos stands. This rocky point is a peninsula joined to the mainland by a sandy spit, which is itself divided by a salt lake. To the east and west of this low sandy spit are small bays. The larger of the two—to the east—has its limits marked by two hills that seem to guard its entrance. The northern hill has remains which Milchhöfer, not surprisingly, thought might belong to a mediaeval castle. On the southern hill, not far from the church of Hagios Nikolaos, there is a large cistern.[93] The site, despite its obvious attractiveness, does not seem to have been used during the classical period. On the western side of the sandy spit we collected sherds of Middle Helladic times. Near by, at the water's

[93]Milchhöfer, *Erläuternder Text* 3–6.21.

edge, we saw the remains of curved walls belonging to apsidal houses. Except for these scanty fragments the settlement lies under water in the shallows of the western bay, where there seem to be considerable remains of walls.[94] This settlement is the earliest so far reported from the area of Anavyssos.[95]

2. The ancient sources make it clear that the deme of Anaphlystos had a harbour. Despite the size of the Bay of Hagios Nikolaos, only a few places on it are entirely suitable for a harbour and installations owing to the flatness of the land immediately behind the shoreline and the consequent danger of flooding. These inconveniences are appreciably less on the eastern side of the bay where the ground rises rapidly from the shore. It is here that the present harbour village of Nea Phokaia is situated. Today there are no obvious remains from antiquity in the village, but such was not the case when Milchhöfer examined this shore before Nea Phokaia was settled; he noted several moles which he assigned to the classical period.[96] He also mentioned fragments of other walls, one of which he suggested might be an *Ufereinfassung*. Despite the tentative quality of these interpretations, there can be no doubt that in the area now occupied by Nea Phokaia there used to be remains of harbour installations. (Presumably these remains were utilized in the building of the modern village.) Since it is clear that there was a harbour in this bay during classical times, since at the most suitable place there have been found the only classical remains noted in the bay, and since these remains belong to harbour works, the conclusion is almost inescapable that the harbour belonging to the deme of Anaphlystos was situated at the present Nea Phokaia. But it does not necessarily follow that there was an important classical settlement at Nea Phokaia near the harbour. No remains from such a centre have been recorded; yet it is unlikely that the present village

[94]The phenomenon of a prehistoric settlement lying under water is not strange in Attika. The same can be seen at Hagios Kosmas, where part of a Late Helladic settlement is now awash. This sinking of the land (a rising of the sea of such magnitude is most unlikely) must have occurred between Late Helladic and late Geometric times and perhaps the same movement accounted for the inundation at both Hagios Nikolaos and Hagios Kosmas (see Mylonas, *Aghios Kosmas* 7–8).

[95]The sherds we secured are in the collection of the American School of Classical Studies.

[96]At least, this is my interpretation of his description. I assume he thought these moles to be classical, otherwise he would not have suggested that they had perhaps served as a shelter for the state triremes or as shipsheds. An earlier reference to "a port, with the remains of some antiquities" can be found in Stuart and Revett, *Antiquities* 3.vii.

would have concealed all traces of an earlier settlement had there been one.[97]

3. The area about Hagios Georgios is worthy of attention. The earliest remains found there are a number of tombs excavated in 1911.[98] The Geometric pottery from one tumulus has been dated within the limits 725–675 B.C.[99] Milchhöfer reported finding parts of a votive relief and of a dedication to Hermes. The latter he said was perhaps from the fifth century B.C., but it is now assigned to the beginning of the fourth century B.C.[100] He also noted remains of walls and suggested that the later village of Anavyso had largely obliterated earlier remains. Some of these earlier ruins can be seen in the gardens and fields adjoining the houses at Hagios Georgios, and they are together with pottery of Hellenistic and Roman times. Hagios Georgios clearly marks the site of a settlement that has been inhabited, perhaps continuously, from at least the eighth century B.C.

4. Just south of the church of Hagios Panteleimon, along both sides of the cart track leading across the plain from the fork in the motor road, remains of an ancient settlement were found by E. Vanderpool and M. Lang in August 1958. They reported that the near-by fields abounded in fragments from pots and tiles and that there was a great

[97]The village of Nea Phokaia is not large and one would expect ceramic remains, if any, to stay visible, especially on the slopes of the hill surmounted by the church, an obvious focal point for an inhabited centre. Vanderpool ("News Letter from Greece" [1961] 300) has recently reported the finding of two graves of the fifth century B.C. near the shore at Phokaia.

[98]Kastriotes and Philadelpheus, "'Ανασκαφαὶ 'Αναβύσου," 110–131. The authors do not record exactly where they excavated, but on 112 they note that the tombs were "ten minutes from the shore" and that "near these tombs was the road, or rather path, that led to Keratea two and a half hours' distance away, and the road to Kamareza." These two roads cross at Hagios Georgios, which is indeed about ten minutes from the sea.

[99]R. S. Young, *Late Geometric Graves* 32 (under item VII.2). Kastriotes and Philadelpheus ("'Ανασκαφαὶ 'Αναβύσου," 124–125) published from the same tomb some handmade pots, which they thought to be Early Helladic. They recognized the strangeness of this combination, even admitted that the pottery from both periods was found together, but still did not think their chronological conclusions impossible. We are better informed and know this handmade ware with incised decoration to be Geometric and so contemporaneous with the other finds (R. S. Young, *Late Geometric Graves* 199 n. 1).

[100]Milchhöfer, "Antikenbericht" (1887) 303–304 and *Erläuternder Text* 3–6.21. U. Köhler (see *IG* II 5.1512c) was not convinced that the inscription was from a dedication and suggested as an alternative that "titulum esse sepulcralem hominis peregrini." Nevertheless, like Kirchner (see *IG* II² 4550), he classified this inscription under "Donaria Reliquorum Deorum et Heroum." Kirchner is the authority for the date in the fourth century B.C.

deal of stone, usually a sign that ancient walls had been reduced to
rubble. One piece of pottery from the late fifth century B.C. was picked
up. In the *Karten* (Sheet XVII) *Grundmauerspuren* is written over
approximately the same area as that referred to above. In 1960 I
visited this site with Vanderpool and we noted a large fragment from
a late Geometric pot.

These remains are of interest for the following reasons. First, a
settlement so placed commanded the main lines of communication
both from and within the plain, and therefore was suited to administer
the area of the plain. Secondly, such a settlement was sufficiently
removed from the sea to be out of reach of pirates, and had hills not
far behind it, a situation reminiscent of Anagyrous. Thirdly, the
farmstead associated with Hagios Panteleimon has been known for
the past several centuries at least as the metochi of Anavyso.

5. North of Ari where the cart road divides, there are extensive
remains from a mining settlement in which the outlines of several
buildings can easily be made out. The most impressive of the remains
lie a few metres to the west of the road, and consist of the well-
preserved walls of at least two houses. In places the walls still stand
to a height exceeding five feet. The masonry is heavy and rectangular
and the coursing tends to be regular. The style is similar to that of
the grave plots of the fourth century B.C. Pottery of the same date
and earlier was picked up, thus confirming habitation of the site
during the classical period. In addition to these houses there are
remains of washing establishments.[101]

In the hills around this northern end of the plain there were several
mines in antiquity. The settlement north of Ari, placed astride a
stream and thus possessing a source of water, was clearly one of the
main centres for the processing of the silver-bearing ore. It would
probably be a mistake to recognize the remains as largely those of
private houses. Rather, the heavy stone walls mentioned above may
have been built in this manner in order to provide strong rooms for
the silver once it had been purified but before it could be taken to
Athens. Other suggestions can justifiably be made: a centre for the
production of silver must have necessitated various large buildings.
Since a settlement like this would have been populated largely by
slaves, the number of private houses would probably have been few,
and the number with substantial foundations even fewer.

[101]Milchhöfer (*Erläuternder Text* 3–6.25) noted a well-preserved washing establishment that had been excavated: it lay northeast of the estate at Ari. This is, however,
too vague a description to admit any precise identification with ruins now existing.

IDENTIFICATION

By the end of the eighteenth century it was recognized that the deme of Anaphlystos must have been located in the region of the Bay of Hagios Nikolaos. Not only had the name survived, but the general area thus indicated confirmed the testimony of Strabo.

However, there is no unanimity of opinion on the location of the village of Anaphlystos within the area. Milchhöfer favoured a position near Hagios Georgios,[102] Löper a site at Velatouri.[103] Concerning the latter, Wrede noted a prehistoric site there,[104] and Milchhöfer's description leaves no doubt that the most prominent ruins on this hill are mediaeval, as can be seen today.[105] Other scholars have been content to mention that Anaphlystos was near Anavyssos.

The ancient sources are quite insistent that Anaphlystos was near the sea. We have seen that one entry in the mining leases suggests that a road joined Anaphlystos and Thrasymos. Both *desiderata* are met in one place if, with Milchhöfer, we locate Anaphlystos at Hagios Georgios. The Geometric graves are evidence for the existence of a village at that period in the neighbourhood: material from the classical and later periods testifies to the continued use of the area as the site for a settlement. Finally, it is worth recalling that this is one of the places that at some time was called Anavyso.

The evidence certainly favours this identification of Hagios Georgios as Anaphlystos. Other possible sites seem too removed from the sea and too lacking in ancient remains of a suitable character. The case for Hagios Georgios is consistently good, even if not overwhelming. It would take the finding of a great deal of new evidence to build up another candidate with equal claims, particularly so when it is obvious that such a large plain must have had several classical settlements.

---

[102]*Die Demenordnung* map facing 48; and *RE* 1 (1894) 2061, s.v. Anaphlystos.

[103]"Die Trittyen," 421.

[104]*Attika* frontispiece.

[105]*Erläuternder Text* 3-6.20. In *RE* 1 (1894) 2061, s.v. Anaphlystos, Milchhöfer refers to sculpture and inscriptions as if they came from Viglaturi (his spelling). The reader is directed to *AM* 12 (1887) 303 ff. On these pages there are items numbered 303-308. They are listed under the general heading "Das Gebiet von Anávyso und Olympos." In each case some indication of the finding place is given and in no case is Velatouri mentioned. In this instance Milchhöfer seems too eager to carry his point. Under this same general heading we can now add the fragment of an archaic stele "found at Anavysos by Mr. Papadimitriou in 1958" (Richter, *Archaic Gravestones* 42-43).

The boundaries of the deme are easy to sketch. The Laureion hills formed the eastern boundary. North of Ari, the edge of the plain was marked by a curving barrier of hills that joined Panion to the Laureion range. These low hills divided the demes of Anaphlystos and Amphi-trope. Another series of low hills joined Panion to Olympos, thus dividing Anaphlystos from Aigilia. Olympos stood as a formidable barrier to the west and south of it there was the sea.

This large plain is almost six kilometres long, too long for a single centre near the sea to provide the only settlement. I imagine that in classical times there were three major centres, one at Hagios Georgios, one near Hagios Panteleimon (the metochi of Anavyso), and the third near Ari. The village at Hagios Georgios was called Anaphlystos, from which the deme took its name: inhabitants of this village would have farmed the southern end of the plain, and looked after the harbour. The inhabitants of the settlement near Hagios Panteleimon would have been interested solely in farming the central and northern parts of the plain, while those at Ari would have been concerned with the mining and production of silver.

IX

AMPHITROPE

ANCIENT REFERENCES

ALTHOUGH there are references to the deme of Amphitrope in several lexica and elsewhere, they do not help us to locate it. One of these references is in Aischines 1.101. The defendant Timarchos is confronted with a list of properties that he has sold in order to avoid liturgies. Those enumerated include an estate in Kephisia, an estate in Amphitrope, and two workshops in the mining area, one in Aulon, the other in Thrasymos.[1] Were it not for the property in Kephisia, one might be tempted to assume that all these holdings were near one another in the mining district. The assumption, however, is obviously unwarranted and this passage really supplies no evidence for the location of Amphitrope.

NAME

The name Amphitrope has survived in the place name Metropisi.[2] This was a village on the south slope of Mount Panion at its eastern end, a village which, to judge from the pottery, flourished in Byzantine and Turkish times. It was seen by Sir George Wheler but he did not associate the name with Amphitrope. Rather, he identified Metropisi as Azenia.[3] Stuart and Revett, however, saw the similarity in names and identified Metropisi as Amphitrope. They wrote: "It stands at the division of the great road going to Sunium from Athens. The left hand leads by Thorikos, and the right by Anaplystus."[4]

[1] The text has ἐπὶ Θρασύλλῳ, which has been emended to ἐπὶ Θρασύμῳ. The corruption of mu to double lambda is very easy.

[2] Although the two words appear at first unlike each other, they share a form of the noun τροπή and in both names the accent falls on the last syllable of τροπή. I can find no explanation of Metropisi other than that it comes from Amphitrope. The ending is that of a normal diminutive, and if we assume that the initial vowel was at some time omitted—a recognized tendency in modern Greek—the remaining consonants would then have had to change, and the simplest change would have been to drop either μ or φ.

[3] *Journey* 449: "*Metropis*: which were probably the *Azenenses*."

[4] *Antiquities* 3.xiv.

This observation of Stuart and Revett raises an obvious question concerning the name Amphitrope: what does it mean? The word is not listed in LSJ[9] but it is clearly a combination of ἀμφί and τροπή, the latter allied to the verb τρέπω. Thus it cannot differ much in sense from the known word περιτροπή, "turning round," "revolution," "diversion." Perhaps the name Amphitrope should be interpreted in this manner: a branching or turning of the main highway. Stuart and Revett, as already quoted, noticed that Metropisi was placed "at the division of the great road going to Sunium from Athens," and that one fork led to Thorikos and the other to Anaphlystos, but they may have overlooked a third road that skirts the foot of Mount Panion and leads to Aigilia.[5] Ardaillon wrote simply: "Le mot Amphitrope vient sans doute de ce que le dème était situé à un carrefour de routes."[6] But Ardaillon was not the first Frenchman to survey Laureion, and on the meaning of Amphitrope he was anticipated by M. Terrier, who wrote:

> L'ancien dème d'Amphitrope, qui était sur l'emplacement du village de Métropisti, était situé à l'extrémité septentrionale de ce district, presque à égale distance entre les deux côtes; il commandait à la fois la route d'Anaphlyste et celle de Thoricos, qui se bifurquaient un peu plus haut. Il suffit de jeter un coup d'œil sur la carte pour s'en assurer. C'est pourquoi je crois que le dème n'a pas dû son nom au circuit qu'on faisait autour de la montagne pour y arriver, mais à cette circonstance que de là on pouvait également se tourner des deux côtés et se diriger sur l'une ou l'autre ville.[7]

The survival of the name, the apparent meaning of the name, and its satisfactory application to the junction of roads near Metropisi all point to the area in which the village of Amphitrope should be sought. As we said of Anavyssos, however, we must not assume that the survival of the ancient place name in an existing place name indicates the precise location of the ancient village.

INSCRIPTIONS

The name Amphitrope appears in the mining leases, though not as frequently as certain other place names. It is preserved as the general location of eight or nine mines, thus indicating that the deme of Amphitrope had mines within its borders.

[5]It is true that the highway branches into two roads, but one of these roads, the one to Anaphlystos, itself branches into two (perhaps three) routes within a kilometre of the main junction, and one of these routes goes to Aigilia.
[6]*Les Mines* 213.
[7]"Mémoire," 100.

There is no unrestored or certain appearance of Amphitrope in the specific locations of mines. Crosby 16a.90–91 is restored] πρὸs ἡλίου [δυομέ: ἡ ὁδὸs ἡ ᾿Αμφιτρο]|[πῆ]θεν Βῆσαζε φέρουσα. This restoration is offered by Miss Crosby with the qualification "perhaps," but I think we can recognize that the supplement is very likely, since there is no other known place name of sufficient length that takes adverbial suffixes. In Crosby 18.45–53, the name Amphitrope can be restored with confidence four times, three of them within five lines. However, in two cases, lines 45 and 49, the name Amphitrope probably describes a general location;[8] in a third case, line 53, the name occurs at the end of a specific location in a position where one often finds a demotic (in this lease abbreviated); and finally in the fourth case, line 46, the name appears in such a mutilated context that no assumptions about its use can be made.

Clearly, the evidence for the position of Amphitrope is not greatly increased by the mining leases. Nevertheless, they indicate that the deme of Amphitrope contained mines and was therefore part of the mining district, and probably that the village of Amphitrope was connected with Besa by a road. We can also add the presumption that the demes of Amphitrope and Besa were contiguous.[9]

According to *IG* II² 1750 Amphitrope supplied two councillors in 334/3 B.C., so we may assume that it was not a large deme.

REMAINS

The name Metropisi is, as we have said, associated with a ruined settlement lying at the foot of the south side of Mount Panion at its eastern end. The ruins lie both north and south of the road that skirts the foot of the mountain, and they include the remains of a church. The settlement is apparently no earlier than Byzantine; yet Milchhöfer noted "antike Bausteine freilich" built into the crumbling walls.[10]

---

[8]Miss Crosby ("Leases," 257) thinks it likely that of the seven leases in lines 40–76 of No. 18 all but the first and last were located at Amphitrope.

[9]The approximate locations of these two demes can be established without difficulty. Amphitrope was near Metropisi, Besa near (but west of) Kamareza. Both were in the mining district; both were in the same trittys. The villages of Amphitrope and Besa were joined by a road, and on three occasions "the road to Besa" is used in the leases to describe a boundary for a mine in the deme of Anaphlystos. Two villages widely separated and themselves far distant from the mine whose location was being described would not have been used as the terminal points of a road that was named as a boundary. The conclusion is demanded by the evidence.

[10]*Erläuternder Text* 3–6.24. In *RE* 1 (1894) 1967, s.v. Amphitrope, Milchhöfer recorded that "the ancient remains are now unimportant."

We did not find these signs of a more ancient village, but the stones may have been carried off to serve more modern buildings elsewhere; nor did we find in the area covered by the destroyed houses any fragments of pottery from the Greek or Roman periods.

To the west of these ruins and a few paces north of the same road we found traces of several graves of the classical period. Graves normally line the roads leading to and from settlements of this period, and, unless we were to assume these graves to belong to some isolated plot, we should infer the presence near by of an ancient road and an ancient settlement. As for the road we have described, it serves today a purpose that must have existed in the past—the linking of the communities at (and near) Metropisi with Olympos (ancient Aigilia).

Metropisi is well situated. It overlooks a small plain which is bounded on the north by Panion, on the west and south by low hills which divide it from the coastal plain of Anavyssos, and on the east by the main Laureion range. Of the hills that form the southern boundary of this small plain, the most prominent is Lulje Kuki, which stands to the east of a gap through which passes a road to Ari and thus to Anavyssos. On the southern slopes of Lulje Kuki, and on both sides of the road, there are impressive remains of large buildings belonging to the fifth and fourth centuries B.C. (F on Figure 7). Several of these buildings have been partially cleared and we may suspect that the work was done in the nineteenth century by those engaged in operating the modern mining company. The position of the settlement,[11] the size and character of the buildings, and the presence of ancient mines in the hills around, all these factors make it obvious that this was no agricultural hamlet but a mining community, to which perhaps the ore was brought to receive its final processing and storing, and from which the neighbouring mines were administered.

Ardaillon gave an account of a third settlement in the area of Metropisi. It lay on the eastern edge of the plain, on the lower slopes of the Laureion range. He described the remains as "nombreuses; les fragments de marbre abondent, et je sais qu'on y a trouvé beaucoup d'antiquités, et même une statue."[12] Despite this full account, we found no traces of antiquities on the slope indicated by Ardaillon on his map;[13] nor, apparently, did Kaupert or Milchhöfer.[14] There are,

[11]Although so close to the plain to the north, this village was entirely divorced from it. Those who determined its position seemingly had no thought for the farming of the plain.   [12]*Les Mines* 213.   [13]*Ibid.* endpiece.

[14]There are no indications of remains on the *Karten* (Sheet XVI) nor are there comments in *Erläuternder Text*.

however, some remains on the low hill to the east of the bridge near
the fork in the road opposite the end of Panion[15] (G on Figure 7).
The modern fences contain worked stones, and there are many broken
roof tiles and fragments of pottery. The settlement dates from the
late Roman period. Whether these are the ruins that Ardaillon described I do not know, but it would be economical to think so. Otherwise,
we must assume the disappearance of the remains of a settlement
which was a few hundred metres away from a settlement whose
remains still exist.

IDENTIFICATION

For two centuries Metropisi has been identified as Amphitrope[16] and
there can be no doubt that the similarity in names favours this identification. Ardaillon, as we have seen, while agreeing that Amphitrope
must be located near Metropisi, associated this ancient deme not with
the ruins at Metropisi but with some remains a little to the east.

The similarity in names, however, cannot by itself be admitted as
conclusive proof that the position of Metropisi represents the position
of Amphitrope. Settlements and their names can both move around.
The name Amphitrope was applied in antiquity to both an area and a
village: Metropisi may have inherited its name from the former. The
most we should assume from the survival of the name alone is that
Metropisi is within the area once called Amphitrope.

The conclusion that the deme of Amphitrope contained within its
borders the area later occupied by the village of Metropisi is suggested
not only by the similarity in names. Other considerations make this
assumption practically mandatory. We have already noted that the
deme of Amphitrope and the deme of Besa were both in the mining
area and were probably adjacent. We know that Amphitrope was in
the same trittys as Aigilia, Anaphlystos, Besa, and Atene. We can be
certain that it was not along the coast. We have already established
the limits of Aigilia and Anaphlystos; we know that Besa was near
(but west of) Kamareza. Since Panion clearly marks the northern
boundary of this trittys[17] and since Laureion seems to be divided

[15]This hill appears on the *Karten* (Sheet XVI) with the height 160 m.

[16]The following are the major authorities who place Amphitrope at, or close to,
Metropisi: Stuart and Revett, *Antiquities* 3.xiv; Milchhöfer, in various places but
esp. *RE* 1 (1894) 1967, s.v. Amphitrope; Löper, "Die Trittyen," 422; Kirchner, in
his commentary to *IG* II² 5606; and Philippson, *Attika und Megaris* 832 n. 1.

[17]The villages north of Panion belong to other trittyes: Keratea = Kephale (coastal
trittys with Thorikos), Kalyvia = Prospalta (inland trittys of Sphettos).

between two trittyes approximately along the north–south line of the chief mountain ridge, the process of elimination makes it obvious that Amphitrope was east of Aigilia, north of Anaphlystos, west of Besa, and south of Panion. We have already shown that the deme of Anaphlystos included the mining area near Ari within its control. Amphitrope, then, must have been north of Ari. These limits mark out with decisive sureness the small plain ringed to the immediate north by Panion, to the east by the Laureion range, and to the west and south by the low range separating it from the plain of Anavyssos. Metropisi was at one time the chief village in this small plain.

The antiquities in this area have been described. Remains of the classical period were found in two places: south of Lulje Kuki, a mining community; west of Metropisi, traces of graves. These graves are of interest because their presence suggests that a classical settlement was near by. East of the graves are the ruins of Metropisi. Here I found nothing from the classical period among the still copious remains, even though Milchhöfer recorded ancient blocks. But this lack of classical materials does not entirely rule out the possibility that an ancient village may lie beneath the present ruins. The same embarrassing lack of fragments of pottery has not invalidated the identification of Lambrika as Lamptrai.[18] There is much to be said in favour of expecting an ancient village at Metropisi. The site is a good one. It is on a road, it is near a main junction, it is on the slopes of a high ridge and thus well protected, it overlooks, but does not encroach upon, a fertile plain which could provide a livelihood for the inhabitants. A site further west would not have been central and would have removed the village still further from the main arterial junction; a site further east would have meant forsaking the slope of Panion and occupying farmland. Those who built Metropisi must have been swayed by some or all of these considerations, some of which would have occurred to those who established the village of Amphitrope. The actual evidence that there was an ancient village on the same site is sparse—a few graves and perhaps a few blocks. But there is even less evidence for any other site in this plain. The settlement south of Lulje Kuki was concerned with mining and not farming. I doubt whether it even existed before the time of Kleisthenes.

I have no hesitation in identifying the plain lying south and east of the eastern end of Panion as the deme of Amphitrope, a deme so

[18]This analogy with Lamptrai is not entirely fair: the remains of inscriptions and sculptural monuments found at Lambrika indicate the existence of an ancient settlement, regardless of the presence or absence of fragments of pottery.

placed that it controlled one of the major junctions on the Athens–
Sounion highway. Within that deme it is clear that the mining activity
recorded in the leases took place among the hills bounding the plain
to the south and had its centre at the settlement south of Lulje Kuki.
As for the identification of the village of Amphitrope, Metropisi is an
attractive candidate in many ways, and what little archaeological
evidence there is supports but does not demand it. This hypothesis
awaits verification.

X

BESA

A REFERENCE to Besa is found in Isaios 3.22: Ξανοκλῆς τοίνυν Βῆσαζε μὲν ἰὼν εἰς τὸ ἐργαστήριον τὸ ἡμέτερον εἰς τὰ ἔργα. The last phrase refers to the mining area and so we are given a general indication of the position of Besa. Strabo (9.4.5) also mentions Besa, but in his description of Lokris, not Attika. There was a Besa in Lokris, and Strabo points out that it was spelt with a double sigma, whereas the Besa in Attika had only one.[1]

The most important reference to Besa is the passage from the περὶ πόρων (4.43–44) of Xenophon, which was discussed in part in chapter VIII above:

I for my part consider that it is possible not to abandon the silver mines in the event of war. Indeed, for the protection of the mines there is a fortification on the south coast in the deme of Anaphlystos, and one on the north coast in the deme of Thorikos. These are separated from each other by about sixty stades. If, therefore, there were between these (ἐν μέσῳ τούτων) a third defence on the topmost part of the deme of Besa, then the miners would assemble in some one of all these fortifications, and if there were some suspicion of war, then shortly every person would retire to a safe position.

If we interpreted the phrase ἐν μέσῳ τούτων literally, we might assume that Xenophon had in mind the placing of a third fort a little south of Synterini on the hill of Kamareza, but there is little to warrant the assumption that he meant to be absolutely precise. The hill of Kamareza is not particularly high, only 252 metres,[2] whereas $2\frac{1}{4}$ kilometres to the north is the highest hill in the Laureion range, Vigla Rimpari, which reaches a height of 372 metres. That the highest hill in Laureion is so close to the theoretical mid-point of a line between the two forts

---

[1]But Stephanos (*Ethnika* s.v. βῆσσα) points out that Herodianos wrote the name of the Lokrian town with one sigma, whereas others used two.

[2]Milchhöfer (*Erläuternder Text* 3–6.25) says that Xenophon planned his fortification for the top of Kamareza hill but that from its appearance the project was never carried out. Milchhöfer does not discuss the logical result of his identification: that all hills in the neighbourhood higher than Kamareza were outside the deme of Besa.

in Anaphlystos and Thorikos is a tribute to Xenophon's accuracy, and
I am convinced that he was advocating a fort located on Vigla Rimpari.
Not only does the hill command an excellent view in all directions, but
it is reasonably flat on top for a considerable area and is defended by
nature on the east where there are sharp cliffs. One might argue that
on one count it does not suit Xenophon's description: it is not well
suited as a place of refuge for the miners, since few would have worked
close by, the majority being further south. This objection, however, is
easily met. Anaphlystos, one of Xenophon's other places of refuge, has
no mines near by, and Thorikos certainly has no more mines in its
immediate surroundings than Besa has (or rather Vigla Rimpari).
Either Xenophon gave little thought to this aspect of his scheme or
else he considered that the miners would get sufficient warning to
enable them to reach these places of refuge.[3]

In the spring of 1954, two members of the American School of
Classical Studies climbed Vigla Rimpari and discovered that, except
where the cliffs made such a bulwark unnecessary, its summit was
surrounded by a low wall which was preserved in places to a height of
one metre. A little pottery was collected both then and in later years.
There is no doubt that this small fort was in use during the classical
period. It is too hazardous to suggest a closer date on the evidence of
fragments of pottery from roof tiles and coarse wares.[4]

One wonders whether the Athenians took Xenophon's advice or
whether it was some other stimulus that prompted them to build the
fort on Vigla Rimpari. The question is somewhat academic because no
decision can be reached without a specific indication of the date of the
fort. Nevertheless, some observations are possible. The fort seems
hardly large enough to have taken care of even one-third of the miners
in Laureion, nor does it appear sufficiently well guarded to have
offered much safety to refugees if an enemy decided to attack the
height. Although I am certain that this is the hill that Xenophon had

[3]The whole plan seems ill conceived. Not only is there this question of the proximity
of the forts if they were to be used as places of refuge, but also the important matter
of their physical size: large enough to contain, shelter, and guard the vast numbers of
miners who worked in the district. Moreover, an attack by land might pass by
Anaphlystos and Thorikos, but surely not an attack by sea; in the latter case two of
the three places of refuge might be subjected to immediate siege and thereby rendered
useless for the purpose envisaged by Xenophon.

[4]There are similarities between this fort and others with rubble walls dated in the
fourth and third centuries B.C. These similarities, however, were found in aspects
that were not characteristic of any particular century, and so I cannot press the
parallel.

in mind, these observations make me suspect that the fortifications were not the result of his advice. Rather, I think he was aware that the top of the hill was lightly fortified and therefore felt that it could easily be adapted to a second purpose. As for the primary purpose, this defended height would have provided an excellent observation post for a small detachment charged with the watching of naval movements in the area between Thorikos and Sounion and in the waters of Anaphlystos. In addition, it could have served as a signalling station linking the forts of Anaphlystos and Thorikos. It is also visible from the fort at Anagyrous, and therefore could have used Anagyrous to relay messages to Athens. Perhaps the Athenians ignored Xenophon's advice because they realized that in the event of an emergency the efficiency of this station would have been greatly reduced by any large groups of refugees.

The references to Besa in the ancient literary sources are thus seen to be very helpful. Xenophon's account enables us to identify a prominent feature that was contained within the deme of Besa. The village of Besa must be looked for in the same area.

NAME

Besa has not survived as a place name in the mining district. Nevertheless, the ancient name is of some interest, since it probably described the setting of the village of Besa. The name appears to be a variant spelling of βῆσσα, which is explained in *Etymologicum Magnum* (s.v. βῆσσαν) as κοιλάδα ὕδωρ ἔχουσαν, καὶ μεσότητα ὀρῶν, συνάγκειαν· ἄλλοι τὸ ἔνυδρον. Strabo (9.4.5) states that the Besa in Lokris (Bessa) was so named because it was a woody place. These notices present a picture of the type of surroundings one might expect of a place named Besa: an upland woody glen, supplied with water.

These features may prove helpful in locating Besa because they are characteristics that would have remained largely unchanged. Laureion is still woody in many parts and one can easily detect the presence of the water courses, which were tapped during the classical period to supply the washing establishments in which the ore was separated from the matrix.

INSCRIPTIONS

The name Besa appears in the mining leases with a frequency which implies that the deme was an important part of the mining district.

The deme of Besa is used as a general location for many mines, and the village of Besa is given as the destination of roads nine times in the specific locations of mines.[5] In addition, various monuments in the deme of Besa provide boundaries for mines. The Herakleion of the people of Besa occurs twice,[6] the Artemision once,[7] the agora once,[8] and the road to the agora possibly three times.[9]

In the case of the village of Besa, the conclusion is inescapable that the village and certain mines were next to one another; mines, in fact, may have been actually within the village. This proximity is suggested by the mention of two of Besa's sanctuaries as boundaries of mines, and is proved by the reference to the agora of the people of Besa as forming the southern boundary of a mine. This knowledge is of great help in locating the village because it immediately supplies certain definite requirements that any proposed site must meet.

But there were also mines outside the village, yet still in the deme of Besa. At least two mines have "the road to Besa" among their specific boundaries.[10] It is mentioned six times (three times of mines in the deme of Amphitrope, twice of mines in the deme of Besa, and once where the general context is now lost). Roads are frequently designated in the leases by the naming of terminal points, for example Thorikos to Besa, Amphitrope to Besa. If we assume that these six references to "the road to Besa" are all to the same road, then I think we must assume further that this road was of such importance that its identity would be obvious despite the short description. ἡ ὁδὸς ἡ]αστικὴ Βήσαζε [φέρουσα (Crosby 4.24) describes just such a road: the road from Athens to Besa, a part of the main highway joining

[5]"The road to Besa" is found in Crosby 7.26, 10.10, 18.15, 18.64, 18.68, and Crosby S 3.8; "the road from Amphitrope to Besa" in Crosby 16a.90–91; "the road from Thorikos to Besa" in Crosby 29.6; "the city (ἀστική) road to Besa" in Crosby 4.24.

[6]Crosby 18.12 and 21.22. In the latter, τὸ Βησαιῶν is restored on the basis of the first reference.

[7]Crosby 18.35–36. Only the first letter of Artemision remains on the stone. The restoration is based on Crosby 5.76–77 (not on Crosby 5.10 as is stated by Miss Crosby in "Leases," 259).

[8]Crosby S 2.31.

[9]The possible places are Crosby 14.33–35, S 2.40, and S 6.6–8. In no case is the complete phrase ἀγορὰν τὴν Βησαιῶν preserved, only the word or the beginnings of the word ἀγοράν. But since there is no mention of any other agora in the lists, the supplements are plausible. Miss Crosby points out ("Fragments," 16–17) that 14.33–35 might be restored in the same way as S 6.6–8, thus supplying two more references to the road to the agora.

[10]Crosby 10.10, 18.15.

Athens and Sounion.[11] The section mentioned in the inscription was not meant to denote the whole stretch from Athens to Besa but only the part that linked Besa with whatever town preceded Besa on the road. I suggest that only this road could be termed "the road to Besa" and still be understood as referring to a specific road.

If this conclusion is correct, then we can add the following to our information about the deme of Besa: some of the mines in the deme were neither within nor close to the village of Besa; the mines which had as one of their boundaries "the road to Besa" were nearer to Athens than the mines at Besa were.

According to *IG* II[2] 1750 Besa supplied two councillors in 344/3 B.C.: it would not have been a large deme.

REMAINS

Since we are confident that the hill Vigla Rimpari was within the limits of the deme of Besa, our attention is drawn to the narrow upland plain running from a little north of Demoliaki to a little south of Synterini. That we should look west of Rimpari and not east is made obvious by a consideration both of the extent of the deme of Thorikos and of the trittys affiliation of Besa.

Within this plain the signs of mining activity are copious. But whereas washing establishments are scattered throughout the area, the mines, broadly speaking, fall into two separate groups—those around Demoliaki and those at Synterini. In addition, there are a few mines near Barbaliaki.

Demoliaki was clearly a major centre for mining operations. The remains of buildings, washing establishments, and cisterns are extensive—testimony to the importance of the near-by mines. However, just as the mines were scattered, so are these remains, and Vanderpool and I formed the opinion that the remains are not from a single village but from a series of separate establishments devoted to a single industry. The remains here are similar to those at Lulje Kuki, and the purposes of these two settlements cannot have been very different. Milchhöfer recorded the discovery in the area of many ancient graves, "anscheinend aus guter Zeit,"[12] but his findings in no way change the character of the ancient remains at Demoliaki.

Let us now turn to Synterini. One notices at once that the mines

[11]See above, chap. VIII, pp. 100–101, for a discussion of roads that came from the city.

[12]*Erläuternder Text* 3–6.25.

form a compact group both among and surrounding the ruins of the most recent village at Synterini. In these ruins various inscriptions and sculptured objects of stone have been found. In addition, Milchhöfer noted the remains of a building of complicated plan and uncertain use but seemingly connected with bathing.[13] There can be no doubt that Synterini represents the site of an ancient settlement. But was it a settlement that owed its existence to mining operations? Ardaillon realized, as does the traveller today, that Synterini commanded an upland plateau that could be (and is) cultivated: "c'est un des coins rares au Laurion qui peuvent se prêter à la culture."[14] Those who established the location of the ancient settlement at Synterini must have done so with a view to the agricultural exploitation of the neighbourhood. They probably were also aware of the strategic location beside the main north–south artery through Laureion at the point where the road turns southeastwards in order to pass over the saddle dividing Synterini from Kamareza. Ardaillon added: "De tout temps, dans l'antiquité comme de nos jours, c'était une position désignée par la nature pour l'établissement d'un centre important." Since the earlier settlements were primarily, if not totally, concerned with agriculture, these considerations make it clear that Synterini was probably founded on this site before the discovery of the local mines.[15] Synterini certainly contained buildings not connected with mining: the sculptural remains suggest places of worship; Milchhöfer noted a bathing establishment (?); and Ardaillon recorded ruins "qui ne sont pas uniquement celles d'ateliers métallurgiques."

IDENTIFICATION

Milchhöfer (as we have seen) placed Besa near Kamareza[16] and Xenophon's fortification on the hill of Kamareza.[17] This view was not shared by Löper, who favoured Barbaliaki or Plaka.[18] Milchhöfer rightly attacked this opinion and reaffirmed his early view.[19] Ardaillon

[13]*Ibid.* The inscriptions and sculpture are collected and described in Milchhöfer's "Antikenbericht" (1887) 284 (No. 185), 294–295 (No. 250), and 300–302 (nos. 282, 291, 294 [?]).

[14]*Les Mines* 213.

[15]The presence of mines among the houses is surely another reason for thinking that the discovery of mines came after the settlement had been established.

[16]*Die Demenordnung* map facing 48.

[17]*Erläuternder Text* 3–6.25.

[18]"Die Trittyen," 422.

[19]*RE* 3 (1899) 323–324, s.v. Besa.

followed neither topographer: he considered Synterini ideally suited
for an ancient village and identified it as Besa.[20] The theories of both
Milchhöfer and Ardaillon have their supporters today: Kirsten follows
the former,[21] LaBarbe the latter.[22] Let us rehearse what is known
about Besa.

Besa was a deme in the mining district; it was part of a trittys that
included Aigilia, Anaphlystos, and Amphitrope; it was probably
adjacent to Amphitrope; it lay approximately midway between the
towns of Anaphlystos and Thorikos; within its borders was a lofty
hill on the top of which Xenophon advocated the placing of a fortification. The village of Besa had mines very close to its agora and to
certain religious buildings; it was not the only centre of mining activity
within the deme; in all probability another centre lay to its north.
Finally, we should add that, since Besa was certainly in existence
before the end of the sixth century b.c.,[23] that is, before the beginning
of the major exploitation of the mining district, its primary reason
for existence at the outset was probably to provide a centre for farmers.

Besa clearly lay on the west side of Laureion rather than the east,
in the northern half rather than the southern. Kamareza really does
not suit these requirements since its outlook is east and south. On the
other hand, Synterini and the lands north and immediately southwest
do fit all the requirements for both the village and the deme of Besa.
Synterini was an ancient village; it had mines around and within it;
sculptural remains suggest the existence of public shrines; it was
ideally placed to provide a centre from which the upland plateau
stretching north to Demoliaki (and even further) might be farmed. As
for the deme, the same area about Synterini contained Vigla Rimpari,
the highest point in Laureion; there are mines at Demoliaki and these
could be identified as the group north of the village of Besa; the
deme's boundaries would march with those of Amphitrope to the
north and northwest and Anaphlystos to the west.

The evidence from Synterini and the neighbouring area fits the
description of Besa that we have assembled from the sources. In my
opinion there can be only one conclusion: Synterini must be identified
as the site of the village of Besa. The extent of the deme is easily

[20]*Les Mines* 213.

[21]Philippson, *Attika und Megaris* 837 n. 2. Kirsten wrote the footnote. He refers the
reader to Milchhöfer and says of Besa that it "vielleicht bei Kamariza lag."

[22]*La Loi navale* map on 27.

[23]The demotic first appears in extant inscriptions, as far as I can discover, in
IG I² 302. This is sufficiently early—418/7 b.c.—to remove any doubts concerning
the Kleisthenic date for its creation as a deme.

established to west and east where hills provide the boundaries: to the east the main ridge of Laureion with its peaks Vigla Rimpari,[24] Mikro Rimpari, and Kaziti; to the west the foothills of Laureion, which here fall to the plain of Anavyssos and in antiquity bordered the deme of Anaphlystos. Forming a ledge between these foothills and the main ridge is the long and narrow belt of land that was the deme of Besa. Its northern limit was probably near Plaka[25] and it would have been here that it adjoined the deme of Amphitrope. South of Synterini Besa was bordered by the hill of Kamareza, which on its southern side joins with other hills to limit the tiny plain southwest of Synterini.

One last observation. This narrow plain set in a ledge between the foothills and the main ridge was well supplied with water, as the number of cisterns shows, and it is still comparatively well wooded. These characteristics recall the meaning of βῆσσα that we established above on the basis of entries in Strabo and *Etymologicum Magnum*. Even now, this name could be applied with ample justification to the area identified as the ancient deme of Besa.

[24]The summit of Vigla Rimpari was certainly on the western side of the watershed and therefore in Besa, not Thorikos.

[25]Plaka is almost two kilometres northeast of Demoliaki and represents the most northern limit of the valley that leads to Demoliaki.

XI

ATENE

THERE are only two references to Atene as far as I know, and one of them depends upon an emendation. Stephanos gives the following entry in his *Ethnika*: Ἀτήνη, δῆμος τῆς Ἀντιοχίδος φυλῆς. Φρύνιχος δὲ τῆς Ἀτταλίδος φησίν. This notice, however, does not help us to locate the deme.

For information of a different kind we must turn to Strabo. He states (9.1.21) that the coastal deme after Anaphlystos but before Sounion was Ἀζηνεῖς.[1] Casaubon recognized that this name was spelled wrong and emended it to Ἀζηνιεῖς. It has been widely assumed ever since that Strabo placed the deme of Azenia between Anaphlystos and Sounion.[2] Its position is therefore established with comparative ease. We know that Anaphlystos controlled the Bay of Hagios Nikolaos and Sounion, the cape on which was the temple of Poseidon. Azenia must have been between the bay and the cape and we can safely assume that the deme was near Legrana. Milchhöfer[3] and Szanto[4] realized independently that this location presented a difficulty because it made Azenia an enclave: its neighbouring demes to the north, Anaphlystos and Besa, belonged to the phyle Antiochis (X), Sounion belonged to Leontis (IV); and Azenia was part of Hippothontis (VIII). This arrangement constituted an exception to Milchhöfer's own thesis that demes within the respective coastal and inland trittyes were contiguous. But Milchhöfer did not challenge Strabo's statement and, despite the serious criticisms of others, maintained in later studies that Azenia was located between Anaphlystos and Sounion, even though a better solution had been proposed.

---

[1]See *Strabonis Geographica* ed. Kramer 2.227: ἀζηνεῖς codd. Tzch. corr. ex coni. Cas. certissima.

[2]In neither the Teubner text (ed. Meineke, Vol. 2 [1853]) nor the Loeb (ed. Jones, Vol. 4 [1927]) is there any suggestion that the text has been emended at this point.

[3]*Die Demenordnung* 32.

[4]"Die kleisthenischen Trittyen," 313–314.

As for Atene, Milchhöfer, after a study of the prytany lists, established that it was probably a deme in the coastal trittys of Antiochis. True to his own thesis, he placed Atene between Thorai and Aigilia, a position indeed excluded from the sea and therefore a deme not mentioned by Strabo.[5] Löper,[6] after reading Milchhöfer's treatise, and von Schöffer,[7] in a critical notice of Szanto's article, both came to the same conclusion: that the problem of the enclave formed by Azenia was easily solved by emending the text of Strabo. Instead of 'Aζηνιεῖς—itself an emendation of 'Aζηνεῖς[8]—they suggested the reading 'Aτηνεῖς. Since Atene was clearly in the coastal trittys of Antiochis, this reading removed the source of the problem. One may wonder with Löper why Milchhöfer did not adopt "this simple correction." That Strabo placed Atene, not Azenia, between Anaphlystos and Sounion is now an accepted fact.[9]

NAME

The name Atene has not survived to the present time, nor does the ancient name appear to be descriptive of the site of Atene.

INSCRIPTIONS

In 334/3 B.C. Atene provided three councillors, according to *IG* II² 1750. This inscription is a list of the members of the prytany of Antiochis for that year. According to Löper[10] the demes are arranged in the inscription by trittyes, and indeed there is no other explanation that accounts both for the order and the space deliberately left beneath the last name under Alopeke. The demesmen from Atene (at

[5]Milchhöfer, although forced to admit the strength of the arguments brought against his position, never conceded victory, even though he hedged with doubts his own theories about Azenia and Atene: see *RE* 2 (1896) 1921–1922, s.v. Atene; *ibid.* 2198, and map facing 2204, s.v. Attika, where Atene is shown (with a question mark) near Olympos, and Azenia between Anaphlystos and Sounion; *ibid.* 2642, s.v. Azenia, where Azenia is located near Eleusis. Kirsten places Azenia in the same area (Philippson, *Attika und Megaris* 863 n. 4), but the evidence is very slight. On the other hand, *IG* II² 2377 might be used to support a view that Azenia was a part of the inland trittys around Dekeleia.

[6]"Die Trittyen," 334–335.

[7]"Bericht über die Litteratur zu Aristoteles' 'Aθηναίων πολιτεία," 49–50.

[8]So Kramer says, followed by Löper. But von Schöffer's text reads 'Aξηνεῖς, which I assume to be an unfortunate misprint.

[9]See e.g. Pritchett, *The Five Attic Tribes* 9, and Kirsten in Philippson, *Attika und Megara* 832 n. 1 and 838 n. 2.

[10]"Die Trittyen," 426.

the bottom of the first column) are between those from Besa (also in the first column) and those from Aigilia (head of the second column). There can be no doubt that the deme of Atene belonged to the coastal trittys of Antiochis.

Between Anaphlystos and Sounion, along the coast, there are only two areas—Charaka and Legrana—that might have supported a village. At Legrana, however, the only early remains are at the eastern edge of the plain on the high ground that separates Legrana from Sounion.[11] These ruins, moreover, clearly fall within the deme of Sounion.

West of Legrana there lies the small plain of Charaka, bordered on the north by the main mass of the Laureion hills, and on the south both by the sea towards the east and by a long high hill towards the west. The other limits of the plain are as easily established. To the east, between it and the flats of Legrana, there are low foothills that form a distinct boundary despite the ease with which they can be crossed. To the west the plain rises steadily until it reaches a ridge joining the main hills to the north and the hill to the south. On the far side of this ridge the land falls abruptly to the sea.

The only remains so far recorded from this area are terrace walls in the western half near the ridge.[12] These walls, which still survive, were built in order to make available for cultivation land where the hills met the plain and where the steep slope made terracing a necessity.[13] Other, and more important, remains have seemingly been overlooked by travellers and scholars. These remains are in two areas, one near the sea at the bay called Charaka, the other on the ridge overlooking the plain and sea.

Before the construction of the Athens–Sounion coastal highway, access to the plain of Charaka was gained by a single cart track that entered from the east, then crossed the plain, and finally ended almost at the ridge. This wagon road runs parallel to the shore and where it passes the bay it is approximately midway between the hills and the

[11] *Erläuternder Text* 3–6.31.

[12] *Ibid.* 3–6.31. Kotzias ("Δημοτικὸν ψήφισμα," 172) mentions "προχείρως" that he knows of three unrecorded sites with well-preserved ruins of fortifications between Anavyssos and Charaka. He does not consider these sites to be necessarily demes but perhaps "οἰκήματα σποράδην κείμενα περὶ τὰ δημοτικὰ ἱερά." I assume that the fortress on the ridge is one of his sites.

[13] Conceivably, these terraces might be classical in date: see Bradford, "Fieldwork on Aerial Discoveries in Attica and Rhodes," 172–180.

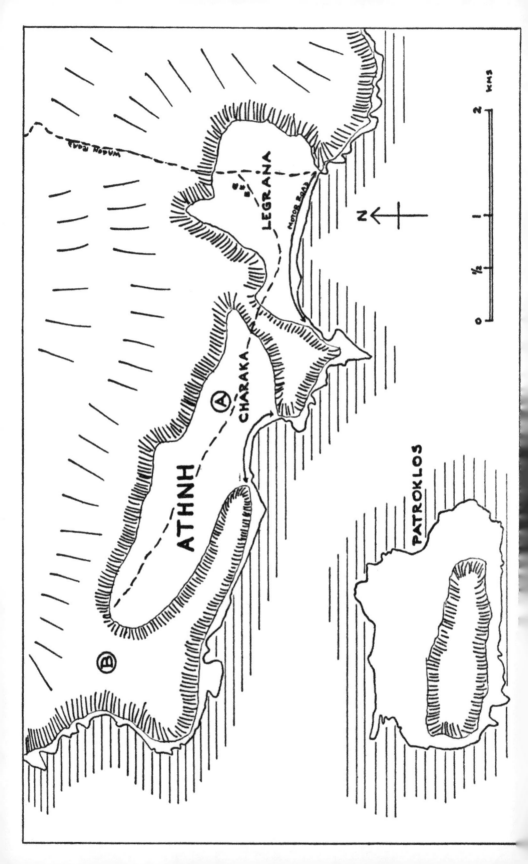

water. At this point, on either side of the road, there are copious fragments of pottery spread over a considerable area, an area certainly large enough for a small village (A on Figure 8). Among the pieces, we noted some that could be assigned to the Hellenistic and Roman periods, a few perhaps to the fourth century B.C. There seemed to be many fragments of imported wine jars, perhaps a natural phenomenon for a village blessed with so fine a harbour. One strange feature was the lack of either worked or large stones, which are customary on the sites of ancient villages. An answer was not hard to find: within the area covered by the sherds was an inactive kiln, which once had been used for making lime. The mere presence of the kiln is proof that at no great distance from it there was at one time an ample supply of reducible material. That the kiln was placed amid the remains of an ancient village suggests that the reducible material was the favourite building stone of those in the Laureiotike—low-grade white marble—the one thing we should expect at such a site, and the one thing missing.

Although final proof is far from complete, it is surely not hazardous to assume that this village controlled the harbour in front of it and the plain around it and had performed these two functions from at least classical times. The size and position of the village suggest to me that the remains are those of a village that controlled an ancient deme.

On the ridge the remains are of a quite different character (B on Figure 8). Surrounding the highest point of the ridge is a walled enclosure within which are traces of many buildings. The *enceinte* is made of rubble, but in most places it is poorly preserved and barely protruding above ground. In addition, one can make out the traces of two towers, both of which were integral parts of the circuit and both of which probably guarded entrances. The tower to the east, which overlooks what may have been the main gate, is the best preserved feature of this settlement: there the walls are quite substantial, built of blocks of a moderate size in the style of masonry termed "rough polygonal." The total area enclosed by the circuit measures approximately ninety metres square. In the northern half of the circuit, two buildings, both containing several rooms, can be made out, but in the southern half there are less obvious traces of small houses.

Although many of the remains are poorly preserved, the over-all picture leaves no doubt about the proper interpretation: these are the remains of a small fort with buildings to house both the equipment and personnel of a garrison. The fort was used in the classical period, certainly during the fifth century B.C. There are many sherds both within and without the walls and a sampling of these produced no fragments definitely Roman or Hellenistic, whereas several could be assigned to the fifth century B.C. with no hesitation.

It is a natural reaction to assume a connection between this fort and the village to its east, and to think that the fort provided a place of refuge for the deme. Yet this line of reasoning seems unsatisfactory: the fort was neither large nor heavily defended—to judge from the remains—and therefore not suited to the task of sheltering the villagers living near by. And what was the pressing reason that caused the villagers to build such a fort? A better approach is to compare this fort with the fort at Anagyrous. Both were sited for maximum range of vision, both were ringed with light defensive walls, both were in operation as early as the fifth century B.C. Perhaps both shared a common purpose, that of providing an observation post for the men detailed to watch the movement of enemy warships and to report to Athens any hostile action, for example an attempted landing.[14]

IDENTIFICATION

Some of the early travellers placed Azenia at Legrana,[15] and, although no one concurs in that opinion today, Atene is sometimes located there.[16] Milchhöfer identified Charaka as Azenia,[17] whereas Löper suggested as a possibility for Atene the western corner of the Bay of Anavyso.[18] This last is most unlikely and, in my opinion, merits no further discussion. The problem is that of making a choice between Charaka and Legrana as the site of Atene.

The case against Legrana is strong. First, there are no ruins suitable for an ancient deme. Secondly, the plain and bay geographically seem to be connected with the land to the east. In fact, Legrana should probably be considered part of the deme of Sounion.

The case for Charaka, on the other hand, is very good. First, it has ruins eminently suitable for identification as the remains of an ancient deme. Secondly, despite their proximity to Sounion, Charaka and its bay seem quite divorced from the area further east. Although the barrier between the plains of Charaka and Legrana is low, it is definite.

Milchhöfer's identification of Charaka as the site of an ancient deme

---

[14]See the appendix to this chapter for further comments.
[15]E.g. Leake, *Demi* 61–62.
[16]Kirsten in Philippson, *Attika und Megaris* 832 n. 1.
[17]*Die Demenordnung* map facing 48; *RE* 2 (1896) map facing 2204.
[18]"Die Trittyen," 422.

(whatever the name) is certainly correct, though it is strange that he overlooked the remains that give substance to the identification. It is an excellent site for a village. The plain is large enough to have provided opportunity for farming; the bay supplied a natural harbour. And all around were hills, thus giving the area seclusion and security.

The deme of Atene has natural limits on all sides. To the south was the sea, to the west sea and hills, to the east a low ridge separating Charaka from Legrana, and to the north two hills, Mikro Baphi and Megalo Baphi.

APPENDIX TO CHAPTER XI

OBSERVATION POSTS IN SOUTHEAST ATTIKA

At the beginning of the winter of 429/8 B.C. the Spartans attacked by night the fort of Boudoron on the island of Salamis (Thucydides 2.93–94). Fire signals were lit and a message was sent to Athens. This message must have gone first to Peiraieus, for the Athenians imagined that the enemy had taken Peiraieus, while the people of Peiraieus assumed that the enemy already possessed Salamis.

Thucydides' account makes several things clear. First, Boudoron was a fort sited to enable its occupants to keep close watch over the movements of enemy shipping to and from Megara. Secondly, Boudoron was not a strong fort and could easily be taken by a sudden and determined attack. Thirdly, those at Boudoron, despite the suddenness of the attack, were able to signal to Peiraieus that the enemy had made a landing: the implication is that those in Peiraieus were on the alert to receive signals at any moment from Boudoron. Fourthly, the code, which would have included a signal for a hostile attack, was still very limited: Peiraieus was able to relay the message to Athens but was unable to make the clarifying addition that the message had as its origin a place other than Peiraieus.

The site of such a fort must have been carefully chosen so that its guardians would command positions from which they could both watch the waters off Megara and signal their findings to Peiraieus. These two considerations would have necessitated the placing of the fort on an elevated ridge or on the summit of a high hill, since the required vistas were in almost opposite directions. Regarding the size, the fort must have been large enough to accommodate not only its garrison but also the crews of the three ships based at Boudoron. (If we assume these to have been triremes, the crews would have totalled about six hundred men.) Presumably the ships were beached near the fort. But whether the landing area was defended, either by walls that formed part of one large circuit or by arms that were joined to the separate circuit of the fort, or whether it was left undefended, we cannot tell. The former would imply a state of strength and preparedness which the account of Thucydides (including 3.51.2) does not suggest; the latter might account for the difficulties met by scholars in identifying the remains of this fort.[1]

But whatever Boudoron's actual position or aspect, its task was obvious: it was an observation post with the duty of following the movements of enemy ships and of reporting to Peiraieus by a pre-arranged code of the simplest sort; as a fort, it was probably not designed to withstand a siege. The Spartans, in sailing from Megara by night, hoped that their ships might escape the observers at Boudoron and thus that the news of the sailing would not reach Peiraieus and Athens ahead of the ships.

[1]W. E. McLeod has recently made a study of remains which he identifies as Boudoron: see his "Boudoron, an Athenian Fort on Salamis," 316–323. His identification is attractive and may prove right. If so, this fort was admirably located for its tasks, even though the peak, from which communication with Peiraieus was secured, was a little above the fort and not contained within its wall. This defence, which McLeod assumes met the sea, encloses a very large area including a stretch of beach suitable for ships. Despite the seeming aptness of some of these features, I am not convinced by the evidence presented and I feel the case to be non-proven. First, if it is difficult to understand why it was necessary for Boudoron to have a length of 1,500 metres, it is even more difficult to explain why the wall was not extended another 250 metres to enclose the peak that was absolutely necessary for signalling to Peiraieus. Secondly, McLeod's assumption that "undeniably both end walls originally began at the sea, even though their lower reaches have been totally effaced" is reasonable only to one who has previously assumed that he knows the purpose of the walls. The complete effacement of walls amounting to about 250 metres in length is worthy of deeper comment. Finally, McLeod has not really proved the antiquity of this rubble wall either from its appearance or purpose. The parallels he cites for walls of this type "accepted as ancient" are misleading because in the main they are not "accepted" on the basis of the character of the wall alone: additional information exists proving or suggesting their antiquity. In the case of Boudoron, no additional reasons are given for the date. To judge from the report, the wall lacks all distinctive features such as towers and gates; no traces of buildings were discovered within the walled area; no pottery was found, at least not of an informative nature. In view of these reservations, and since my remarks about Boudoron do not require its positive identification, I have not used McLeod's conclusions about Boudoron.

Thucydides closes his account of this section by remarking that the Athenians took steps to make the harbour of Peiraieus less vulnerable to attack. But the possibilities of attack from the sea were neither new nor limited to a single quarter. Peisistratos had landed at Marathon and successfully marched on Athens: his son had led the Persians to the same place but with different results. Even so, the Athenians must have been acutely conscious of the danger of sea-borne attack from the east as well as from the south. And perhaps they showed something of their appreciation of the situation when they built large forts at Rhamnous and Sounion in the second half of the fifth century B.C., forts which certainly did more than merely ensure the safe passage of corn ships (Thucydides 8.4). But forts however large, if widely spaced, do not provide safeguards against sudden and unexpected military action on the parts of the coast not visible to them.

The forts at Anagyrous and Atene are very similar. Both are located on high ground a little removed from the sea, and, as a consequence of their siting, they command excellent views of the open waters off the Attic coast from Anagyrous to Atene. They are about the same size and both are defended by light walls more suited to ensure privacy from the villagers than security from the enemy. Finally, both forts appear to have been first occupied in the fifth century B.C.

These similarities in design and location suggest a similarity in purpose, but a purpose seemingly unconnected with the near-by villages, since neither fort was large enough to act as a place of refuge nor sufficiently defended to stand siege. In addition, such a connection would leave unexplained why Anagyrous and Atene needed forts for their protection while other demes in the vicinity did not. If the siting is not to be explained by the proximity of inhabited centres, then it must be related to some strategic advantage that these forts gained by being placed on these particular heights. This advantage is not hard to find. Between Peiraieus and Sounion there are two major changes in direction in the coastline, the first after Cape Zoster, the second after Cape Charaka, thus making it impossible to keep the whole coast under surveillance from centres at Peiraieus and Sounion. The fort at Anagyrous is placed after Cape Zoster in such a way that from it one can see not only the open waters from Zoster to Charaka but also Peiraieus and the open waters from Peiraieus to Halai Aixonides. The fort at Atene is just north of Cape Charaka, but because of its siting one can see from it not only the open waters from Charaka to Zoster but also the fort and sanctuary at Sounion and some water to the south of Sounion. One cannot see, however, the waters between

Charaka and the island of Patroklos, but this strait is visible from Sounion. It is probable that these locations—at Anagyrous and Atene —were chosen because forts placed there would command a view of the greatest possible extent of coastline.

Let us now recall the salient features of Boudoron as deduced from Thucydides. It was a lightly defended fort placed on a ridge or hill so that its guardians could keep watch on naval traffic off Megara. Thus, in siting, defence, and date Boudoron must have been similar to the forts at Anagyrous and Atene. These similarities imply a further similarity, that of purpose, and I have no doubt that the primary task given to those who held these forts was to keep careful watch over the movements of ships along the southeast coast of Attika. Between capes Zoster and Charaka only the deep bays of Porto Lombardo and Hagios Nikolaos would have been hidden, but even there ships would have been unable to approach or leave without coming under observation. A further task, one also shared by Boudoron, would have been to inform Athens by signalling of any emergency created by hostile forces. Sounion also must have had this duty.

Even as Boudoron was unable to signal direct to Athens, so it would have been impossible for the forts at Anagyrous, Atene, and Sounion to signal to Athens without some relay stations. Peiraieus, since it is visible from the fort at Anagyrous, could have received messages from Anagyrous and then have passed them on to Athens. From Atene one can see the main ridge of Hymettos, so messages from Atene could have reached Athens with only one intermediate station if a watch had been placed on the correct part of Hymettos. But a station meant to be operated day and night would not likely have been established on a ridge that is frequently covered with cloud from autumn to spring. It is better to assume that Atene signalled its messages to the fort at Anagyrous, which was clearly visible and which already had a full-time guard. The same is true of Sounion. Whereas in theory Sounion could have signalled its messages to one of the near-by peaks of Laureion, to be relayed from there to Hymettos and thence to Athens, to do so would have meant the setting up of other posts to be operated alongside the observation posts at Anagyrous and Atene. This procedure would have been dangerous because of weather conditions on Hymettos and wasteful because the fort at Atene is easily visible from Sounion. Messages could have been sent from Sounion to Atene and from there by stages to Athens.

The forts at Anagyrous and Atene, according to these arguments, were established as observation posts from which a constant watch might be kept upon all shipping passing within sight along the south-east coast, particularly between capes Zoster and Charaka. Since Sounion and Anagyrous were visible from Atene, and since Peiraieus was visible from Anagyrous, this chain of observation posts also constituted a chain of signalling stations from Sounion to Athens (and vice versa). News of hostile action could be sent to Athens from any one of these posts without the establishment of other posts on the peaks or ridges of mountains.

In the demes studied above there was one other that contained a fort like those at Anagyrous and Atene. The top of Vigla Rimpari in the deme of Besa is defended by a low rubble wall of light construction and there is an obvious similarity between this fort and the others. It could well have served the same purpose. From Vigla Rimpari, the highest peak in the Laureiotike, there is a clear view east from Thorikos to near Sounion, and west from Anaphlystos to Anagyrous. The area from Sounion to Charaka is hidden by the hills immediately north of Sounion; nevertheless, no better site could have been chosen to survey movement of shipping around the southern end of Attika. Nor would such a fort have lacked organized means for communication with Athens: from Vigla Rimpari the fort at Anagyrous is visible. It could have been used also by Thorikos as a relay station for messages to Athens. From the similarities of these three forts, I am certain that they must have been closely related in design and purpose.

Thucydides' account of the Spartan attack on Boudoron shows that Athens in the late fifth century B.C. had established an observation post at a strategic point on Salamis to watch enemy shipping and, with the help of relay stations, to report vital information to Athens. Because of their similarities with Boudoron, we can now identify certain other posts that were set up along the southeast coast of Attika between Peiraieus and Sounion at Anagyrous, Atene, and Besa. These, combined with the forts at Sounion, Thorikos, and Anaphlystos, would have provided a constant watch over the waters off this coast, and because no one fort was out of sight of all the others they were able to report their observations to Athens.

XII

CONCLUSION

διένειμε δὲ καὶ τὴν χώραν κατὰ δήμους τριάκοντα μέρη, δέκα μὲν
τῶν περὶ τὸ ἄστυ, δέκα δὲ τῆς παραλίας, δέκα δὲ τῆς μεσογείου,
καὶ ταύτας ἐπονομάσας τριττῦς, ἐκλήρωσεν τρεῖς εἰς τὴν φυλὴν
ἑκάστην ὅπως ἑκάστη μετέχῃ πάντων τῶν τόπων.

SO Aristotle (*Ath. Pol.* 21.4) describes the creation of the thirty
Kleisthenic trittyes and tells us something of their nature. Of
these thirty trittyes, the ten demes studied in this book constitute three adjacent coastal trittyes. Since so little is known of the
trittyes in general, the detailed investigation of the constituent parts
of these three may give us a better understanding of the remaining
seventeen coastal and inland trittyes. Thus this study may make it
possible to interpret more accurately the statement of Aristotle that
is quoted above. The ten city trittyes present special problems, since
the demes belonging to a trittys were not necessarily contiguous and
many of them had boundaries established by man, not by nature;
the city trittyes are therefore excluded from this survey.

The ten coastal demes examined in this book belong, as we have said,
to three adjacent coastal trittyes: Aixone and Halai Aixonides form
the coastal trittys of Kekropis; Anagyrous and Lamptrai (Upper and
Lower) belong to the coastal trittys of Erechtheis;[1] Thorai, Aigilia,
Anaphlystos, Amphitrope, Besa, and Atene constitute the coastal
trittys of Antiochis, probably called Anaphlystos.[2] The names of the
other two coastal trittyes have not been preserved, so for convenience
they will be referred to as [Aixone] and [Lamptrai]. On the basis of
the boundaries of the ten demes as established by our study, and
since the demes forming each of the three trittyes adjoin one another,
it is now possible to define the limits of these trittyes.

---

[1]The question whether Kedoi and Pambotadai also belong to this trittys is discussed
above, chap. v, pp. 58–59, n. 31. Even if it could be shown that they did, this
would not necessarily change the over-all boundaries of the trittys because one or
both could be accommodated in the more remote parts of the trittys without imping-
ing upon Anagyrous or Upper and Lower Lamptrai.

[2]For the names of the thirty Kleisthenic trittyes, see the appendix to this chapter.

[Aixone] was the first coastal trittys east of the city district. Because the most easterly of the city demes was Halimous with its centre near Hagios Kosmas, the boundary between the city and the coastal districts must have reached the sea between Hagios Kosmas and Glyphada. Midway between these two are several wide *reumata* that run from Mount Hymettos to the coast and start at the Gyrismos, a deep gully that breaks into Hymettos directly east of Hagios Kosmas. The eastern limit of the city trittyes followed the line of the northern section of Hymettos from the Stauro to the Gyrismos, then from the Gyrismos to the coast it followed one of the *reumata* setting out from the mouth of the gully, thus continuing the direction of the first part of Hymettos. This, the eastern boundary of the city trittyes from the Gyrismos to the sea, also formed the western boundary of [Aixone]. The other limits of this trittys are more obvious. To the southwest was the sea, while to the north and east was Hymettos, which reaches the sea between the villages of Vouliagmene and Varkiza and there forms the eastern prong of Zoster.

Of [Lamptrai] two boundaries are easily defined. To the west lay Hymettos, to the south the sea. The northern limit is not quite so obvious. It followed a chain of hills that starts immediately south and west of Koropi and extends to a point south of Markopoulo, where there is a wide gap separating this chain from the large mass of Mount Merenda. This group of hills formed the division between the coastal area and the inland plain. The eastern limit is the most difficult to establish. The crucial area is the valley in which lies the hamlet of Hagios Demetrios. This valley is bounded on both east and west by hills that reach the sea; thus either set of hills could form the eastern limit of the trittys. The eastern hills, however, seem to form a more natural boundary for the trittys, since they run from the sea towards Markopoulo and there join the hills that form the northern limit. In addition, just as the gap separating the northern hills from Merenda marks a clear division, so the gap between the north–south continuation of these hills (i.e. those to the east of Hagios Demetrios) and Mount Panion marks another obvious division.

The trittys of Anaphlystos lay to the east of [Lamptrai] and so shared the latter's eastern boundary. Its other limits are clearly defined. To the north the long mass of Mount Panion–Keratea formed a natural border. The hills of Laureion lay to the east, and at the north-eastern corner only a slight gap separated them from the eastern end of Keratea. The eastern border passed along the main north–south ridge of Laureion composed of Vigla Rimpari and Kamareza and then proceeded along the heights immediately west of the Legrana Valley, reaching the sea at the promontory forming the west side of the Bay of Legrana.

In these three trittyes the boundaries follow the natural limits, which in most cases are very prominent. I suggest that when the new trittyes were established by Kleisthenes at the end of the sixth century B.C., these three were so formed because they were seen to be natural geographic entities. Any other combination of these same demes would have produced trittyes that were geographically unnatural. This use of natural limits had one immediate result: three trittyes were created that were unequal in area. Anaphlystos is larger than [Lamptrai], and [Lamptrai] is larger than [Aixone]. Since all three trittyes were coastal and shared a similar topography and economy, it can be assumed, other things being equal, that the one with the greatest area of cultivable land—Anaphlystos—supported the greatest number of people, the one with the smallest area—[Aixone]—the smallest number.

This study of the boundaries of three trittyes makes it possible to draw these two important conclusions: these three trittyes had boundaries that followed natural limits; they differed so much in size that we must assume they differed also in population. The latter difference is really an inevitable result of the former: nature has not divided Attika into units either equal in area or equal in population.

It is beyond the scope of this study to prove whether or not similar conclusions hold true for the remaining seventeen coastal and inland trittyes. We can, however, take the findings obtained by Gomme[3] and Kirsten[4] and on this evidence determine the boundaries of the coastal and inland trittyes. The results are shown on Figure 9. In many cases, too many to be explained by coincidence, the probable political boundary corresponds to geographical limits. On the other hand, there are a few trittyes with limits established where no natural boundaries existed; these trittyes are in the large plains where the areas contained by natural boundaries were too large for inclusion in single trittyes.

[3] *Population* 56–65 and map (endpiece).

[4] Kirsten's work is in two places: Philippson, *Attika und Megaris* 986–988 and 1065–1068; and "Der gegenwärtige Stand der attischen Demenforschung," 168–171 and Pl. 26. The latter depends heavily on the earlier study. The plate noted in the second study is very like my Figure 9. Unfortunately it is on so small a scale that I cannot benefit from it. I have not always followed identifications made by Kirsten. From my own studies I know that some of them are wrong and that some are doubtful. Figure 9 is therefore a cautious representation of current opinion based on Gomme and Kirsten but incorporating minor corrections of them

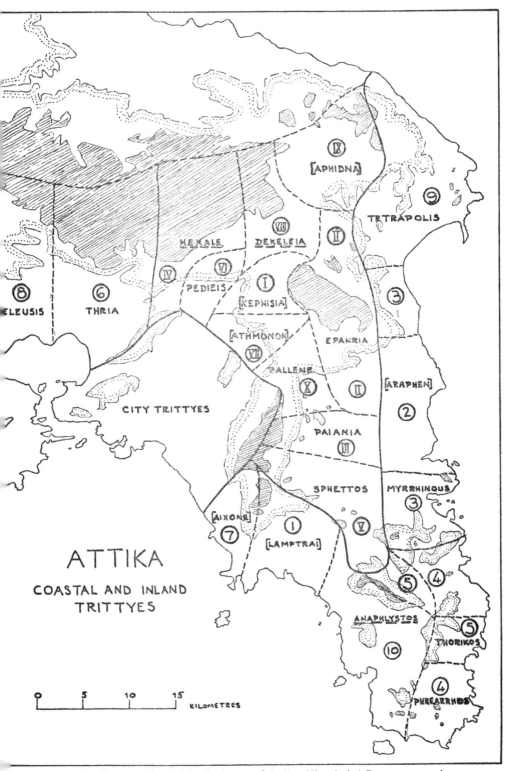

FIGURE 9. The coastal and inland trittyes of Attika. The circled Roman numerals indicate the tribal affiliations of the inland trittyes, the circled Arabic numerals the tribal affiliations of the coastal trittyes.

From an examination of the generally accepted boundaries of the trittyes not studied in this book, it seems fair to conclude that most of the remaining coastal and inland trittyes were natural units with easily defined and easily understood boundaries; that where obvious boundaries existed they were used; but that occasionally nature's boundaries were not sufficient and in these circumstances limits were drawn with little relation to topographical features.

We can also see from Figure 9 that disparity in size is not just an isolated feature of the three trittyes studied above, but is part of the Kleisthenic system of trittyes. It is true that a difference in size need not always denote a corresponding difference in population, especially when we compare trittyes that are physically dissimilar, yet there are sufficient differences in size between trittyes of similar character to force us to assume that the trittyes supported populations of varying sizes.

Thus, on the evidence of Gomme and Kirsten, the conclusions we have reached about three coastal trittyes would appear to hold true for the remaining seventeen coastal and inland trittyes. Yet two factors must always be kept in mind: our study concerns only three trittyes and, however detailed, is insufficient to determine the general characteristics of twenty; the studies of Gomme and Kirsten depend frequently upon the findings of earlier scholars, who were themselves sometimes in error. It must be admitted, therefore, that these conclusions are unproved and will remain so until more trittyes have been thoroughly studied and their borders accurately located.

But even tentative conclusions are of importance when they concern a subject as little understood as that of the Kleisthenic trittyes. The following quotations from the works of two well-known scholars illustrate typical misconceptions: N. G. L. Hammond writes, "Cleisthenes then grouped the demes within each region into ten 'trittyes' in such a way that the demes of a single trittys were for the most part not contiguous one with another";[5] and E. M. Walker claims, "A system more artificial than the tribes and trittyes of Cleisthenes it might well pass the wit of man to devise."[6] And yet it is clear from the studies of Milchhöfer and Löper that the demes making up each trittys were for the most part contiguous,[7] and it now seems a just conclusion from this study that the trittyes of the coast and interior were not artificial but natural units. And if natural, then many (perhaps

[5]*History of Greece* 189.
[6]*CAH* 4 (1926) 143.
[7]See above, chap. v, pp. 47 and 49 for a discussion of this point.

all) of the twenty coastal and inland trittyes were unequal in size and almost certainly unequal in population. This inequality would render impossible the normal interpretation of Aristotle's description of the distribution of the trittyes among the ten tribes. In *Ath. Pol.* 21.4, after noting the creation of thirty trittyes, ten from the city, ten from the coast, and ten from the interior, Aristotle concludes by saying: ἐκλήρωσεν τρεῖς [τριττῦς] εἰς τὴν φυλὴν ἑκάστην ὅπως ἑκάστη μετέχῃ πάντων τῶν τόπων.

The simplest method of using the lot as a means of establishing the tribal groupings would have been to place the names of the ten city trittyes in one container, the names of the ten coastal trittyes in a second, and the names of the ten inland trittyes in a third. Then some appointed person would have drawn a name from each of the three containers and the three trittyes chosen would have constituted a phyle. This operation would have been repeated until all ten phylai had been formed.

Such a simple system would have achieved the results that Kleisthenes envisaged only if either all the thirty trittyes were equal in population or if the ten trittyes in each of the three divisions of the city, coast, and interior were equal, for undoubtedly he had in mind the formation of ten phylai each of which would contain approximately one-tenth of the total number of citizens. Although there is no direct proof of practical equality in the number of citizens contained in each phyle, this assumption must be considered highly probable because any radical inequality would have undermined the basis of too many institutions in the state that were organized around ten approximately equal phylai.[8] The use of the lot, then, entailing an accidental arrangement of trittyes to form ten equal phylai, would have been impossible unless the ten trittyes in each of the three divisions were equal.

Since we have already concluded that the trittyes were of different sizes, the system of distribution outlined above would not have achieved the results that Kleisthenes wanted. If the lot had been employed without any checks, the draw might have combined three large trittyes, thus constituting a phyle much larger than many others, or three small trittyes, thus forming a phyle small in comparison with other phylai. Since Kleisthenes intended the ten phylai to be as nearly as possible equal, to secure such a result he might have had to tamper with the lot. It is therefore probable that the lot was not employed at this stage.

[8]Cf. Gomme, *Population* 49; Hignett, *History of the Athenian Constitution* 137–138; and Larsen, *Representative Government* 5.

Since the basic problem is how to distribute unequal trittyes to form equal phylai, we must first consider the differences in the trittyes. Some idea can be obtained from the prytany and bouleutic lists of the fourth and third centuries B.C., from which we can calculate the number of representatives sent by each deme to the Council of 500. Since it is assumed that the representation of a deme in the Boule was related to its population,[9] by adding up the number of representatives sent by the demes making up the individual trittyes we can establish a figure for each trittys that is related to its population. Even though the figures will have been drawn from documents of the fourth and third centuries B.C., this does not mean that they cannot tell us something about conditions at the close of the sixth century B.C. Since Kleisthenes made membership in a deme hereditary, the population of each deme was little affected by movement within Attika either to or from each deme. Because the figures for representation remain practically unaltered during the fourth and third centuries B.C. despite opportunities to make changes and reasons for so doing, it has been suggested that the figures had become traditional by the beginning of the fourth century B.C., and that their origin should be dated to the time of Kleisthenes.[10] It is impossible with the evidence at our disposal to prove or disprove this suggestion. Nevertheless, since this study has argued that the trittyes were natural units and therefore probably unequal in population from the time of their creation at the close of the sixth century B.C., the figures from the fourth and third centuries B.C. may be used (with the caution that the numbers of councillors from individual demes may not be exactly those of the sixth century B.C.) to form some general conclusions about the relative population of trittyes at the time of Kleisthenes, and how ten phylai could have been constituted from such unequal units.

From these lists it is clear that, of the thirty trittyes, ten were represented by either 16 or 17 members in their respective prytanies, two by 18 members, and one by a minimum of 15. In the remainder, there were a group of larger trittyes represented by between 20 and 25 members each, a group of smaller trittyes represented by between 9 and 13 members each, and one trittys represented by 27 members.[11]

[9]Larsen, *Representative Government* 5–9, and the authorities quoted there (192 n. 9).
[10]*Ibid.* 8–9.
[11]The figures are taken from two sources: Gomme, *Population* 56–65, and Carroll, "Representation in the Athenian Boule of Five Hundred." I have used Carroll's figures for the tribes where Gomme gives none and for Antiochis where Gomme wrongly assigns three demes.

Assuming that no important distinctions of size were made between trittyes with representations differing by only a few members, for example between one trittys represented by 9 members and another by 13, we can see at once that there were in fact only four definite sizes, which can be described as extra-large, large, medium, and small. A grading of the trittyes in this way would have made their distribution to form ten equal phylai a relatively simple matter, but not through use of the lot. The one extra-large trittys could have been combined with two small trittyes from the appropriate parts of Attika, the large trittyes combined with one medium and one small trittys apiece, and the remaining medium trittyes combined in threes. The resulting ten phylai would have been approximately equal, thus fulfilling Kleisthenes' needs. Although more work needs to be done on the bouleutic and prytany lists, enough is known and accepted to justify the very general table that follows.

Phyle	I	II	III	IV	V	VI	VII	VIII	IX	X
City	M	S	S	M	M	M	S	M	S	S
Coast	L	M	L	M	M	S	M	L	L	EL
Interior	S	L	M	M	M	L	L	S	M	S

Whatever the precise steps that Kleisthenes took to establish the ten phylai, one step must have been taken first. It is impossible to imagine the establishment of demes, trittyes, and phylai without a complete survey of Attika, both cadastral and censual, for it is only on such a basis that Kleisthenes could have divided Attika into natural units and then combined them to form ten approximately equal phylai. Next, he would have had to determine the trittyes, then grade them according to size, and finally set out the possible combinations that would result in equal phylai. Obviously, we cannot maintain that he graded the trittyes according to the scheme presented above. But I do insist that some such scheme was used[12] and that the trittyes, once graded, were arranged to form phylai not by accident but by design.

There is, I believe, other evidence to show this careful design. Figure 9 makes it clear that in each of the phylai Aigeis (II), Akamantis (V), and Aiantis (IX) the coastal trittys was partly contiguous to

[12]Kleisthenes was certainly not expecting to create ten exactly equal phylai, and so we do him no disservice by suggesting that he approximated the sizes of the trittyes. We merely assume that he did what would be natural to anyone creating political units based on population.

the inland trittys. Of the other seven coastal trittyes, two (IV and VIII) had no real contact with any inland trittys, while three (I, VII, and X) were in contact only with the inland trittys of phyle V, which however already had a common border with the coastal trittys of the same phyle. These five trittyes, then, could never have shared borders with the inland trittyes of the same phylai. This leaves two coastal trittyes, Myrrhinous and Thria. The former was very near the inland trittys of the same phyle but did not, I think, share a border with it; the latter, where it came in contact with an inland trittys, seems to have shared a border with a trittys from a different phyle. Of the five coastal trittyes that could possibly have shared a border with the inland trittys of the same phyle, three certainly did so, in each case forming a large continuous area of land belonging to one phyle. The occurrence of such contiguity in three out of five cases is not in my opinion accidental but shows that Kleisthenes preferred to have the coastal and inland trittyes contiguous within a phyle where it was topographically possible and where these combinations did not run contrary to the creation of ten approximately equal phylai.[13]

On Figure 9 one can also see that two of the coastal trittyes— Tetrapolis and Myrrhinous—were divided, that is, not made up of contiguous demes. The trittys of Tetrapolis was composed of four demes, the most northerly of which was Rhamnous. A more ancient grouping also called the Tetrapolis had included Probalinthos but not Rhamnous. Why then was Probalinthos placed in the trittys of Myrrhinous? I think the answer lies in the size of trittys that would have been formed had Probalinthos been admitted to the trittys that contained Marathon, Oinoe, Trikorynthos, and, there being no other coastal trittys to which it could belong, Rhamnous. Without Probalinthos, this trittys was large; with Probalinthos, it would have been larger than the extra-large trittys of Anaphlystos. Had Probalinthos been grouped with the demes immediately to the south, then [Araphen], which would have become a large trittys with this addition, could not have been combined with Epakria, also large, and we have already seen that Kleisthenes wanted coastal and inland trittyes of the same phyle to be contiguous where possible.[14] So Probalinthos was

[13]Bradeen ("The Trittyes," 28) had noted some of these instances of a common border between the coastal and inland trittyes of the same phyle. However, he ascribed this occurrence to chance.

[14]Some may feel that a better method of determining the affiliation of Probalinthos might have been to give it up to [Araphen] and, in order to balance this addition, to redraw the boundary between [Araphen] and Myrrhinous so that some (or all) of the demes in the southern end of [Araphen] might have been included in Myrrhinous. Such a distribution would have ensured that the inland and coastal trittyes of phyle

placed with the demes forming the trittys of Myrrhinous, the nearest trittys it could join without seriously disrupting the system imposed by Kleisthenes.[15]

In southeastern Attika, where the Kleisthenic arrangement seems to have produced enclaves in the two trittyes of Phrearrhos and Thorikos, nature divided this area into two groups of demes that would have formed a smallish small trittys and a largish large trittys. The groupings established by Kleisthenes, however, made two medium trittyes. I conclude that, in order to balance other trittyes that could not be changed, Kleisthenes needed more medium trittyes than were provided by nature, and that in this corner of Attika he found a way of creating them without too violent a dislocation of natural limits.

The evidence that the trittyes were grouped together by careful design and not by accident to form the phylai seems to me overwhelming, even after we admit that the basis of the theory—the inequality of the trittyes in population—is a matter of inference rather than demonstration. Precisely how Kleisthenes went about organizing the trittyes and phylai we do not know. Of one thing, however, we can be sure: he did not use the lot. Aristotle was wrong in saying that Kleisthenes "assigned by lot three trittyes to each phyle," the obvious meaning of the received text.[16]

In a recent article on Attika, R. Sealey finds it difficult to accept the

---

III, Paiania and Myrrhinous, had a common border for some distance. But it would have also added to Myrrhinous demes geographically quite divorced from it. The consideration that the boundary between [Araphen] and Myrrhinous be drawn along the line of a range of hills that runs eastwards from south of Kato Vraona and meets the sea on the southern side of the bay of Vraona was obviously felt to be of greater importance than the placing of Probalinthos in one of its two neighbouring coastal trittyes.

[15]It might be argued that Kleisthenes had no such thoughts when he broke up the old organization of the Tetrapolis but merely wanted to weaken its traditional influence. While I do not think we should deny that he may have been pleased with this result, indeed wanted it, we must not overlook the fact that the position of Rhamnous and the size of the old Tetrapolis made a division necessary. There is no discredit to the thesis that Kleisthenes arranged Attika according to certain overriding principles in showing that at the same time he achieved some personal ends of a political nature. Something similar may have affected the assigning of trittyes to the phyle Antiochis. If the Alkmaionidai at one time possessed influence in Aigilia and still retained that influence, though not necessarily residence, at the close of the sixth century B.C. (see p. 74, n. 21), is it fortuitous that Alopeke formed the city trittys of the phyle Antiochis, while the coastal trittys of the same phyle contained Aigilia? Was Kleisthenes trying to gain for the Alkmaionidai control of one of the ten new phylai? I owe this point to discussion with W. G. Forrest and to his article "Themistokles and Argos," 234.

[16]Some may feel that my statement that "Aristotle was wrong" is regrettably

traditional chronology of Kleisthenes' reforms; he advocates dating
the reforms to 502/1 B.C. and their coming into force at the beginning
of 501/0 B.C.[17] Apart from any other consideration, Sealey, by allowing
less than one year, perhaps no more than six months, for the work
involved in establishing ten new phylai with their trittyes and demes
—a necessary prelude to the Council of 500—has shown little realiza-
tion of the magnitude of the task that Kleisthenes accomplished.
Indeed, I am far from convinced that those who place Alkmaion's
archonship in 507/6 B.C., and who thus allow a period of less than two
years for this rearrangement, have left sufficient time.[18] Perhaps this

---

final. But the alternatives do not encourage the adoption of another point of view.
We should have to assume one of two things. Either we have misinterpreted his words,
which were somehow intended to describe the assignment by lot of the names of the
ten tribal heroes to the ten groups of three trittyes each—an act that would have
marked the formal creation of the ten phylai—or we have inherited a defective text.
But any interpretation of this passage other than the obvious one strains the meaning
of the Greek, and there is nothing to suggest textual corruption. It is better to convict
Aristotle of a mistake than to defend him on such flimsy grounds: the *Ath. Pol.*
is not free of errors.

[17]"Regionalism," 175–177. Sealey does not actually say the beginning of 501/0
B.C., but it is a reasonable assumption that the oath was administered at the opening
of the conciliar year.

[18]It is of course extremely difficult to judge the length of time needed for such an
undertaking. While it was to Kleisthenes' advantage to get the reforms carried out as
quickly as possible, it was also to his advantage to get the job done well. And to do
it well he needed a great deal of information. We should remember, however, that
Kleisthenes may have been able to use earlier surveys. The administration of
Peisistratos' tithe on produce (Aristotle, *Ath. Pol.* 16.4) must have demanded
extensive knowledge of rural conditions throughout the whole of Attika, perhaps
even a cadastral survey. The revision of the citizen rolls after the expulsion of Hippias
(*ibid.* 13.5), if carried out methodically, may have been the equivalent of a censual
survey. If Kleisthenes merely had to bring these surveys up to date and adapt them
for his purposes, then his task was much lighter than if he had had to institute
surveys and await the collection of the needed information.

The only possible indications of absolute time that we have are as follows. The ten
new phylai came into being in the archonship of Alkmaion (the normal interpretation
of Pollux 8.110), but unfortunately this archonship cannot be associated with any
particular year. Alkmaion might have been archon in 507/6, 506/5, 505/4, 503/2,
or 502/1 B.C. Aristotle (*ibid.* 22.2), as generally understood, places in the year 501/0
B.C. the first oath taken by the Council of 500 and the first board of ten generals
elected by the phylai (for the most recent discussion of the chronological problems
involved in this passage, see Sumner, "Chronological Problems," 35–37). Is it a
coincidence that both these events took place for the first time in 501/0 B.C. and that
both depended on the creation of the ten phylai, the former indirectly, the latter
directly? Should we assume that the oath was administered at the first opportunity,
that is, at the first meeting of the new council, and that the board of ten generals

conclusion to a study of certain demes gives some idea of the complex problems that Kleisthenes faced when he chose to form ten equal phylai on the basis of natural units, and suggests some of the means he may have used to solve them. It should leave little doubt that much time was needed for such a careful and extensive reorganization of the fundamental political framework, a reorganization in no way entrusted to the lot but skilfully designed by the mind of Kleisthenes.

---

was first constituted in this way as soon as the ten new phylai had replaced the old four? If so, we should place Alkmaion's archonship in 502/1 B.C. and in the same year the actual establishment of the ten new phylai. It would then follow that at the beginning of the following year, 501/0 B.C., the new council entered office for the first time and the first board of ten generals elected by the phylai assumed its duties. In this reconstruction the reforms of Kleisthenes concerning the formation of demes, trittyes, and phylai take about six years to put into effect. Some may argue that six years is too long for the operation, that the new council met for some years without an oath, and that the board of ten generals was chosen by another method for some time after the new phylai had been formed. And I acknowledge the length of time to be a valid objection especially if Kleisthenes inherited much detailed information about Attika collected during the tyranny and immediately after the expulsion of Hippias. But Kleisthenes may not have found this body of prepared material. Moreover, there would still be no answer to the question of why the Athenians should suddenly introduce two new features into their constitution in the same year, 501/0 B.C., both of which demand the existence of the ten new phylai.

APPENDIX TO CHAPTER XII

THE NAMES OF THE THIRTY KLEISTHENIC TRITTYES

The names of the thirty Kleisthenic trittyes have not been preserved in extant literary sources, although some believe that Aphidna is an exception.[1] Epigraphic material, however, supplies many names but these are sometimes incomplete and therefore need supplements, not all of which are self-evident.

The evidence for the names has been assembled by H. Hommel and

---

[1]The evidence for Aphidna is discussed below. For what it is worth, I draw attention to an entry in the *Lexica Segueriana* (259, s.v. Ἐπακρία): ὄνομα χώρας πλησίον τετραπόλεως κειμένης. Are these references to the trittyes of Epakria and Tetrapolis, which marched together for some distance?

published in two articles, the first in 1939, the second in 1940.[2] His conclusions are not the same in both because more information was available when he wrote the second article, and because he used different methods of establishing the names of those trittyes for which there was no evidence from antiquity. Since 1940 there has been a small increase in the amount of evidence.

There can be no doubt about most of the names of trittyes that are preserved on stone. The following names are firmly established: *city*—Skambonidai[3] IV, Cholargos[4] V, Lakiadai[5] VI, Peiraieus[6] VIII, Alopeke[7] X; *coastal*—Myrrhinous[8] III, Phrearrhioi[9] IV, Thorikos[10] V, Thria[11] VI, Eleusis[12] VIII, Tetrapolis[13] IX; *inland*—Epakria[14] II, Paiania[15] III, Sphettos[16] V, Pedieis[17] VI, Pallene[18] X. Less certain are Dekeleia[19] (inland) VIII, and Kydathenaion[20] (city) III; indeed, the

[2]*RE* 7 (1939–1948) 330–370, s.v. Trittyes; and "Die dreissig Trittyen."

[3]Meritt, "Greek Inscriptions" (1961) 265: No. 82.

[4]*IG* I[2] 900.

[5]*IG* I[2] 884.

[6]*IG* I[2] 897. The trittys Peiraieus has also been restored in *IG* I[2] 885, but since we know that another trittys had a name beginning with Pe—Pedieis—the restoration is not necessarily correct.

[7]Meritt, "Greek Inscriptions" (1961) 264: No. 81.

[8]*IG* I[2] 898.

[9]Meritt, "Greek Inscriptions" (1940) 54: No. 2.

[10]Meritt, "Greek Inscriptions (14–27)" (1939) 50–51: No. 16.

[11]*IG* I[2] 899.

[12]*IG* I[2] 897. The trittys Eleusis has also been restored in *IG* I[2] 885, but the restoration is entirely dependent upon the identification of the second trittys as Peiraieus, a matter which is not certain (see n. 6 above).

[13]*IG* I[2] 900.

[14]*IG* II[2] 2490. The trittys Epakria was at one time restored in *IG* I[2] 899, but Wade-Gery has proved this supplement incorrect (see n. 17 below).

[15]*IG* I[2] 898 and *IG* II[2] 1748.

[16]Meritt, "Greek Inscriptions" (1940) 53: No. 1.

[17]*IG* I[2] 899 as restored by Wade-Gery, "Horos," 884–886, and Meritt, "Greek Inscriptions" (1940) 55: No. 3. Gomme (*Commentary* 2.73) accepts Wade-Gery's supplement and is not troubled by any apparent contradiction between *pedion* and Acharnai in Thucydides 2.20.1.

[18]Meritt, "Greek Inscriptions" (1940) 55–56: No. 4.

[19]*IG* I[2] 901 as restored by Wade-Gery, "Horos," 886–887, where the inland trittys of Hippothontis is shown to begin with Tε or Zε and contains about nine letters. The obvious name for this trittys, were it not for the first letter, is Dekeleia, which would fit the available space. Hommel, in fact ("Die dreissig Trittyen," 185), accepts this as the trittys name and suggests as one possibility that a scribal error is involved. I too feel that the best, though obviously not the neatest, solution is to regard the T or Z as a mistake for Δ.

[20]*IG* II[2] 1748 (line 22), where only the initial K is preserved.

latter might conceivably be Kytheros[21] or a name beginning with K other than that of a deme.

In addition, we have the inscription *IG* I² 883 which reads according to Hiller and Meritt]αμέον [τρ]ιττύς.[22] Δι]ομέον, Ποτ]αμέον, and Κερ]αμέον have all been suggested.[23] The first supplement is clearly inadmissible. Not only is the form unexpected,[24] but, more important, the restoration demands an omicron where the stone has an alpha. The second suggestion is equally impossible. Meritt[25] has already pointed out that its form is inappropriate, but this alone would not rule it out as a possibility. The real objection is that we know for certain that the Potamioi demes did not provide the name of the city trittys of the phyle Leontis because that trittys was called Skambonidai. Furthermore, it is no help to argue that the Potamioi demes were coastal, not city, since the coastal trittys of Leontis was Phrearrhioi.[26] The third possibility is epigraphically sound and, if one is going to apply the name of a deme to the trittys, the only remaining candidate. But the supplement leads to a great difficulty. The city trittys of Akamantis, which included the deme Kerameis, is clearly recorded on another stone (*IG* I² 900) as Cholargos, and it is hard to believe that either there were four trittyes in this one phyle or that the city trittys was known by two names, whether or not contemporaneously.[27] In my

[21]It has not been firmly established whether Kytheros was a city or inland deme. Gomme (*Population* 51 n. 2) favours the former, Pritchett (*Five Attic Tribes* 7 with reference to Solders) the latter.

[22]Meritt, "Greek Inscriptions" (1940) 53–54.

[23]Hommel (*RE* 7 [1939–1948] 366–370, s.v. Trittyes) suggested the first two, and it was Szanto who first proposed the third ("Die kleisthenischen Trittyen," 314).

[24]The name of the deme is Διόμεια and one would not expect the second iota to drop out, especially as the demotic was normally Διομειεύς.

[25]"Greek Inscriptions" (1940) 54.

[26]Gomme (*Population* 59) feels that all the Potamioi demes should be placed in one trittys and it must be admitted that they all appear under a single heading in a recently published bouleutic list (Charitonides, "First Half of a Bouleutai List," 36). Nevertheless, one should note Pausanias 1.31.3: Ἴωνος δὲ τοῦ Ξούθου . . . τάφος ἐν Ποταμοῖς ἐστι τῆς χώρας. Pausanias' addition of the information τῆς χώρας (one would naturally presume from the demes he mentions that they are in the country, not the city) has little meaning unless there was a Potamioi deme that was *not* τῆς χώρας.

[27]Raubitschek ("Gates," 281 n. 4), unless I infer too much from what he writes, believes that about the middle of the fifth century B.C. the name of the city trittys of Akamantis was changed from Cholargos to Kerameis. Does he think that the problem of *IG* I² 901 can be answered in a similar way—that the name of the trittys of Hippothontis beginning Τε or Ζε was an earlier name for either the city or the coastal trittys later known as Peiraieus or Eleusis? I do not consider that such a

opinion the dilemma occasioned by this restoration is insoluble and until such time as we have evidence to the contrary we should consider the supplement impossible, especially as it is not mandatory for a trittys to bear the name of a deme. Of the eighteen names that are reasonably certain, three—Tetrapolis, Epakria, and Pedieis—are not connected with demes, and there is nothing to guarantee that other names in the same category were not used. We should therefore assign this broken name to one of the trittyes that would otherwise remain nameless.

Two other inscriptions should be noted, Agora I 5564 and Agora I 2197. In both cases the name of one of the two trittyes recorded has entirely disappeared, leaving only an indication of its length (in the genitive case). Agora I 5564, published by Meritt,[28] named two trittyes of the phyle Leontis, the second of which is Phrearrhioi. With regard to the name of the first, from the stone we know that it contained about six letters (or seven if the final epsilon of δεῦρε was elided[29]). That it is the name of the inland trittys and not the city is proved by the recent discovery that the city trittys of Leontis was Skambonidai, a name far too long to fit the available space.[30]

In his first article Hommel very tentatively proposed the name Kropia for this trittys, but in his second he changed to Eupyridai. The latter has too many letters for the space on the stone, and the former has a minimum of seven, perhaps more if the name of the trittys was derived from Kropidai.[31] Neither name makes a satisfactory supplement. Two other deme names are possible: Hybadai (if we can be certain that it was an inland deme) and Hekale. The genitive of the former has six letters and would fill the space admirably. The genitive

drastic solution, defying as it does the traditional conservatism of the Athenians in matters such as nomenclature, is justified by the facts. It has never been established that at any time the city trittys of Akamantis was called Kerameis. All we know is that one (theoretically) possible restoration of this inscription involves the word Kerameis, assuming the alpha to be correctly inscribed. Hommel in fact ("Die dreissig Trittyen," 183–184) brings forward the possibility of an error in the inscribing. Only when we can say with much more certainty than at present what name was supposed to have been inscribed can we decide whether or not an error was made.

[28]"Greek Inscriptions" (1940) 54: No. 2, and (1961) 265 under No. 82.

[29]Cf. IG I² 897, 899.

[30]The order of the trittyes, inland followed by coastal, is the normal one for these inscriptions according to Raubitschek, "Gates," 280–281 n. 4. But see n. 36 below.

[31]A derivation from the name Kropidai would be more normal since it seems to have been the official name of the deme. The name Kropia is used, however, by Thucydides (2.19.2) but it may represent a distinction between the village itself and the area administered by the village (see Gomme, *Commentary* 2.71).

of the latter has seven or eight letters depending upon the spelling,[32] and the shorter form would satisfy all epigraphic requirements if elision were introduced to make lines of equal length.[33] Given these alternatives, but remembering that the name of a non-deme is always a possibility, I should choose Hekale as the name of the inland trittys of Leontis. Hybadai has the disadvantage of being almost unknown (and perhaps not even a part of the inland trittys), whereas Hekale, although small, was well known on account of the legend of Theseus and boasted a rural cult in honour of the heroine Hekale, a rite attended by people from the surrounding demes.[34] Since the worship of Hekale was an activity common to those who lived at and near the deme of Hekale, it would be a most suitable name for a trittys which included demes whose members participated in the Hekalesia.

The second inscription is Agora I 2197, also published by Meritt, which records the names of two of the trittyes of the phyle Antiochis, the second of which is the inland trittys Pallene.[35] Nothing of the first name is preserved but Meritt says that the name "contained approximately ten letters." The inscription is non-stoichedon and "ten letters" probably represents a minimum. Thus the supplement Ἀλοπεκέον, the name of the city trittys, is very doubtful. It is likely then that we are dealing with the name of the coastal trittys. Meritt points out that Ἀναφλυστίον "may plausibly be restored." With his judgment I agree and merely add that Anaphlystos is a most suitable name for a trittys in which the deme of Anaphlystos was the largest of the six demes making up the trittys.[36]

To sum up the epigraphic data: we have firm evidence for sixteen names, less certain for two others, and we know that one name in the genitive ended with]αμέον. To these we may add my suggestion of Hekale and Meritt's of Anaphlystos, thus making a total of twenty-one names.

We must now turn to the name Aphidna and consider the literary

[32]The following adjectival forms exist: Ἑκάλιος, Ἑκάλειος, Ἑκαλεύς, Ἑκαλειεύς.
[33]This point cannot be pushed too far since the inscription is non-stoichedon and irregularities in the length of line and in the spacing are not uncommon features of this category of inscription.
[34]Plutarch, Theseus 14.2: ἔθυον γὰρ Ἑκαλήσια οἱ πέρι δῆμοι συνιόντες Ἑκάλῳ Διί, καὶ τὴν Ἑκάλην ἐτίμων. . . .
[35]"Greek Inscriptions" (1940) 55–56: No. 4, and (1961) 264 under No. 81.
[36]That it violates the rule of thumb that the order of the trittyes was city, inland, coastal, is of no consequence. There are now enough known exceptions to make one question the usefulness of assuming a "normal order" (see Raubitschek, "Gates," 280–281 n. 4).

evidence that some believe proves it to be the name of a trittys. Hesychios (s.v. Περρίδαι) records that Perrhidai was τῆς Ἀττικῆς δῆμος ἐν Ἀφίδναις. That Perrhidai was a deme in the constitutional sense appears clear from Harpokration (s.v. Θυργωνίδαι) and Stephanos (s.v. Περρίδαι) where the deme is given a tribal assignment. Epigraphic evidence for the existence of Perrhidai is inconclusive.[37] Since a Kleisthenic deme can hardly be said to be within another deme, the argument runs that in this case Aphidna cannot be the name of a deme and must therefore represent the next larger unit, a trittys.[38] F. Jacoby was not entirely convinced by this argument: "I do not feel able to acknowledge Aphidna as having documentary evidence, though this explanation by Kirchner . . . seems probable enough."[39]

Jacoby's doubts seem to me justified. Not only are our suspicions roused by this unique appearance of a trittys name in an extant literary text, but we know that in the fourth century B.C. there were communities (or districts) within the deme of Aphidna that later became demes in their own right. Two inscriptions list properties located Ἀφίδνησι ἐν Πεταλιδῶν or Ἀφιδ ἐν Πεταλίδωι and one records several Ἀφιδ (or Ἀφιδν) ἐν Ὑπωρείαι.[40] From the rest of both inscriptions it is abundantly clear that the properties are located with reference to

---

[37]As far as I know, there are only two inscriptions that possibly carry the name Perrhidai. Dow (*Prytaneis* 36–38 and particularly 38–39 n. 2) suggests that Athenian Agora I 2553, line 11, can be restored with the deme heading Περρεῖδαι; and it appears thus in his formal text with the initial letter misleadingly aligned with the left margin of the column and merely dotted even though the "snick" presumably justifying the dot is not well placed for part of a letter and could be incidental to the inscription. Indeed, it is a very unsatisfactory supplement for other reasons: Dow has shown that this inscription is a prytany list probably of the phyle Oineis; yet Perrhidai is usually associated with Aiantis on the good evidence of Nikandros (Harpokration, s.v. Θυργωνίδαι) and later with Ptolemais. Stephanos says that Perrhidai belonged to Antiochis (s.v. Περρίδαι), but his assignments are not always trustworthy (see also Pritchett, review of S. Dow, *Prytaneis* in *AJP* 60 (1939) 258–259). Dow under-estimates the difficulties inherent in his supplement, especially when he writes: "This solution, which involves an irregularity by the mason, seems preferable." Perhaps we should assume an even greater measure of irregularity by the mason and try to restore a deme of Oineis. The second inscription is *IG* II² 2362, a catalogue of Attic demes, where Perrhidai is usually restored in line 52. Pritchett, however, rightly points out that the restoration is not mandatory ("An Unfinished Inscription," 166).

[38]See Kirchner's commentary on *IG* II² 5719.

[39]*FGrH* 3b Supplement (Leiden 1954) 2.291 n. 20.

[40]For Petalidai see Meritt, "Greek Inscriptions" (1936) 393–413: No. 10, line 155, and *IG* II² 1594, lines 46 and 48. For Hyporeia see *IG* II² 1594, lines 29, 31 (?), 33, 35, 37, and 39.

demes, not to trittyes.[41] In the fourth century B.C. Petalidai and Hyporeia were recognizable parts of the deme of Aphidna. Later both were demes in the phyle Ptolemais, which also included the deme of Aphidna. This change in their status may well have taken place at the close of the third century B.C. when Ptolemais was created.[42]

I feel that Perrhidai had the same type of history, and that Hesychios' entry, quite unlike his almost formulaic statements about other demes, has somehow preserved the fact that Perrhidai, even though a deme,[43] was once part of the deme of Aphidna, like Petalidai and Hyporeia. But there is a difference. Perrhidai existed as a deme before the creation of Ptolemais, because Harpokration (s.v. Θυργωνίδαι) says that it was transferred to Ptolemais from Aiantis along with the demes Aphidna, Titakidai, and Thyrgonidai. We should perhaps date the formation of Perrhidai as a deme (as well as Titakidai and Thyrgonidai?) to 307/6 B.C., when the Athenians added two new phylai—Antigonis and Demetrias. We know that at that time some new demes were created for these new phylai by dividing already existing ones: however, in these cases the new demes bore the same names as the demes from which they were detached. I suggest that the same process took place in the deme of Aphidna, but that since the new demes were not assigned to the new phylai but remained in Aiantis along with Aphidna they took different names.

These considerations are sufficient, I believe, to deny the existence of evidence proving that Aphidna was the name of a trittys. However, this conclusion should not be misunderstood: Aphidna may yet be shown to be the name of a trittys, but at this moment we do not possess any evidence to claim that in fact it was.

The count, therefore, still stands at twenty-one names. For the remaining nine we have no evidence at all. Hommel tried to fill the gap, larger than nine in 1939, in various ways. He suggested that almost all the names of the Twelve Towns had been used for the twelve pre-Kleisthenic trittyes and that Kleisthenes had re-used most of them for his trittyes.[44] On the basis of this theory and of the list of the Twelve Towns recorded by Philochoros (*FGrH* 3b, 328 F 94), he proposed the following as names of trittyes: *city*—Phaleron IX (which he added as

[41]This does not seem to have been Meritt's view ("Greek Inscriptions" [1936] 406), but agrees with Pritchett's (*Five Attic Tribes* 26, particularly n. 54).

[42]Pritchett, *Five Attic Tribes* 26–27.

[43]It is, I think, impossible to assume that here Hesychios is using δῆμος in a non-Kleisthenic sense. Should one substitute τόπος for δῆμος (cf. Hesychios, s.v. Βραυρών)?

[44]Hommel, *RE* 7 (1939–1948) 338–339 and 366, s.v. Trittyes.

the twelfth name in Philochoros' list, which lacks one name[45]); *coastal*—Philaidai II (in earlier times called Brauron); *inland*— Kephisia I, Kropia IV (an emendation of the text, which reads Kekropia). In addition he proposed Thorikos V (coastal), Sphettos V (inland), and Dekeleia VIII (inland), all of which have since proved either correct or most probable. Had Hommel entertained my views about Aphidna, he would have added Aphidna as the name of the inland trittys of Aiantis because Aphidna is listed among the Twelve Towns. The only name in Philochoros' list that Hommel did not use (apart from Brauron, which he equated with Philaidai) is Kytheros. Here he argued that this name had become very insignificant by the time of Kleisthenes and was therefore dropped in favour of either Myrrhinous or Paiania.[46] In this earlier article he did not attempt to assign names to the several trittyes that remained nameless.[47]

In his later article, Hommel developed another method of establishing possible names. He noticed that, in the trittyes named after demes, the deme with the same name as the trittys was practically always the largest of the demes within the trittys. The one exception he admitted was Lakiadai, which appears from the figures drawn by Gomme from Kirchner's *Prosopographia Attica* to be slightly smaller than Oie.[48] This difference in size is also made clear by their respective bouleutic representations, which suggest, however, that the difference was not slight but considerable.[49] Despite this, Hommel formulated the theory that almost without exception in every trittys the largest deme (which he determined by the number of extant recorded members) provided the name of the trittys,[50] except of course in the cases of Epakria, Tetrapolis, and Pedieis, which were known to have names other than those of demes. The following names were proposed in addition to those already established, it being no difficult matter to name all thirty trittyes on this basis: *city*—Euonymon I, Kollytos II, Leukonoe IV, Melite VII, Phaleron IX (thus vindicating its earlier choice); *coastal*—Lamptrai I, Halai Araphenides II (instead of Philaidai or Brauron), Phrearrhioi IV (later proved correct), Aixone VII, Anaphlystos X (now accepted as very probable); *inland*—Kephisia I

[45]Jacoby, *FGrH* 3b Supplement 1.393 and 2.287–289, makes it clear that Phaleron is a most unlikely choice for Philochoros' twelfth name since it was part of the Tetrakomia.

[46]See n. 21 above.

[47]See the list in Hommel, *RE* 7 (1939–1948) 367, s.v. Trittyes.

[48]Gomme, *Population* 61.

[49]Oie sent six representatives, Lakiadai two or three.

[50]"Die dreissig Trittyen," 194–195.

(thus vindicating its earlier choice), Eupyridai[51] IV (instead of Kropia, a doubtful choice in the first place), Phlya VII.[52] Regarding Aphidna, since it was the largest, if not the only, deme in its trittys,[53] Hommel would have chosen it on the same basis for the name of the inland trittys of Aiantis (thus vindicating its choice on the basis of the Twelve Towns), had he doubted the value of the literary evidence for this name.

Neither of Hommel's methods of assigning names to otherwise unnamed trittyes is entirely satisfactory. The first system, the use of the names of the Twelve Towns, has been vigorously attacked by F. Jacoby,[54] who rightly objects to Hommel's premise that the twelve pre-Kleisthenic trittyes preserved the names of the Twelve Towns. What little evidence we have for the names of the former suggests that they were quite different.[55] Jacoby's major questions then follow naturally: does Philochoros' list have any real validity? does it present unimpeachable evidence for the names of the Twelve Towns? Jacoby's analysis of the evidence shows convincingly that very little reliance should be placed on the list, since it is most unlikely that it represents an unbroken tradition from pre-classical times to its author's; rather, "Philochoros (or whoever preceded him) selected twelve names from a greater number of well-known Attic places (there were really more than twelve) which for reasons no longer recognizable he considered to be the oldest and which in his opinion must have made up the territory of ancient Attica, whether or not he dealt with their extent and boundaries."[56]

Hommel's second method of assigning names is also open to criticism.

---

[51]*Ibid.* 196 n. 7; Hommel saw a difficulty concerning Eupyridai and Aithalidai, because he reported that Eupyridai sent five representatives to the Boule, Aithalidai seven. If this were so, then it would be hard to argue that Eupyridai was bigger than Aithalidai. But in fact both sent two representatives. Had Hommel used the bouleutic representations as an indication of relative size, he might have noted that Paionidai sent three representatives, a number which suggests that Paionidai might have been larger than either Eupyridai and Aithalidai.

[52]See the list *ibid.* 198–199.

[53]Aphidna was always the largest deme in its trittys until the end of the fourth century B.C. Certainly there is no evidence for the existence of Thyrgonidai and Titakidai before that date.

[54]*FGrH* 3b Supplement 1.393–396 and 2.290–293.

[55]Ferguson, "Athenian Law Code," 151–158.

[56]*FGrH* 3b Supplement 1.396. One might wonder whether Philochoros, somewhat in the manner of Hommel, picked out his Twelve Towns on the assumption, perhaps, that some of the names of the Kleisthenic trittyes preserved the names of the pre-Kleisthenic trittyes and so had a claim to great antiquity.

Not only did he have to admit at least one exception to his rule, but there are several others as well. More names of members of the deme of Kerameis are known than of Cholargos, yet Cholargos was the name of the trittys that contained both these demes.[57] Hommel's suggestion that the city and inland trittys of Leontis were named Leukonoe and Eupyridai has been proved wrong: the city trittys was Skambonidai, a deme about the same size as Leukonoe,[58] and the inland trittys had a name with fewer letters in it than Eupyridai.[59] I have proposed to call this inland trittys Hekale. Whether my proposal is right or wrong does not alter the fact that, if this trittys was named after a deme, it must, despite Hommel's argument, have been after a deme smaller than Eupyridai.[60] On the other hand, recently found evidence has proved the correctness of Hommel's choice of Alopeke, Phrearrhioi, and most likely of Anaphlystos. Nevertheless, the number of exceptions is too high for any confident application of the rule formulated by Hommel. And one must also remember that his rule does not admit of names of trittyes from sources other than deme names, whereas we know that at least three, probably four, such names existed.

We must conclude that there is no certain method of assigning names to trittyes for which no name is recorded. Only by finding the names inscribed on stone or mentioned in ancient literary texts yet to be discovered can we be confident that the correct names have been established. Some of Hommel's suggestions may in time be proved right: certainly in many cases the chief deme in a trittys did supply the name of that trittys. But there is no guarantee that this happened in the cases of the trittyes whose names are so far unknown: and there is always the chance that a trittys had a name that was not a deme name.

We should stop, therefore, with the names that are firmly or partly established and leave the rest to be determined by future discoveries.

[57]But see above, n. 27, for a consideration of the evidence for the existence of the trittys Kerameis.

[58]Indeed smaller if we were to accept that the number of names preserved for each is a certain indication of their relative size. But, more important, we should note that Leukonoe and Skambonidai both sent three representatives to the Boule, a suggestion that both were about the same size.

[59]See p. 150 above.

[60]In n. 51 above, I have pointed out that the evidence for the relative size of the demes of the inland trittys of Leontis does not conclusively establish Eupyridai as the largest. We can be certain, however, that it was bigger than the demes that sent only one bouleutic representative and probably bigger than some of those that sent two.

TABLE I
NAMES OF THE KLEISTHENIC TRITTYES*

PHYLE	I ERECHTHEIS	II AIGEIS	III PANDIONIS	IV LEONTIS	V AKAMANTIS
City trittys	?	?	*Kydathenaion*	**Skambonidai**	**Cholargos**
Coastal trittys	?	?	**Myrrhinous**	**Phrearrhos**	**Thorikos**
Inland trittys	Kephisia	Epakria	**Paiania**	*Hekale*	**Sphettos**

PHYLE	VI OINEIS	VII KEKROPIS	VIII HIPPOTHONTIS	IX AIANTIS	X ANTIOCHIS
City trittys	**Lakiadai**	Melite	**Peiraieus**	Phaleron	**Alopeke**
Coastal trittys	**Thria**	Aixone	**Eleusis**	**Tetrapolis**	*Anaphlystos*
Inland trittys	**Pedieis**	?	**Dekeleia**	Aphidna	**Pallene**

*To this list we must add one unassigned trittys with the name (in the genitive)]αμέον.

Yet, a number of Hommel's proposals for names of otherwise unnamed trittyes seem too reasonable to ignore, although I recognize that even these may be proved incorrect. I should include as good possibilities Melite,[61] Phaleron,[62] Aixone,[63] Kephisia,[64] and Aphidna,[65] assuming that Hommel would have proposed the last mentioned had he shared my scepticism of the literary evidence for its existence as a trittys name.

Table I shows the results of this investigation. The names in bold type are established, those in italic are probable and in each case there exists some pertinent epigraphic evidence, and those in roman are, I believe, reasonable guesses.

[61]Melite was one of the most important of the city demes and certainly would have been a natural choice for a trittys that took a deme name.

[62]Phaleron was the single deme in the city trittys of Aiantis. Had a deme name been chosen for the trittys, it could not have been other than Phaleron. We must remember, however, that Acharnai was the single deme in its trittys and that the trittys was named Pedieis. Hommel, "Die dreissig Trittyen," 189–192 and 196–197, tried to find proof for the trittys name Phaleron (as well as several other trittys names) in the demotics carried by the tribal epimeletai, the suggestion being that these officers represented one of the three trittyes making up a phyle and that the demotic was actually a "trittytic." Hommel finally and rightly concluded that this thesis could not be maintained. Even so he did not ask the question how a differentiation could possibly be made between a demotic and trittytic in the case of a trittys made up of a single deme where both trittys and deme had the same name.

[63]Aixone and Halai Aixonides made up the coastal trittys of Kekropis. Again, if a deme name was chosen for the name of the trittys, the trittys could hardly be called anything else but Aixone.

[64]Kephisia as a trittys name would be a natural choice. Not only was it the name of the largest deme within the trittys, but it was also the name of the river that formed one of the boundaries of the trittys. And, though this point is perhaps of uncertain relevance, the name is clearly of great antiquity.

[65]Again, unless a name other than that of a deme was picked, the choice must have fallen on Aphidna.

BIBLIOGRAPHY

This bibliography is a list of the works to which I have referred, with the exception of the annual archaeological reports in *AA* and *BCH*, and of Pittakys' contributions to the early numbers of *ArchEph*. As far as I know, it omits nothing of significance for a study of the ten coastal demes from Aixone to Atene.

1. ANCIENT AUTHORS AND TEXTS CITED

AISCHINES. *Orationes*. Edited by F. BLASS after F. FRANK. Second edition. Leipzig 1908.

AISCHYLOS. *Tragoediae*. Edited by G. MURRAY. Second edition. Oxford 1955.

ANDROTION. *FGrH* 3b, No. 324. Edited by F. JACOBY. Leiden 1950.

ARISTOPHANES. Scholia to *Lysistrata*. *Comoediae*. Edited by G. Dindorf. Vol. 4, Part 3. Oxford 1838.

ARISTOTLE. *Atheniensium respublica*. Edited by F. G. KENYON. Oxford 1920.

ATHENAIOS. *The Deipnosophists*. Translated by C. B. GULICK. 7 vols. Loeb Classical Library. London and New York 1927–1933, London and Cambridge, Mass. 1937–1941.

DEMOSTHENES. *Orationes*. Edited by S. H. BUTCHER and W. RENNIE. 3 vols. Oxford 1903–1931.

Etymologicum Magnum. Edited by T. GAISFORD. Oxford 1848.

HARPOKRATION. *Harpokration et Moeris*. Edited by I. BEKKER. Berlin 1833.

HERODOTOS. *Historiae*. Edited by C. HUDE. Third edition. 2 vols. Oxford 1927.

HESYCHIOS. *Lexicon*. (1) Edited by K. LATTE. Vol. 1 (letters A–D). Copenhagen 1953. (2) Edited by M. SCHMIDT. Second edition. Jena 1867.

ISAIOS. *The Speeches of Isaeus*. Edited by W. WYSE. Cambridge 1904.

Lexica Segueriana. Edited by I. BEKKER in *Anecdota Graeca*. Vol. 1. Berlin 1814.

PAUSANIAS. *Graeciae descriptio.* Edited by F. SPIRO. 3 vols. Leipzig 1903.

PHILOCHOROS. *FGrH* 3b, No. 328. Edited by F. JACOBY. Leiden 1950.

PLUTARCH. *Vitae parallelae.* Edited by K. ZIEGLER. Vol. 1, Part 1. Leipzig 1957.

POLLUX. *Onomasticon.* Edited by E. BETHE. 3 parts. Leipzig 1900–1937.

PTOLEMY. *Geographia.* Edited by C. F. A. NOBBE. 3 vols. Leipzig 1843–1845.

SKYLAX. *Periplus.* Edited by C. MÜLLER in *Geographi Graeci Minores.* Vol. 1. Paris 1855.

STEPHANOS. *Ethnika.* Edited by A. MEINEKE. Berlin 1849, photographically republished at Graz 1958.

STRABO. *Geographica.* (1) Edited by G. KRAMER. 3 vols. Berlin 1847. (2) Edited by A. MEINEKE. 3 vols. Leipzig 1852–1853. (3) Translated by H. L. JONES. 8 vols. Loeb Classical Library. London and New York 1917–1932.

SUIDAS. *Lexicon.* Edited by A. Adler. 5 vols. Leipzig 1928–1938.

THEOKRITOS. *Theocritus.* Edited by A. S. F. Gow. 2 vols. Cambridge 1950.

―――― *Scholia in Theocritum vetera.* Edited by C. WENDEL. Leipzig 1914.

THUCYDIDES. *Historiae.* Edited by H. S. JONES and J. E. POWELL. Second edition. 2 vols. Oxford 1942.

XENOPHON. *Opera omnia.* Edited by E. C. MARCHANT. 5 vols. Oxford 1900–1920.

2. MODERN AUTHORS

ARDAILLON, E. *Les Mines du Laurion dans l'antiquité.* Paris 1897.

ARVANITOPOULOS, A. S. "'Ἀττικαὶ ἐπιγραφαί 14: 'Επίγραμμα 'κούρου,' πεσόντος ἐν πολέμῳ· τὰ κατὰ τόπους σήματα καὶ τὸ κοινὸν ἐν τῷ κεραμεικῷ δημόσιον σῆμα," *Polemon* 2 (1934–1938) 81–88.

BAEDEKER, K. *London and Its Environs.* Leipzig 1911.

BEAZLEY, SIR J. D. *Attic Black-Figure Vase-Painters.* Oxford 1956.

BERGK, T. "'Kritische Bemerkungen,' I Xenophon," *Zeitschrift für die Altertumswissenschaft* 12 (1854) 432.

BLÜMEL, C. *Staatliche Museen zu Berlin, Katalog der Sammlung antiker Skulpturen.* Vol. 2, Part 1: *Griechische Skulpturen des sechsten und fünften Jahrhunderts v. Chr.* Berlin 1940.

BÖCKH, A. *Corpus Inscriptionum Graecarum.* Vol. 1. Berlin 1828.

BRADEEN, D. W. "The Trittyes in Cleisthenes' Reforms," *TAPA* 86 (1955) 22–30.

BRADFORD, J. "Fieldwork on Aerial Discoveries in Attica and Rhodes. Part 2. Ancient Field Systems on Mt. Hymettos, near Athens," *Antiquaries Journal* 36 (1956) 172–180.

—— *Ancient Landscapes: Studies in Field Archaeology*. London 1957.

CARROLL, H. J. "Representation in the Athenian Boule of Five Hundred: A Summary of Results, November 1955." Unpublished manuscript.

CHANDLER, R. *Travels in Asia Minor, and Greece: or, An Account of a Tour Made at the Expense of the Society of Dilettanti*. Third edition. 2 vols. London 1817.

CHARITONIDES, S. "The First Half of a Bouleutai List of the Fourth Century B.C.," *Hesperia* 30 (1961) 30–57.

CHASE, G. "An Archaic Greek Sphinx in Boston," *AJA* 50 (1946) 1–5.

CONZE, A. *Die attischen Grabreliefs*. Vols. 1 and 2. Berlin 1893–1900.

CROSBY, M. "Greek Inscriptions: A Poletai Record of the Year 367/6 B.C.," *Hesperia* 10 (1941) 14–27.

—— "The Leases of the Laureion Mines," *ibid.* 19 (1950) 189–312.

—— "More Fragments of Mining Leases from the Athenian Agora," *ibid.* 26 (1957) 1–23.

CURTIUS, E. and KAUPERT, J. A. *Karten von Attika*. Berlin 1881–1900.

DAVIES, O. "The Ancient Mines of Laurium in Attica," *Man* 21 (1931) 6–7.

DAY, J. "Cape Colias Phalerum and the Phaleric Wall," *AJA* 36 (1932) 1–11.

DODWELL, E. *A Classical and Topographical Tour through Greece, During the Years 1801, 1805, and 1806*. 2 vols. London 1819.

DOW, S. *The American Excavations in the Athenian Agora, Hesperia Supplement 1: Prytaneis: A Study of the Inscriptions Honoring the Athenian Councillors*. Athens 1937.

DUPRÉ, L. *Voyages à Athènes et à Constantinople*. Paris 1825.

ELIOT, C. W. J. *See* Jones

ESPÉRANDIEU, E. "Renseignements inédits sur la collection du comte de Choiseul-Gouffier," *MSAF* 58 (1899) 161–211.

FERGUSON, W. S. "The Athenian Law Code and the Old Attic Trittyes" in *Classical Studies Presented to Edward Capps on His Seventieth Birthday* (Princeton 1936) 144–158.

FINE, J. V. A.   *The American Excavations in the Athenian Agora,*
  Hesperia Supplement 9: *Horoi: Studies in Mortgage, Real Security,*
  and Land Tenure in Ancient Athens. (Athens) 1951.
FORBES, R. J.   *Studies in Ancient Technology.* Vol. 3. Leiden 1955.
FORREST, W. G.   "Themistokles and Argos," *CQ* 54 (1960) 221–241.
FRAZER, J. G.   *Pausanias's Description of Greece.* Second edition.
  6 vols. London 1913.
FROMHOLD-TREU, M.   "Die Telephos-Trilogie des Sophokles," *Hermes*
  69 (1934) 324–338.
FURTWÄNGLER, A.   *Beschreibung der Vasensammlung im Antiquarium.*
  Berlin 1885.
———— and LÖSCHCKE, G.   *Mykenische Vasen vorhellenische Thonge-*
  fässe aus dem Gebiete des Mittelmeeres. Berlin 1886.
GARDIKAS, G. K.   "Δῆμοι 'Αττικῆς," *Praktika* (1920) 29–79.
GARDNER, E. A.   "Archaeology in Greece, 1894–5," *BSA* 1 (1894–
  1895) 55–66.
GELL, Sir WILLIAM.   *The Itinerary of Greece; Containing One Hundred*
  Routes in Attica, Boeotia, Phocis, Locris, and Thessaly. London
  1819.
GENNADIOS, P. G.   Λεξικὸν φυτολογικόν. Athens 1914.
GOMME, A. W.   *The Population of Athens in the Fifth and Fourth*
  Centuries B.C. Oxford 1933.
———— *A Historical Commentary on Thucydides.* Vol. 2. Oxford 1956.
GUARDUCCI, M.   *See* Richter (third item)
HAMMOND, N. G. L.   "The Battle of Salamis," *JHS* 76 (1956) 32–54.
———— *A History of Greece to 322 B.C.* Oxford 1959.
HANRIOT, C.   *Recherches sur la topographie des dèmes de l'Attique.*
  Napoléon-Vendée 1853.
HARRISON, E. B.   "Archaic Gravestones from the Athenian Agora,"
  Hesperia 25 (1956) 25–45.
HELDREICH, T. VON.   Τὰ δημώδη ὀνόματα τῶν φυτῶν προσδιοριξόμενα
  ἐπιστημονικῶν. Second edition. Athens 1925.
HERWERDEN, H. VAN.   "Lectiones Xenophonteae," *Revue de philo-*
  logie de littérature et d'histoire anciennes 4 (1880) 17–24.
HIGNETT, C.   *A History of the Athenian Constitution to the End of*
  the Fifth Century B.C. Oxford 1952.
HILLER VON GÄRTRINGEN, F.   *Inscriptiones Atticae Euclidis anno*
  anteriores. (*IG* I editio minor.) Berlin 1924.
HOMMEL, H.   "Die dreissig Trittyen des Kleisthenes," *Klio* 33 (1940)
  181–200.
———— *See also* Wissowa *et al.,* Vol. 7 (second series)

HONDIUS, J. J. E. "A New Inscription of the Deme Halimous,"
BSA 24 (1919–1920, 1920–1921) 151–160.

—— and RAUBITSCHEK, A. E. *Supplementum Epigraphicum
Graecum.* Vol. 10. Leiden 1949.

HOPPER, R. J. "The Attic Silver Mines in the Fourth Century
B.C.," *BSA* 48 (1953) 200–254.

JACOBY, F. *Die Fragmente der griechischen Historiker.* Berlin 1923–
1930, Leiden 1940–   ·

—— *Atthis: The Local Chronicles of Ancient Athens.* Oxford 1949.

JEFFERY, L. H. "A Sixth-Century Poros Inscription from Attica,"
BSA 39 (1938–1939) 90–93.

—— *The Local Scripts of Archaic Greece.* Oxford 1961.

JONES, J. E.; SACKETT, L. H.; and ELIOT, C. W. J. "TO ΔEMA: A
Survey of the Aigaleos-Parnes Wall," *BSA* 52 (1957) 152–189.

KAHRSTEDT, U. *Das wirtschaftliche Gesicht Griechenlands in der
Kaiserzeit.* Berne 1954.

KARO, G. *See* Wissowa *et al.,* Supplement 6

KARUSOS [KAROUZOS], C. *Aristodikos.* Stuttgart 1961.

KASTRIOTES, P. and PHILADELPHEUS, A. "'Ανασκαφαὶ 'Αναβύσου,"
Praktika (1911) 110–131.

KASTROMENOS, P. *Die Demen von Attika.* Leipzig 1886.

KAUPERT, J. A. *See* Curtius

KERAMOPOULLOS, A. D. "'Ανασκαφαὶ ἐν Αἰξωνῇ 'Αττικῆς," *Praktika*
(1919) 32–46.

KINNARD, W. *See* Stuart (second item)

KIRCHNER, J. *Inscriptiones Atticae Euclidis anno posteriores.* (*IG*
II–III editio minor.) Berlin 1913–1940.

KIRSTEN, E. "Der gegenwärtige Stand der attischen Demenforschung" in *Atti del terzo congresso internazionale di epigrafia greca
e latina* (Rome 1959) 155–172.

—— *See also* Philippson

KOCK, T. *See* Wissowa *et al.,* Vol. 12

KÖHLER, U. *Inscriptiones Atticae aetatis quae est inter Euclidis
annum et Augusti tempora.* (*IG* II, Part V.) Berlin 1895.

KOLBE, W. *See* Wissowa *et al.,* Vol. 7

KOTZIAS, N. C. "Δημοτικὸν ψήφισμα 'Αλῶν τῶν 'Αραφηνίδων," *ArchEph*
(1925–1926) 168–177.

—— "'Ανασκαφαὶ τῆς βασιλικῆς τοῦ Λαυρεωτικοῦ 'Ολύμπου," *Praktika*
(1952) 92–128.

KOUMANOUDES, S. "'Αττικῆς ἐπιγραφαὶ ἀνέκδοτοι," 'Αθήναιον 1 (1873)
1–19.

KOUROUNIOTES, K. "Τὸ ἱερὸν τοῦ 'Απόλλωνος τοῦ Ζωστῆρος," *Deltion* 11 (1927–1928) 9–53.

KROLL, W. *See* Wissowa

KYPARISSIS, N. "'Εξ 'Αθηνῶν καὶ 'Αττικῆς," *Deltion* 11 (1927–1928) (Παράρτημα τοῦ 'Αρχαιολογικοῦ Δελτίου 1927–1928) 44–66.

———— and PEEK, W. "Attische Urkunden," *AM* 66 (1941) 218–239.

LABARBE, J. *La Loi navale de Thémistocle.* Paris 1957.

LAMPROS, S. P. 'Η ὀνοματολογία τῆς 'Αττικῆς, καὶ ἡ εἰς τὴν χώραν ἐποίκησις τῶν 'Αλβανῶν. Athens 1896.

LANG, M. "Epigraphical Note," *AJA* 65 (1961) 62.

LARSEN, J. A. O. *Representative Government in Greek and Roman History.* Berkeley and Los Angeles 1955.

LEAKE, W. M. *The Topography of Athens and the Demi. 2. The Demi of Attica.* Second edition. London 1841.

LEGRAND, P. E. "Biographie de Louis-François-Sébastien Fauvel, antiquaire et consul (1753–1838)," *RA* 30 (1897) 41–66, 185–201, 385–404, and *RA* 31 (1897) 94–103, 185–223.

LIDDELL, H. G. and SCOTT, R. *A Greek-English Lexicon.* Ninth edition revised and augmented by H. S. JONES assisted by R. McKENZIE. 2 vols. Oxford 1940.

LOLLING, H. G. "Inschriften aus Nordgriechenland," *AM* 4 (1879) 193–227.

LÖPER, R. "Die Trittyen und Demen Attikas," *AM* 17 (1892) 319–433.

LÖSCHCKE, G. *See* Furtwängler

MCLEOD, W. E. "Boudoron, an Athenian Fort on Salamis," *Hesperia* 29 (1960) 316–323.

MANN, S. E. *A Historical Albanian and English Dictionary.* London 1948.

MERITT, B. D. "Greek Inscriptions," *Hesperia* 5 (1936) 355–430.

———— "Greek Inscriptions (14–27)," *ibid.* 8 (1939) 48–82.

———— "Greek Inscriptions," *ibid.* 9 (1940) 53–96.

———— "Greek Inscriptions," *ibid.* 30 (1961) 205–292.

MICHON, E. "Notes sur quelques monuments du Département des Antiquités grecques et romaines au Musée du Louvre," *MSAF* 58 (1899) 27–117.

MILCHHÖFER, A. "Antikenbericht aus Attika," *AM* 12 (1887) 81–104, 277–330, and *AM* 13 (1888) 337–362.

———— *Karten von Attika, Erläuternder Text.* Parts 3–6. Berlin 1889.

———— *Untersuchungen über die Demenordnung des Kleisthenes.* Berlin 1892.

———— *See also* Wissowa *et al.*, vols. 1, 2, 3 and 6

MILLER, E. "Inscription grecque nouvellement découverte aux environs d'Athènes," *RA* 11 (1865) 154–159.

MITSOS, M. T. "'Επιγραφαὶ ἐξ 'Αθηνῶν," *ArchEph* (1957) 44–49.

———— and VANDERPOOL, E. "Inscriptions from Attica," *Hesperia* 19 (1950) 25–30.

———— and VANDERPOOL, E. "Inscriptions from Attica," *ibid.* 22 (1953) 177–181.

MITTELHAUS, K. *See* Wissowa

MYLONAS, G. E. *Aghios Kosmas: An Early Bronze Age Settlement and Cemetery in Attica.* Princeton 1959.

OMONT, H. *Missions archéologiques françaises en Orient aux xviie et xviiie siècles.* Vol. 1. Paris 1902.

ORLANDOS, A. K. "La Basilique paléochrétienne de Glyphada," Πρακτικὰ τῆς 'Ακαδημίας 'Αθηνῶν 5 (1930) 258–265.

———— Τὸ ἔργον τῆς 'Αρχαιολογικῆς 'Εταιρείας κατὰ τὸ *1957.* Athens 1958.

PAPADIMITRIOU, I. "Μυκηναϊκοὶ τάφοι 'Αλυκῆς Γλυφάδας," *Praktika* (1954) 72–88, and *ibid.* (1955) 78–99.

PAPAGIANNOPOULOS-PALAIOS, A. "'Αττικαὶ ἐπιγραφαί 7: "Εργα 'Εκφαντίδου, Κρατίνου, Τιμοθέου καὶ ἡ Σοφοκλέους Τηλέφεια," *Polemon* 1 (1929) 161–173.

———— "'Αττικά· τὸ θέατρον Αἰξωνῆσιν," *ibid.* 4 (1949–1950) 138.

———— "'Ενδείξεις περὶ τῆς εἰς Αἰξωνὴν ἀποβιβάσεως τοῦ 'Αποστόλου Παύλου," Αἰξώνη 1 (1950–1951) 131–136.

PARSONS, A. W. "The Klepsydra and the Paved Court of the Pythion," *Hesperia* 12 (1943) 191–267.

PEEK, W. "Attische Inschriften," *AM* 67 (1942) 1–217.

———— *See also* Kyparissis

PHILADELPHEUS, A. *See* Kastriotes

PHILIPPSON, A. *Die griechischen Landschaften.* Vol. 1, Part 3. *Attika und Megaris.* With "Beiträge" by E. KIRSTEN. Frankfurt 1952.

PICKARD-CAMBRIDGE, Sir ARTHUR. *The Dramatic Festivals of Athens.* Oxford 1953.

PLEKET, H. W. *The Greek Inscriptions in the "Rijksmuseum van Oudheden" at Leyden.* Leiden 1958.

PRITCHETT, W. K. Review of S. Dow, *The American Excavations in the Athenian Agora, Hesperia Supplement* 1: *Prytaneis: A Study of the Inscriptions Honoring the Athenian Councillors* in *AJA* 60 (1939) 257–260.

———— "Greek Inscriptions," *Hesperia* 11 (1942) 230–249.

———— *The Five Attic Tribes after Kleisthenes.* Baltimore 1943.

———— "An Unfinished Inscription, *IG* II² 2362," *TAPA* 85 (1954) 159–167.

———— "Toward a Restudy of the Battle of Salamis," *AJA* 63 (1959) 251–262.

PROKESCH VON OSTEN, A.   *Denkwürdigkeiten und Erinnerungen aus dem Orient.* 3 vols. Stuttgart 1836–1837.

PROTOPSALTES, E. G.   Ὁ Γεώργιος Χριστιανὸς *Gropius* καὶ ἡ δρᾶσις αὐτοῦ ἐν Ἑλλάδι. Athens 1947.

RANGABÉ, A. R.   *Antiquités helléniques ou répertoire d'inscriptions et d'autres antiquités découvertes depuis l'affranchissement de la Grèce.* 2 vols. Athens 1842–1855.

RAUBITSCHEK, A. E.   "The Gates in the Agora," *AJA* 60 (1956) 279–282.

———— *See also* Hondius

REISCH, E.   "Heraklesrelief von Lamptrae," *AM* 12 (1887) 118–130.

REVETT, N.   *See* Stuart

RICHTER, G. M. A.   *Catalogue of Greek Sculptures in the Metropolitan Museum of Art.* Cambridge, Mass. 1954.

———— *Kouroi, Archaic Greek Youths: A Study of the Development of the Kouros Type in Greek Sculpture.* Second edition. London 1960.

———— *The Archaic Gravestones of Attica.* With "An Appendix with Epigraphical Notes" by M. GUARDUCCI. London 1961.

ROSS, L.   *Archäologische Aufsätze.* 2 vols. Leipzig 1855–1861.

ROTTIERS, B. E. A.   *Monumens de Rhodes.* Brussels 1828.

RUSOPOULOS, A. S.   "Scavi attici di Aixone," *Bullettino dell'Instituto di Corrispondenza Archeologica* (1864) 129–132.

SACKETT, L. H.   *See* Jones

SCHÖFFER, V. VON.   "Bericht über die im Jahre 1891 und der ersten Hälfte des Jahres 1892 erschienene Litteratur zu Aristoteles' Ἀθηναίων πολιτεία," *Jahresbericht über die Fortschritte der classischen Altertumswissenschaft* 75 (1893) 1–54.

SCOTT, R.   *See* Liddell

SCRANTON, R. L.   *Greek Walls.* Cambridge, Mass. 1941.

SEALEY, R.   "Regionalism in Archaic Athens," *Historia* 9 (1960) 155–180.

SELTMAN, C. T.   *Athens: Its History and Coinage before the Persian Invasion.* Cambridge 1924.

SMYTH, H. W.   *Greek Grammar.* Revised by G. M. Messing. Cambridge, Mass. 1956.

SOURMELES, D.   Ἀττικά, ἢ περὶ δήμων Ἀττικῆς, ἐν οἷς καὶ περί τινων μερῶν τοῦ Ἄστεως. Athens 1855.

STACKELBERG, O. M. VON. *Die Gräber der Hellenen*. Berlin 1837.

STAÏS, V. "Περὶ τῶν ἐν Βάρῃ ἀνασκαφῶν," Δελτίον ἀρχαιολογικόν 6 (1891) 28–32.

STAUROPOULLOS, P. "Ἱερατικὴ οἰκία ἐν Ζωστῆρι τῆς 'Αττικῆς," *ArchEph* (1938) ('Αρχαιολογικὰ χρονικά) 1–31.

STEVENS, G. P. and VANDERPOOL, E. "An Inscribed Kouros Base (with Supplementary Note by D. M. ROBINSON)" in *Commemorative Studies in Honor of Theodore Leslie Shear, Hesperia Supplement* 8 (1949) 361–364.

STUART, J. and REVETT, N. *The Antiquities of Athens Measured and Delineated by James Stuart F.R.S. and F.S.A. and Nicholas Revett, Painters and Architects*. Vol. 3. London 1794.

—— *Antiquities of Athens and Other Places in Greece, Sicily, Etc., Supplementary to the Antiquities of Athens by James Stuart, F.R.S., F.S.A. and Nicholas Revett, Delineated and Illustrated by C. R. Cockerell, A.R.A., F.S.A., W. Kinnard, T. L. Donaldson, W. Jenkins, W. Railton, Architects*. London 1830.

STUBBINGS, F. H. "The Mycenaean Pottery of Attica," *BSA* 42 (1947) 1–75.

SUMNER, G. V. "Notes on Chronological Problems in the Aristotelian ΑΘΗΝΑΙΩΝ ΠΟΛΙΤΕΙΑ," *CQ* 55 (1961) 31–54.

SZANTO, E. "Die kleisthenischen Trittyen," *Hermes* 27 (1892) 312–315.

TERRIER, M. "Mémoire sur les ruines de Sunium et de la côte de l'Attique, depuis la baie de Vari jusqu'à la presqu'île de Courouni," *Archives des missions scientifiques et littéraires* 3 (second series) (printed 1866) 55–129.

THEOCHARIS, M. D. "A Knossian Vase from Attica," *Antiquity* 34 (1960) 266–269.

THOMPSON, H. A. "Excavations in the Athenian Agora: 1949," *Hesperia* 19 (1950) 313–337.

URE, P. N. *The Origin of Tyranny*. Cambridge 1922.

VANDERPOOL, E. "News Letter from Greece," *AJA* 58 (1954) 231–241, *AJA* 59 (1955) 223–229, and *AJA* 65 (1961) 299–303.

—— See also Mitsos, and Stevens

VULLIAMY, L. *Examples of Ornamental Sculpture in Architecture. Drawn from the Originals of Bronze Marble and Terra Cot[ta] in Greece Asia Minor and Italy. By Lewis Vulliamy Arch[t] in the Years 1818, 1819, 1820, 18[21] and Engraved by Henry Moses*. London. (The 40 Plates are dated between Nov. 15, 1823 and Dec. 20, 1827.)

WADE-GERY, H. T. "Horos" in *Mélanges Gustave Glotz* Vol. 2 (Paris 1932) 876–887.

WALKER, E. M. "Athens: The Reforms of Cleisthenes," *CAH* 4: *The Persian Empire and the West* (Cambridge 1926) 137–172.

WALTER, O. "Zur Heraklesbasis von Lamptrai," *Mitteilungen des deutschen archäologischen Instituts* 3 (1950) 139–147.

WALTERS, H. B. *Catalogue of the Bronzes, Greek, Roman, and Etruscan, in the Department of Greek and Roman Antiquities, British Museum.* London 1899.

WHELER, G. *A Journey into Greece by George Wheler Esq.; in Company of Dr Spon of Lyons.* London 1682.

WILHELM, A. "Inscription attique du Musée du Louvre," *BCH* 25 (1901) 93–104.

———— "Ein Grabgedicht aus Athen," *Annuaire de l'Institut de Philologie et d'Histoire orientales* 2 (1934) 1007–1020.

WINTER, F. "Grabmal von Lamptrae," *AM* 12 (1887) 105–118.

WISSOWA, G.; KROLL, W.; WITTE, K.; MITTELHAUS, K.; and ZIEGLER, K. *Paulys Real-Encyclopädie der classischen Altertumswissenschaft.* Stuttgart. Vol. 1 (1894), s.v. Aigilia (1), Amphitrope, Anagyrus, Anaphlystos (A. MILCHHÖFER). Vol. 2 (1896), s.v. Atene, Attika (1), Azenia (A. MILCHHÖFER). Vol. 3 (1899), s.v. Besa (A. MILCHHÖFER). Vol. 6 (1909), s.v. Euonymon (A. MILCHHÖFER). Vol. 7 (1910–1912), s.v. Halai (1) (W. KOLBE). Vol. 12 (1924–1925), s.v. Lamptrai (T. KOCK). Vol. 6 (second series, 1936–1937), s.v. Thorai (W. WREDE). Vol. 7 (second series, 1939–1948), s.v. Trittyes (H. HOMMEL). Supplement 6 (1935), s.v. Mykenische Kultur (G. KARO).

WITTE, K. *See* Wissowa

WOLTERS, P. In *Brunn-Bruckmann's Denkmäler griechischer und römischer Sculptur, fortgeführt und unter Mitwirkung von Fachgenossen mit erläuternden Texten versehen von Paul Arndt und Georg Lippold.* Texte und Register zu den Tafeln 651–700. Munich 1926.

WOODHEAD, A. G. *Supplementum Epigraphicum Graecum.* Vol. 15. Leiden 1958.

———— *The Study of Greek Inscriptions.* Cambridge 1959.

WREDE, W. *Attika.* Athens 1934.

———— "Die Heraklesbasis von Lamptrai," *AM* 66 (1941) 160–165.

———— *See also* Wissowa *et al.*, Vol. 6 (second series)

YOUNG, J. H. "Greek Inscriptions: A Poletai Record of the Year

367/6 B.C. Addendum: A Topographical Note," *Hesperia* 10 (1941) 28–30.

—— "An Epigram at Sunium" in *Studies Presented to David Moore Robinson on His Seventieth Birthday* Vol. 2 (St. Louis 1953) 353–357.

—— "Studies in South Attica," *Hesperia* 25 (1956) 122–146.

—— "Greek Roads in South Attica," *Antiquity* 30 (1956) 94–97.

YOUNG, R. S. *The American Excavations in the Athenian Agora, Hesperia Supplement* 2: *Late Geometric Graves and A Seventh Century Well in the Agora.* Athens 1939.

ZIEGLER, K. *See* Wissowa

ZSCHIETZSCHMANN, W. "Die Darstellungen der Prothesis in der griechischen Kunst," *AM* 53 (1928) 17–47.

Catalogue sommaire des marbres antiques. Paris 1922.

Les Antiquités égyptiennes, grecques, étrusques, romaines et gallo-romaines du Musée de Mariemont. Brussels 1952.

INDEXES

I. INDEX OF GENERAL SUBJECTS

II. REGISTER OF PLACE NAMES

III. INDEX OF SCHOLARS AND OTHER PERSONS

IV. INDEX OF ANCIENT REFERENCES CITED

(The asterisks mark discussions important either for this study or for the reference.)

V. INDEX OF INSCRIPTIONS CITED

(The asterisks mark discussions important either for this study or for the reference.)